God's ...y

God's Body

The Anthropomorphic God in the Old Testament

Andreas Wagner

Translated from *Gottes Körper*
by Marion Salzmann

t&tclark
LONDON · NEW YORK · OXFORD · NEW DELHI · SYDNEY

T&T CLARK
Bloomsbury Publishing Plc
50 Bedford Square, London, WC1B 3DP, UK
1385 Broadway, New York, NY 10018, USA

BLOOMSBURY, T&T CLARK and the T&T Clark logo are trademarks of Bloomsbury
Publishing Plc

First published in Germany 2010 as *GOTTES KÖRPER: Zur alttestamentlichen
Vorstellung der Menschengestaltigkeit Gottes*

Copyright © 2010 by Gütersloher Verlagshaus, Gütersloh, in der Verlagsgruppe
Random House GmbH, Munich

First published in Great Britain 2019
Reprinted 2019

Copyright © Andreas Wagner, 2019

Cover design: Terry Woodley
Cover images © clockwise from top: Ivy Close Images, www.BibleLandPictures.com,
Heritage Image Partnership Ltd, Peter Horree / Alamy Stock Photo

A catalogue record for this book is available from the British Library.

A catalogue record for this book is available from the Library of Congress.

ISBN: HB: 978-0-5676-5599-8
PB: 978-0-5676-5598-1
ePDF: 978-0-5676-5597-4
eBook: 978-0-5676-5596-7

Typeset by Deanta Global Publishing Services, Chennai, India
Printed and bound in Great Britain

To find out more about our authors and books visit www.bloomsbury.com and
sign up for our newsletters.

CONTENTS

LIST OF ILLUSTRATIONS

PREFACE

Martin Luther once said that every age has to work on its own translation and understanding of the Bible; times change, and we change with them. New questions challenge old readings of the texts while old questions may require different approaches. New insights and new notions afford new knowledge. However, when basic concepts change, our perceptions may be channelled in other and diverse directions.

These aspects apply to our discussion of God's human figure in the Old Testament. On the one hand, our modern understanding of the body hampers our understanding of Old Testament phenomena. On the other hand, academic discussion of these concepts can lead to new approaches. The issue of portrayal, which is closely related to the body, is similar. Our modern understanding of images is so deeply ingrained that an intense process of reflection is necessary to understand images from the time of the Old Testament, which function in such a completely different manner. To put it another way, if modern recipients are confronted with Ancient Oriental concepts and representations of the body – and therefore with the Old Testament concept of God's human form – without any process of reflection, then misunderstandings are inevitable.

The purpose of this book is to unfold the Old Testament concept of God's human form in light of modern understanding of Ancient Oriental images and corporeal concepts. This process will introduce readers to a far off, strange, but always fascinating world. Only then will we be able to appreciate the intention of the Old Testament conceptualization of God's human form and to convey its theological substance.

It is not hard to recognize that the premises underlying Old Testament concepts are of quite a different character. However, it is much more of a challenge to grasp and to describe the results of this analysis from our modern vantage point. We need to be aware of our own preconceptions, many of which are subconscious. Therefore, the *attempt* to understand Old Testament phenomena must begin with an attempt to understand our own world. Hopefully, this will cause us to marvel at the world around us and to revel in it. In learning to understand others, we learn to understand ourselves. Although this is by no means an easy process, there is no alternative, nor should there be, and we must endeavour to try.

I would like to describe this book as an 'attempt', as an 'essay'. Much of it is tentative and readers must allow themselves to become immersed in various discussions, and to be led along some seemingly erroneous paths. They can be sure, however, that in the end an overall picture will emerge.

In trying to fulfil the publishers request for a comprehensible style, without giving up my own ideals of writing objectively and precisely. References to further academic literature and discussion can be found in the text and footnotes.

Many colleagues took part in the discussions which led to this book. G. Braulik and U. Rüterswörden (on legal form), A. Berlejung (cult images), H. Bredekamp (image analysis), B. Janowski (anthropology), O. Keel (image concepts), M. Oeming (Old Testament theology), S. Schroer (body symbolism), S. Weyer-Menkhoff (metaphors and image concepts), Chr. Wagner (image analysis), D. Wildung (Egyptian art), A. Behrens, J. F. Diehl, A. Kropp, R. G. Lehmann, M. Mark, A. Müller, J. Vette and many others were always available for discussion.

Professor Diethelm Michel, who died in 1999, introduced me to many issues in Old Testament anthropology and was an important partner in discourse. Were he alive today, he would say that experts would recognize this inheritance.

Without the support of the institutions with whom I have had the honour to work, I would not have been able to do this research. Thus, this book is gratefully dedicated to the faculties of protestant theology in Mainz, Basel, Heidelberg, Darmstadt and Bern.

I would also like to thank the Deutsche Forschungsgemeinschaft (DFG) who supported the research project entitled *Stabilitas Dei – Die Gestaltbeständigkeit des alttestamentlichen Gottes im Vergleich mit außeralttestamentlichen Göttern*. This book is the first large publication arising from this project.

Many people were extremely helpful with the necessary research: my thanks to K. Adam, S. Appelfeller, D. Benz, Chr. Schefe and S. Shokrzadeh, and to the students and assistants who sought out literature and pertinent examples. K. Müller, in particular, helped prepare the manuscript and organize the project while at the same time keeping tabs on all the various tasks and on the final publication itself.

I am especially grateful to D. Steen from the Gütersloh Verlagshaus and A. A. Diesel. Both patiently encouraged and supported the author and the book, through all its difficulties.

PREFACE FOR ENGLISH EDITION

It is a great honour and pleasure for me to prepare a redacted English version of my book *Gottes Körper*. The first decade of the twenty-first century saw the publication of several books exploring related themes. One can assume that this is a reflection of the *Zeitgeist*, and I for one am very pleased to see this new global interest in anthropomorphism.

The following two (or three) books in particular, all of which have pushed different subjects of discussion, are worthy of further mention:

E. J. Hamori, *When Gods Were Men: The Embodied God in Biblical and Near Eastern Literature* (BZAW 384, Berlin and Boston: deGruyter, 2008).

B. D. Sommer, *The Bodies of God and the World of Ancient Israel* (Cambridge: Cambridge University Press, 2009).

For religions in Mesopotamia see:

B. N. Porter, *What is a God? Anthropomorphic and Non-anthropomorphic Aspects of Deity in Ancient Mesopotamia* (Transactions of the Casco Bay Assyriological Institute 2, Eisenbrauns/The Casco Bay Assyriological Institute, 2009).

Hamori's book focuses on the stories of God's 'acting' in the Old Testament, in other words 'anthropopragmatism'. Sommer's work engages with different aspects of anthropomorphism in the texts of the Old Testament. He tries to illustrate how 'fluidity', including both anthropomorphism (God's body) and anthropopragmatism (God's acts and forms of presence), is fundamental to the conception of God in the Old Testament. In my book, I tried to delineate the main aspects and the functions of the body of God arising from the study of the body parts present in the texts (direct anthropomorphisms). Lastly, in the book of Porter, the author questioned if anthropomorphism is an essential part of the real nature of gods (in ancient Mesopotamia).

In this new English version of *Gottes Körper*, I will endeavour to respond to some of the issues raised in the works of Sommer and Hamori, which were published subsequent to my writing of *Gottes Körper* in 2007/08. Further, I will also try to engage with publications made between 2009 and 2015.[1]

In *Gottes Körper*, the discussion of anthropomorphism in the Old Testament depends on the discussion of that, which is known in Continental Europe as 'Alttestamentliche Anthropologie'. This is now a booming field of research in the area of Old Testament studies. The classic text in the field is *Anthropologie des Alten Testaments* by Hans Walter Wolff first published 1973.

H. W. Wolff, *Anthropologie des Alten Testaments, mit Zwei Anhängen neu herausgegeben von Bernd Janowski* (Gütersloh: Gütersloher Verlag, 2010); English: *Anthropology of the Old Testament* (Mifflintown, Pennsylvania: Sigler Press, 1996).

Much time has passed since then and there have been countless new publications in anthropology in general,[2] as well as in the field of anthropology of the Old Testament,[3] particularly since the turn of the millennium.

---

[1]Such as the following recently published books and articles: E. Martin (ed.), *Tiergestaltigkeit der Göttinnen und Götter zwischen Metapher und Symbol* (BThSt 129; Neukirchen-Vluyn: Neukirchener 2012; A. K. Knafl, *Forming God: Divine Anthropomorphism in the Pentateuch* (Siphrut: Literature and Theology of the Hebrew Scriptures 12; Winona Lake, IN: Eisenbrauns, 2014); A. Wagner (ed.), *Göttliche Körper – göttliche Gefühle: Was leisten anthropomorphe und anthropopathische Götterkonzepte im Alten Orient und Alten Testament?* (OBO 270; Fribourg: Academic Press Fribourg; Göttingen: Vandenhoeck & Ruprecht, 2014), with the following parts: A. Wagner, *Menschenkörper – Gotteskörper: Zur Einführung*, pp. 1–28; I. Wunn, *Die Entstehung der Götter*, pp. 31–47; A. Nunn, *Mesopotamische Götter und ihr Körper in den Bildern*, pp. 51–66; P. Machinist, *Anthropomorphism in Mesopotamian Religion*, pp. 67–99; B. Pongratz-Leisten, *Entwurf zu einer Handlungstheorie des altorientalischen Polytheismus*, pp. 101–16; M. S. Smith, *Ugaritic Anthropomorphism, Theomorphism, Theriomorphism*, pp. 117–40; H. Niehr: *Körper des Königs und Körper der Götter in Ugarit*, pp. 141–67; C. M. Maier, *Körperliche und emotionale Aspekte JHWHs aus der Genderperspektive*, pp. 171–89; M. Köhlmoos, '*Denn ich, JHWH, bin ein eifersüchtiger Gott' Gottes Gefühle im Alten Testament*, pp. 191–217; K. Müller, *Lieben ist nicht gleich lieben. Zur kognitiven Konzeption von Liebe im Hebräischen*, pp. 219–37.
[2]Overviews include the following: G. Dressel, *Historische Anthropologie. Eine Einführung* (Wien: Böhlau, 1996); R. van Dülmen, *Historische Anthropologie. Entwicklung, Probleme, Aufgaben* (Köln: Böhlau, 2001); A. Assmann (ed.), *Positionen der Kulturanthropologie* (Stw 1724, Frankfurt: Suhrkamp, 2004); C. Wulf, *Anthropologie. Geschichte, Kultur, Philosophie* (Rowohlts Enzyklopädie 55664; Reinbek: Rowohlt Taschenbuch Verlag, 2004); J. Tanner, *Historische Anthropologie zur Einführung* (2nd edn, Zur Einführung 301, Hamburg: Junius, 2008); R. Habermas, J. Tanner and B. Wagner-Hasel (eds.)., Thema: 20 Jahre Zeitschrift Historische Anthropologie 20 (2012).
[3]Literature on Anthropology: Cf. for research building on H. W. Wolff, see for example; Hedwig-Jahnow-Forschungsprojekt (ed.), *Körperkonzepte im Ersten Testament: Aspekte einer Feministischen Anthropologie* (Stuttgart: Kohlhammer, 2003); S. Schroer, Feministische Anthropologie des Ersten Testaments: Beobachtungen, Fragen, Plädoyers, in: *lectio difficilior* 1 (2003). Available online: http://www. lectio.unibe.ch/03_1/schroer.htm; S. Schroer and T. Staubli, *Die Körpersymbolik der Bibel* (2nd edn, Gütersloh: Gütersloher Verlagshaus, 2005). English: *Body Symbolism in the Bible* (trans. Linda M. Maloney; Collegeville, Minn.: Liturgical

In the German speaking scientific community especially, 'Anthropologie' has come to denote all issues, themes, subjects and so on, concerning the human being, self-understanding, the human ways of thinking, mentalities and so on, in different cultures and times. It is often called 'Historische Anthropologie/Historical Anthropology' and it encompasses impulses from the French history school of the Annales, the 'Mentalitätsgeschichte' and a lot of input from different kinds of social history.[4] Again, one can see the *Zeitgeist* at work. The boom-time of 'Historical Anthropology' (in Europe) were the two decades either side of the turn of the millennium. In the context of this 'crossing point' from the second to the third millennium, people (in 'Western' cultures) have again the particular need to define: 'What is a human being?', 'What are the possibilities, the limits of human doing and thinking?' and so on. One way to find one's own position is to look back in history or to look to other cultures, which define these questions in their own manner. Comparing these varied positions with the varied positions within 'our' own traditions could perhaps lead to the discovery of new and exciting answers.[5]

Not least the Christian and Jewish traditions have conveyed anthropological ideas and opinions which are based on outdated interpretations of biblical texts and thoughts. So new results in biblical or Old Testament anthropology will provide fresh impetus to contemporary Christian and Jewish thought.

Particularly significant in this regard is the research into 'body' and 'body concepts'. We learnt in the last century that the 'body' is not a natural but a

---

Press, 2001). Cf.: In addition, the body and body part related literature: A. Wagner, *Anthropologische Aufbrüche: Alttestamentliche und interdisziplinäre Zugänge zur historischen Anthropologie* (FRLANT 232; Göttingen: Vandenhoeck & Ruprecht, 2009); T. Krüger, *Das menschliche Herz und die Weisung Gottes. Studien zur alttestamentlichen Anthropologie und Ethik* (AThANT 96; Zürich: Theologischer Verlag, 2009); B. Janowski and K. Liess, *Der Mensch im alten Israel: Neue Forschungen zur alttestamentlichen Anthropologie* (Freiburg im Breisgau: Herder, 2009); J. van Oorschot (ed.), *Der Mensch als Thema theologischer Anthropologie. Beiträge in interdisziplinärer Perspektive* (BthSt 111, Neukirchen-Vluyn: Neukirchener, 2010); C. Frevel (ed.), *Biblische Anthropologie: Neue Einsichten aus dem Alten Testament* (QD 237; Freiburg im Breisgau: Herder, 2010); A. Berlejung (ed.), *Menschenbilder und Körperkonzepte im Alten Israel, in Ägypten und im Alten Orient* (ORA 9; Tübingen: Mohr Siebeck, 2012); B. Janowski, *Der Ganze Mensch: Zur Anthropologie der Antike und ihrer europäischen Nachgeschichte* (Berlin: Akademie Verlag, 2012); S. Schroer, and T. Staubli, *Menschenbilder der Bibel* (Ostfildern, Patmos, 2014); J. van Oorschot and A. Wagner (eds.), *Anthropologie(n) des Alten Testaments* (2nd edn, VWGTh 42, Leipzig: Evangelische Verlagsanstalt, 2015), pp. 11–21.

[4]Cf.: A. Wagner, Emotionen in alttestamentlicher und verwandter Literatur: Grundüberlegungen am Beispiel des Zorns, in: R. Egger-Wenzel and J. Corley (eds.), *Emotions from Ben Sira to Paul* (DCL.Y 2011; Berlin and Boston: deGruyter, 2012), pp. 27–68.

[5]Cf.: A. Wagner, Anthropologie(n) des Alten Testaments im 21. Jahrhundert, in: Oorschot and Wagner (eds.), *Anthropologie(n) des Alten Testaments*, pp. 11–21.

cultural concept[6] that differs from culture to culture.[7] Similarly, other parts of the human being are subject to different cultures: emotions, the concept of human being and so on.

However, if 'body' is a cultural concept, what kind of 'body concept' do we find in the culture and the texts of the Old Testament? Further, if there is a special body concept, what about the body of God? What are the consequences for the understanding of God's body, if we try to understand his body from the specific Israelite/Ancient Near East (ANE) body concept? What is different to an understanding aligned to a modern (Western) body concept? These questions were at the heart of my work leading up to *Gottes Körper*. So the understanding of the '(human) body' as a part of 'anthropology (in the European tradition)' turns into 'theology', the understanding of God's body. Thus, in a fashion one can read the book too as a history of the body in Old Testament times and cultures.

A very important part of my reasoning is to begin by analysing images of the body, both human and God. We have two kinds of images which we can use: (a) images in speech, in texts, and (b) images we have found on materials. Both are illustrating bodies and body parts. Both kinds of images have their own peculiarities, but both are key to understanding the (one) concept of the body in the Old Testament and the Israelite culture(s). This explains the focus of my book on the visual body and the visual body parts. Images on materials can mainly represent the visual body. If you want to compare images in the speech with those found on materials, you have to narrow down the body to the visual aspects (Chapter 1) and consider the idea of 'images' (Chapter 4) carefully. If we consider the body concept in general, we can try to use it to describe the body of God (Chapters 5 and 7).

In the Christian and Jewish traditions, the prohibition of images depicting God has often muddied the issue of God's anthropomorphic body, correlating with ideas and conceptions of God, influenced by Hellenism,

---

[6]Cf.: B. Duden, *Geschichte unter der Haut. Ein Eisenacher Arzt und seine Patientinnen um 1730* (Stuttgart: Klett-Cotta, 1987). English: *The Woman Beneath the Skin: A Doctor's Patients in Eighteenth-Century Germany* (trans. T. Dunlap; Cambridge, MA and London: Harvard University Press, 1991); B. Duden, *Der Frauenleib als öffentlicher Ort. Vom Mißbrauch des Begriffs Leben* (Hamburg: Luchterhand, 1991), English: *Disembodying Women. Perspectives on Pregnancy and the Unborn* (trans. L. Hoinacki; Cambridge, MA and London: Harvard University Press, 1993); J. Butler, *Gender Trouble. Feminism and the Subversion of Identity* (New York: Routledge, 1990); J. Butler, *Bodies that Matter: On the Discursive Limits of "sex"* (New York: Routledge, 1993); D. J. Haraway, *Primate Visions: Gender, Race and Nature in the World of Modern Science* (New York: Routledge, 1989); D. J. Haraway, *Simians, Cyborgs, and Women: The Reinvention of Nature* (New York: Routledge, 1990); P. Sarasin, 'Körpergeschichte', Historisches Lexikon der Schweiz 7 (2009), pp. 412–13.
[7]A. Wagner, Die Gestalt(en) Gottes und der Mensch im Alten Testament, in: B. Janowski and C. Schwöbel (eds.), *Dimensionen der Leiblichkeit*. (ThID 16; Neukirchen-Vluyn: Neukirchener, 2015), pp. 46–68 (In particular see pp. 46–49); A. Wagner, Menschenkörper – Gotteskörper: Zur Einführung, in Wagner (ed.) *Göttliche Körper – göttliche Gefühle*, pp. 1–28.

which had a huge impact on the New Testament and later times. Benjamin Sommer has described this phenomenon brilliantly in his work (see also Chapter 3). For a long time, nobody wanted to see and observe the anthropomorphic facts found in the Old Testament, but they are simply too numerous and too obvious to be overlooked. The Old Testament texts outline an anthropomorphic body image of God. We have to understand that in the Old Testament the prohibition of images meant the prohibition of statues, not the prohibition of ideas about the image and body of God (Chapter 2). In a new light, we have to reconsider the unique opinion of the priestly codex (Gen. 1) on mankind as an image of God (Chapter 6).

This book could not have been published without great help and support. First of all, many thanks go to Marion Salzmann for the translation and to Dominic Mattos for the publisher, both of whom promoted the translation project from the beginning. Also, I would like to thank Leeladevi Ulaganathan, who coordinated the project on behalf of the publisher, and the copy-editing department.

On the other hand, I sincerely thank my co-workers Susanne Gräbner, Liam Myerscough and Nikolett Móricz for their proof-reading and project management support. Above all, my thanks go to Daniel Benz, who has been in charge of supplementary research and coordination.

1

Introduction – An investigation into the external body of God as it can be portrayed pictorially

1.1 God's external form as the focus of our investigation

No one can talk about God without having an 'image' of God in mind. When we talk to or with God, an implicit or explicit concept of God is always present. Many of these concepts claim to be abstract, and consider God as the greatest good, as a force, as an impersonal numinous phenomenon: but in prayer we fall back instinctively on an intimate 'you'.

Biblical tradition is characterized by the conviction that God encounters mankind as a personal, embodied counterpart. We should not be too quick to transpose this concept into our modern times. We must bear in mind that the biblical concept came into being in a completely different cultural world. Therefore, it must be approached and understood, at least initially, in that context.

Indeed, Old Testament tradition consistently assumes that the concept of the body is the same for humans as it is for God. In Gen. 1, 'man' is made in the image of God. Numerous texts reflect the concept of God in human form, painting a 'verbal picture' of 'his' figure, that is, the body of God. The external image, the (visible/optical) 'image' of God, therefore corresponds with the human form, the (visible/optical) 'image' of 'man'. Feelings and actions correspond likewise, as do perception of the organic inner world of God and humans.

This book concentrates on observing *God's external form*, which appears in human form anthropomorphically. Connections to other fields such as feelings/emotions/impulses (anthropopathisms[1]), behaviour and action (anthropopragmatisms[2]) and so on will be treated in future works. The methodical approach adopted here thus restricts our observation to the *external* form. The line of argumentation in this book concentrates on the depiction of the incarnate body in material and verbal pictures. Depictions of the body open up a new understanding of God's body. As far as I can see, depictions of whole bodies in the material pictorial world of the Ancient Orient or the Old Testament do not include 'inner organs'. Further, some concepts such as the rûaḥ (*spirit*) were not, or could not be, depicted in material images. The external bodily form, the figure, therefore appears to be a definable field of research.

This does not mean that we should not be aware of possible connections between the results of our investigation on the external form and the results from investigations on the inner parts of the body (e.g. *ræ'hæm*), and other aspects which constitute God and humans. This is also true for the previously mentioned anthropopathisms and anthropopragmatisms. Since a publication cannot hope to encompass all these aspects, I rely on a step-by-step approach and focus solely upon the external form.

1.2 God's external form between the poles of recent research on depictions and the body

For a new approach to biblical discourse on God in (pictorially conceivable) human form, we must assume a connection between verbal images and material drawings (also called 'flat images'), statues (sometimes called 'round images') and so on. I shall call non-linguistic depictions 'material images' to distinguish them from 'verbal images'. Previous investigations of anthropomorphism have not considered material images sufficiently.

Material images reveal clearly how the external form was 'seen' in the Ancient Orient and in Old Testament times. Thus, they are particularly suitable as source material for the concept of the figure and for understanding the (depicted) body. The characteristics of material depictions converge well with those of verbal images.

As we shall see, the way in which a (human) body is understood and portrayed cannot be taken for granted, nor is it the same at all times. Our

[1]Cf.: A. Wagner, *Emotionen, Gefühle und Sprache im Alten Testament* (2nd edn, KUATU 7, Spenner: Waltrop, 2011); Egger-Wenzel and Corley (eds.), *Emotions from Ben Sira to Paul.*
[2]Cf.: H. M. Kuitert, *Gott in Menschengestalt: Eine dogmatisch-hermeneutische Studie über die Anthropomorphismen der Bibel* (BEvTh 45; Munich: Kaiser, 1967), pp. 12–13; F. Christ, *Menschlich von Gott reden: Das Problem des Anthropomorphismus bei Schleiermacher* (ÖTh 10; Einsiedeln et al.: Gütersloh; Benziger: Mohn, 1982), pp. 15–16; Machinist, *Anthropomorphism in Mesopotamian Religion*, p. 68.

understanding of the functions of *parts* of the figure or the body and their portrayal is just as varied today. The understanding of the figure or the body in a given culture is reproduced in their portrayals of figure and body. Further, the understanding of the figure and body in a given culture, in turn, influences their perception of the *human figure* of God.

One might ask how we can consult material images, in addition to verbal images, for our understanding of 'pictures' of God when there are none available (or hardly any[3]) from the Ancient Israelite context and certainly none from the Old Testament. One possibility is to draw on material human depictions from Ancient Israel as well as on material depictions of humans, and of gods, from non-Old Testament contexts, provided by recent research. Both give a good indication of the conception of image and form in the Old Testament, including the 'image' of God.

Two impulses are of particular importance for this new approach:

First, we see an 'orientation towards pictures' on two accounts, which are in turn interconnected. The last decades of the twentieth century were characterized, according to many new publications, by an 'iconic turn'. Academic attention has trained on the medium of pictures in many disciplines and subjects, and indeed new disciplines (such as media science, film science, etc.) have emerged.[4] The iconic turn correlates with the enormously increased importance of pictures (photos, film, TV, etc.)

---

[3]Cf.: C. Uehlinger, Exodus, Stierbild und biblisches Kultbildverbot, in C. Hardmeier, R. Kessler and A. Rume (eds.), *Freiheit und Recht* (Festschrift F. Crüsemann, Gütersloh: Gütersloher Verlagshaus, 2003), pp. 42–77. For an image of the completely anthropomorphic figure on the throne on the unique 'Drachma of Yehud' see H. Gitler, and O. Tal, *Coinage of Philistia of the 5th and 4th Centuries BC: A Study of the Earliest Coins of Palestine* (Collezioni Numismatiche 6, Milan and New York: Ennere and Amphora Books, 2006), p. 230.

[4]Cf. for iconic turn: W. J. T. Mitchell, *Picture Theory: Essays on Verbal and Visual Representation* (Chicago: University of Chicago Press, 1994); H. Belting, *Bild und Kult: eine Geschichte des Bildes vor dem Zeitalter der Kunst* (7th edn, Munich: C. H. Beck Verlag, 2011). English: *Likeness and Presence: A History of the Image before the Era of Art* (trans. E. Jephcott, Chicago: University of Chicago Press, 1997); H. Belting, *Bild-Anthropologie. Entwürfe für ein Bildwissenschaft* (4th edn, Munich: Willhelm Fink Verlag, 2011). English: *An Anthropology of Images. Picture, Medium, Body* (trans. T. Dunlap; Princeton: Princeton University Press, 2011); G. von Graevenitz et al. (eds.), *Die Unvermeidlichkeit der Bilder* (Literatur und Anthropologie 7, Tübingen: Gunter Narr Verlag, 2001); H. Burda and C. Maar (eds.), *Iconic turn. Die neue Macht der Bilder* (2nd edn, Köln: DuMont Buchverlag, 2004), Online available: http://www.iconicturn.de, Hubert Burda Stiftung (München); H. Burda (ed.), *The digital Wunderkammer: 10 chapters on the iconic turn* (Munich: Willhelm Fink Verlag, Paderborn: Petrarca, 2011); E. Nordhofen (ed.), *Bilderverbot: Die Sichtbarkeit des Unsichtbaren* (Ikon: Bild + Theologie, Paderborn: Schöningh Verlag, 2001); B. Janowski and N. Zchomelidse (eds.), *Die Sichtbarkeit des Unsichtbaren: Zur Korrelation von Text und Bild im Wirkungskreis der Bibel* (AGWB 3; Stuttgart: Deutsche Bibelgesellschaft, 2002); R. M. E. Jacobi, B. Marx and G. Strohmaier-Wiederanders (eds.), *Im Zwischenreich der Bilder* (EuG 35; Leipzig: Evangelische Verlagsanstalt, 2004); A. Wagner, V. Hörner and G. Geisthardt (eds.), *Gott im Wort - Gott im Bild: Bilderlosigkeit als Bedingung des Monotheismus?* (2nd edn, Neukirchen-Vluyn: Neukirchener, 2008).

in the last century. Alongside the general move towards pictures – not independent of it but rather encouraged by it – we find an increased interest in material pictures within Old Testament exegesis in the last third of the twentieth century. This is due, of course, to the increasing availability of source material from the temporal and geographical context of the Old Testament, and the discovery of further pictorial material.[5] One can safely conclude that material images have become an important topic in Old Testament studies.

Secondly, new research on the body and concepts of the body provided the decisive impetus for this investigation of the image of God in the Old Testament. The body has become an important topic for the humanities and cultural science in an era where its partial 'technical reproduction' has become possible. It has been shown that basic corporeal concepts are subject to cultural and historical change. Attitudes towards the body (friendly or hostile) differ historically and culturally. We have become aware of the connection between parts of the body and communication, the relation between corporeal and non-corporeal parts of humans, the variance of body ideals according to social class, the body as a necessary precondition for recognition and so on. A transdisciplinary field has opened up that has also borne fruit in Old Testament studies.[6]

---

[5]Cf. for material pictures in Old Testament context: O. Keel, *The Symbolism of the Biblical World. Ancient Near Eastern Iconography and the Book of Psalms* (trans. T. J. Hallett; New York: Seabury Press, 1978); O. Keel and C. Uehlinger, *Gods, Goddesses, and Images of God in Ancient Israel* (Minneapolis, MN: Fortress Press, 1998); O. Keel and C. Uehlinger, *Altorientalische Miniaturkunst. Die ältesten visuellen Massenkommunikationsmittel: Ein Blick in die Sammlungen des Biblischen Instituts der Universität Freiburg Schweiz* (Darmstadt: P. von Zabern Verlag, 1990); Schroer and Keel, *Die Ikonographie Palästinas/Israels und der Alte Orient. Eine Religionsgeschichte in Bildern*; and many other studies connected with O. Keel, S. Schroer, C. Uehlinger et al.; cf. for A. Berlejung, *Die Theologie der Bilder: Herstellung und Einweihung von Kultbildern in Mesopotamien und die alttestamentliche Bilderpolemik* (OBO 162; Göttingen: Vandenhoeck & Ruprecht Verlag, 1998). Further reading: T. Podella, 'Bild und Text: Mediale und historische Perspektiven auf das alttestamentliche Bilderverbot', in: *SJOT* 15 (2001), pp. 205–56; J. Ebach, Die Einheit von Sehen und Hören: Beobachtungen und Überlegungen zu Bilderverbot und Sprachbildern im Alten Testament, in Jacobi, Marx and Strohmaier-Wiederanders (eds.), *Im Zwischenreich der Bilder*, pp. 77–104; I. J de Hulster and J. M. LeMon (eds.), *Image, Text, Exegesis. Iconographic Interpretation and the Hebrew Bible* (LHB.OT 588; London and New York: Bloomsbury, 2014).
[6]Important literature on corporeal concepts: General: H. Schmitz, *System der Philosophie, Vol. 3.1: Der leibliche Raum* (Space of the Felt Body) (3rd edn, Bonn: Bouvier, 1998); H. Schmitz, *System der Philosophie, Vol. 3.2: Der Gefühlsraum* (The Space of Emotions) (3rd edn, Bonn: Bouvier, 1998); H. Schmitz, *System der Philosophie, Vol. 3.5: Die Wahrnehmung* (Perception) (2nd edn, Bonn: Bouvier, 1989). Further reading: C. Benthien, *Haut: Literaturgeschichte – Körperbilder – Grenzdiskurse* (Rohwolts Enzyklopädie 55626, Reinbek: Rowohlt Verlag, 1999); C. Benthien, *Im Leibe wohnen: Literarische Imagologie und historische Anthropologie der Haut* (Körper, Zeichen, Kultur 4; Berlin: Berlin Verlag Spitz, 1998); M. Egidi et al. (eds.), *Gestik. Figuren des Körpers in Text und Bild* (Literatur und Anthropologie 8, Tübingen: Narr-Verlag, 2000), pp. 11–41; E. Fischer-Lichte and A. Fleig (eds.), *Körper-Inszenierungen: Präsenz*

Increased interest in depictions and the availability of Ancient Oriental-Old Testament material, as well as new considerations and knowledge of interpreting the body, are crucial keys for understanding the figure of God. To explain more clearly:

a   The comprehension of depictions is subject to historical change. If we want to understand Ancient Oriental-Old Testament depictions then we must immerse ourselves in their pictorial world, since it produced an understanding not congruent with ours. We must inquire into the 'seeing' which differs from ours.[7]

It is not easy to discern what constitutes 'our' understanding and 'our' view of images. Without intending to generalize too much we can say that both the phenomenon of pictures and our reactions to them are varied and complex. Characteristic of our pictorial world is a flood of images and our methods of critique, both of which are influenced by European/Western traditions.

We are all familiar with a flood of images, which greet us on a daily basis. Most of us consume huge quantities every day – TV images, film, photos, advertisements, art and so on. Our experience is that all these pictures, whether they move or not, are initially seen

---

und Kultureller Wandel (Tübingen: Attempto Verlag, 2000), pp. 7–17; J. Funk and C. Brück (eds.), *Körper-Konzepte* (Literatur und Anthropologie 5; Tübingen: Gunter Narr, 1999); A. Hübler, *Das Konzept "Körper" in den Sprach- und Kommunikationswissenschaften* (UTB 2182: Linguistik, Tübingen and Basel: Francke, 2001); M. Schmitz-Emans, 'Der Körper und seine Bindestriche: Zu Analysen der Ambiguität des Körperlichen und zur Dialektik seiner Modellierungen im wissenschaftlichen Diskurs der Gegenwart', in: *KulturPoetic* 1/2 (2001), pp. 275–89. Cf.; for literature in English in preface footnote no. 6. For Old Testament/Ancient Oriental: G. Baumann, Die 'Männlichkeit' JHWHs: Ein Neuansatz im Deutungsrahmen altorientalischer Gottesvorstellungen, in F. Crüsemann (ed.), *Dem Tod nicht glauben: Sozialgeschichte der Bibel* (Festschrift für Luise Schottroff zum 70. Geburtstag, Gütersloh: Gütersloher Verlag, 2004), pp. 197–213; G. Baumann, JHWHs Körper und die Gender-Frage, in Hedwig-Jahnow-Forschungsprojekt (ed.), *Körperkonzepte im Ersten Testament: Aspekte einer Feministischen Anthropologie*, (Stuttgart: Kohlhammer, 2003, pp. 220–50); J. Ebach, Gott ist kein Mann – aber warum? in Crüsemann (ed.), *Dem Tod nicht glauben: Sozialgeschichte der Bibel*, pp. 214–32; F. Hartenstein, 'Das Angesicht JHWHs: Studien zu seinem höfischen und kultischen Bedeutungshintergrund in den Psalmen und in Exodus 32–34', (FAT 55; Tübingen: Mohr Siebeck, 2008); F. Hartenstein, Die unvergleichliche 'Gestalt' JHWHs: Israels Geschichte mit den Bildern im Licht von Dtn 4,1–40, in Janowski and Zchomelidse (eds.), *Die Sichtbarkeit des Unsichtbaren*, pp. 49–77; Hedwig-Jahnow-Forschungsprojekt (ed.), *Körperkonzepte im Ersten Testament: Aspekte einer Feministischen Anthropologie* (Stuttgart: Kohlhammer, 2003); T. Podella, *Das Lichtkleid JHWHs: Untersuchungen zur Gestalthaftigkeit Gottes im Alten Testament und seiner altorientalischen Umwelt* (FAT 15; Tübingen: Mohr Siebeck, 1996); A. Schart, 'Die «Gestalt» YHWHs: Ein Beitrag zur Körpermetaphorik alttestamentlicher Rede von Gott', in: *ThZ* 55 (1999), pp. 26–43; Schroer and Staubli, *Body Symbolism in the Bible*.
[7]Cf.: Hartenstein, *Die unvergleichliche 'Gestalt' JHWHs*, p. 50: 'Are the senses, in particular seeing, appreciated in the texts of the Hebrew bible in the same way as we do today and do they have the same semantic field?' Cf.: Belting, *An Anthropology of Images. Picture, Medium, Body.*

on a flat surface, a screen, a canvas or paper. These two-dimensional
materials provide the information we need in order to convert them
into three dimensional depictions in our heads. This process is so
familiar that we do not realize that we had to learn how to do it.

The critique starts at this point of our normal, unconscious
process. Images in the mass media do not demand 'a complex
understanding process'; the television picture 'relies on a passive
attitude on the part of the consumer; it wants to impress our
emotions and senses and does not demand sophisticated cognitive
processing', as Bettina Hurrelmann relates when drawing on the
work of Neil Postman.[8]

Blanket rejection of images should be handled with care.
Similarly, we should be cautious about polarizing between 'bad'
or deceptive pictures, which rely on passive consummation, and
the 'good' heard or written word. Pictures do not threaten human
or theological rationality per se. Mindful of the non-pictorial
Protestant tradition, we should be wary of such denigrations.
Moreover, considering the peculiarities of Ancient Oriental
pictorial 'language', such blanket denigration makes little sense
(see Chapter 4). 'Images are first and foremost artefacts, which
confront the gaze with particular aspects of a concrete or virtual
reality. ... [T]he viewing of images – in the sense of examination,
contemplation, and analysis – is not a facility inherent to the human
being. Like speaking, viewing is a culturally mediated competence
that needs to be developed and cultivated.'[9] If this 'culturally
mediated competence' or skill is imparted culturally, then it differs
according to the culture. This skill is my concern here; learning to
understand a culture that is not our own demands a certain amount
of effort. We have grown up with a perspective pictorial culture,
but in order to understand pictures from Ancient Oriental cultures,
we must first agree to the conditions necessary for understanding
this very different pictorial culture. Then we will gain a new
understanding of the image of God.

b   The perception of man and his body varies in different cultures and
at various times within one culture. Modern historical anthropology
has discovered a new, broad field of research. The understanding
of the 'depiction of the body as an act of communication' valid for

[8]B. Hurrelmann, Kinder und Medien, in: K. Merten, S. J. Schmidt and S. Weischenberg (eds.),
Die Wirklichkeit der Medien. Eine Einführung in die Kommunikationswissenschaft (Opladen:
Springer VS, 1994), pp. 377–407.
[9]L. Giuliani, *Bild und Mythos: Geschichte der Bilderzählung in der griechischen Kunst* (Munich:
C. H. Beck, 2003). English: *Image and Myth. A History of Pictorial Narration in Greek Art*
(trans. by J. O'Donnell, Chicago: University of Chicago Press, 2013), p. xii.

the Ancient Orient and the Old Testament varies substantially from modern understanding of the body.[10]

The understanding of the body has of course a great influence on anthropomorphic concepts. Each anthropomorphic concept must be understood on the basis of the anthropological context of its respective culture and time. To put it another way, since images of humans change with the times, anthropomorphism is not always the same. If we try to understand Old Testament anthropomorphism with our modern preconceptions of the human form, then misunderstanding is certain. Here, too, we must work at acquiring the knowledge necessary to facilitate understanding.

1.3 Anthropomorphisms, role ascriptions and comparisons

In order to set parameters, I point out here that I will concentrate on anthropomorphisms which concern God's body directly. Roles ascribed to God will not be taken into account, such as God as the father (2 Sam. 7.14, Deut. 32.6, Isa. 63.16 i.a.), God as the king (Isa. 43.15, Isa. 44.6, Ps. 97.1), God as a war hero (Exod. 15.3), God as judge (Ps. 58.12), God as shepherd (Ps. 23.1), God as midwife (Ps. 22.10–11, Job 10.18) and many others. These could be called anthropomorphisms and verbal images in a wider sense. However, as the short previous overview has shown, they depict God in manifold roles, not specified by gender.

In addition, I shall also not consider explicit comparisons that use a comparative particle, for example comparisons involving 'as' or 'like' (Hebr. *k/kn* etc.).[11]

Ps. 103.13 *As a father has compassion on his children, so the Lord has compassion on those who fear him.*

Isa. 66.13 *As one whom his mother comforts, so I will comfort you. You will be comforted over Jerusalem.*

---

[10]A. Wagner, Das synthetische Bedeutungsspektrum hebräischer Körperteilbezeichnungen, in: K. Müller and A. Wagner (eds.), *Synthetische Körperauffassung im Hebräischen und den Sprachen der Nachbarkulturen* (AOAT 416; Münster: Ugarit Verlag, 2014), pp. 1–11.
[11]Here, the newer metaphor theory goes in another direction, as in: G. Lakoff and M. Johnson, *Metaphors We Live By* (Chicago: University of Chicago Press, 1980), where comparisons with comparative particles are included in the phenomenon of metaphor theory. However, I do not wish to go into this in further detail here.

Hos. 5.14 *For I will be **like** a lion to Ephraim and **as** a young lion to the house of Judah. I, even I, will tear and go away; I will carry away and no-one will rescue.*

Hos. 5.12 *And I am **like** pus for Ephraim and **as** rottenness for the house of Judah.*

A great distance prevails between the things with which God is compared, and God himself. This same distance is not found in terms used directly for God's body. Thus, terms used directly for God's body are clearly distinct from comparisons and, as such, can be seen as 'direct anthropomorphisms'.

1.4 The structure of this book

The structure of this book builds on what has been established previously. Chapter 2 provides a first attempt to unravel the correlation between the depiction of God's body and the picture of the human body. This presupposes that we take into account just how open the Old Testament really was to verbal images, in light of the prohibition on images. Chapter 3 discusses anthropomorphism as seen to date. Chapter 4 is an introduction to the specific understanding of images and of the body in the Ancient Orient and the Old Testament. Chapter 5 then turns to the theological assertions of Old Testament anthropomorphism. Chapter 6 investigates the correlation between depictions of God in human form and humans who are made in the image of God, that is, where God's anthropomorphism and human's theomorphism confront each other. Chapter 7 considers the significance of Old Testament speech about and with God in human form.

2

The 'picture' of God – Yhwh in the corporeal form of man

2.1 Images of God and the prohibition of images

Prohibitions have an essential function in life and thought. We must, therefore, reflect on the character of prohibitions and their Old Testament linguistic forms before we discuss the prohibition of images.

Prohibitions create distinctions	*Prohibitions open up spaces*
Prohibitions erect borders, erect prohibited zones which nobody may enter without being sanctioned. Prohibitions restrict human action and curtail freedom.	*Prohibitions act as fences which protect the area they enclose. They protect spheres of life, thought and understanding without which life would not be possible in this world.*

The Old Testament prohibition of murder – 'You shall not murder' (Exod. 20.13/Deut. 5.17) – forbids killing humans.[1] Nobody may commit murder without having to answer for his action. A limit is set and violation of it is sanctioned. This prohibition, however, also provides sheltered space for all. Within this sheltered space, the law applies, no one is at the mercy of others

---

[1]The prohibition of killing 'prohibits "illegal," "wrongful," "non-communal," unlawful-unjustified, "unauthorized" killing', W. H. Schmidt (with H. Delkurt and A. Graupner), *Die Zehn Gebote im Rahmen alttestamentlicher Ethik* (EdF 281, Darmstadt: Wissenschaftliche Buchgesellschaft, 1993), p. 109. Cf.: C. Dohmen, *Exodus 1-18/19-40* (HthKAT, Freiburg im Breisgau: Herder, 2004), p. 122; T. Veijola, *Das fünfte Buch Mose: Deuteronomium* (ATD 8,1, Göttingen: Vandenhoeck & Ruprecht, 2004), pp. 166–7; M. Köckert, *Die Zehn Gebote* (BSR 2430; München: C. H. Beck, 2007); D. Markl (ed.), *The Decalogue and Its Cultural Influence* (HBM 58; Sheffield: Sheffield Phoenix Press, 2014).

nor may any person murder another. The prohibition of murder makes this place for living dependable, indeed it makes it possible for humans to live together. No one need fear that he or she will be killed when a conflict rears its ugly head or when someone feels like committing murder. The prohibition on murder is the basis for coexistence. *You shall not murder* secures life.[2]

The exact forms of speech with which the Old Testament expresses prohibitions must be observed closely.[3] As in the Decalogue, in the Ten Commandments, prohibitions are generally found in connection with legal statements and collections of laws. There are vast numbers of legal statements of all kinds in the Old Testament (Decalogue in Exod. 20/Deut. 5, Book of the Covenant in Exod. 20–23, Holiness Code in Lev. 17–26, Deuteronomy Law in Deut. 12–26 etc.). Legal statements like the following appear often:

Exod. 21.18–19

v.18 *If men quarrel and one hits the other with a stone or with his fist and he does not die but is confined to bed, v.19 and recovers and walks around outside with his staff,*	Statement of the facts
the one who struck the blow will not be held responsible but he must pay the injured man for the loss of his time and for the medical costs.	Statement of the consequences

This type of legal statement, which concerns a single case with an *if*-formula, is called *casuistic*. Casuistic legal statements are intended to facilitate justice and are a manual for adjudicating on individual cases.[4]

---

[2]The differentiation and opening up of space refers to the 'Mosaic differentiation' described by Jan Assmann, cf.: J. Assmann, *Moses der Ägypter: Entzifferung einer Gedächtnisspur* (München: Hanser, 1998) English: *Moses the Egyptian: The Memory of Egypt in Western Monotheism* (Cambridge, MA: Harvard University Press, 1997); J. Assmann, Monotheismus und Ikonoklasmus als politische Theologie, in E. Otto and J. Assmann (eds.), *Mose: Ägypten und das Alte Testament* (SBS 189; Stuttgart: Verlag Katholisches Bibelwerk, 2000), pp. 121–39; J. Assmann, *Die Mosaische Unterscheidung: oder der Preis des Monotheismus* (Edition Akzente München: Carl Hanser, 2003). English: *The Price of Monotheism* (trans. R. Savage; Stanford, CA: Stanford University Press, 2010). The verbal picture of space not only characterizes the manner in which prohibitions function but also the particular character of the Israelite Yhwh-religion, at least in the later form which determined the Old Testament in the form we know. Comparative formulations for Old Testament prohibitions exist, cf.: P. Mommer, W. H. Schmidt and H. Straus (eds.), *Gottes Recht als Lebensraum* (Festschrift für Hans Jochen Boecker, Neukirchen-Vluyn: Neukirchen, 1993).
[3]Cf.: H. J. Boecker, *Recht und Gesetz im Alten Testament und im Alten Orient* (NStB 10; Neukirchen-Vluyn: Neukirchener, 1976). English: *Law and the Administration of Justice in the Old Testament and Ancient East* (trans. J. Moiser; London: Society für Promoting Christian Knowledge, 1980); T. Frymer-Kensky, Israel, in: R. Westbrook (ed.), *A History of Ancient Near Eastern Law* (HdO 1,72; The Near and Middle East, Leiden: Brill, 2003), pp. 975–1046.
[4]Frymer-Kensky, Israel, p. 978, which refers to the classic study by A. Alt, *Die Ursprünge des israelitischen Rechts* (BVSAW 86,1; Leipzig: Hirzel, 1934). English: *Origins of Israelite Law* in: Id (ed.), *Essays on Old Testament History and Religion*, (Garden City, NY: Doubleday, 1966); Casuistic legal statements are still given today, cf.: Dohmen, *Exodus*, p. 149.

Legal statements of the sort found in the Ten Commandments differ distinctly. The phrasing is completely different; let us consider Exod. 20.17: *You shall not murder*. The elements of the offence are not ascertained here, nor any consequences drawn. The sentence is not divided into two parts but is unilinear. In Hebrew, it is formed with a verb form negated by the particle *l'o* (preformative conjunction), the strongest type of negation in Hebrew. The phrase *You shall not murder* must be understood as a fundamental rule, it irrefutably forbids (unlawful, see fn.1) murder without any evasive option. Legal statements of this kind are therefore called *apodictic*.[5] Unlike casuistic legal statements which settle individual cases, apodictic statements regulate basic issues fundamentally.

Sometimes an explanation is added to make a statement more understandable, for example, Exod. 23.9 *Do not oppress an alien for you yourselves know how it feels to be aliens, because you yourselves were aliens in Egypt*. Such explanations are most apparent in apodictic statements. In the Decalogue, too, the prohibition of imagery and the prohibition against working on the Sabbath are substantiated. If we consider the reasoning given for apodictic legal statements, we find two aspects: (a) admonitory recollections of historical experiences and (b) general social motivation. These are *specific* to Israel and are not found in comparable Ancient Oriental legal statements. This once again underlines their importance.[6]

Apodictic legal statements in the Old Testament are often compiled in series (cf. Dodecalogue in Lev. 18, also Lev. 19, Exod. 34.10–35, Deut. 27).

The observation of the correct legal form in the Ten Commandments of the Decalogue is immensely important since it indicates that the legal statements in Exod. 20.1–17/Deut. 5.6–21 are apodictic statements, absolute and universal prohibitions which are understood as expressing the divine

---

[5]This term can be traced to Alt, *Die Ursprünge des israelitischen Rechts*. English: *Origins of Israelite Law*. For more on this issue, cf.: Boecker, *Recht und Gesetz im Alten Testament und im Alten Orient*, pp. 191–207; Otto: 'Dekalog. I. Altes Testament', in RGG⁴ 2 (1999) pp. 625–28. English: 'Decalogue. I. Old Testament', RPP 3 (2007), pp. 709–12. Sometimes such statements are named 'prohibitive', but there is no uniform linguistic form, cf. for example: Dohmen, *Exodus*, p. 91. Dohmen calls 'apodictic' legal statements in the Decalogue 'prohibitives' (preformative conjugation, negated with *lo*ʾ), other grammarians name preformative conjugations negated with ʾ*al* as prohibitive, cf.: R. Meyer, *Hebräische Grammatik* (Berlin and New York: deGruyter, 1992), p. 75. I do not intend to make further derivations with the term 'apodictic' as far as their roots in divine law are concerned; I consider 'apodictic' the best term to express the unconditional validity of this type of legal statement.

[6]Therefore Boecker says: 'The motive deprives OT law of the authoritarian stamp which legal principles normally bear'. Boecker, *Recht und Gesetz im Alten Testament und im Alten Orient*, p. 205; cf.: Frymer-Kensky, *Israel*, p. 979: 'Fifty percent of biblical laws have a clause attached that may underline the origin of the law, make a promise for keeping it, explain the reason for it, hold out threats, and give purpose for the laws'. For the justification of the prohibition of imagery see subsequent notes.

will. They are cardinal indicators of standpoint, and orientation in belief
and conduct for mankind.[7]

The prohibition of imagery creates distinctions

Our contemplation of the 'picture' of God in the Old Testament must begin
with the apodictic Old Testament prohibition of imagery. From a present-
day perspective, 'the' prohibition of imagery is one of the most formative
characteristics of the Old Testament concept of God.[8] The Old Testament
God desires to be revered without images. The prohibition of imagery, in
particular in the Decalogue, makes this very clear. Indeed, the absence of
images becomes the symbol by which the Old Testament God is recognized.
It becomes the distinctive criterion.[9]

As with the prohibition of murder, we should not only emphasize
the restrictive aspect of the prohibition of imagery, nor the fundamental
prohibition of images of God, pictures of Yhwh. The prohibition of imagery
rather also holds possibilities through this distinction, in the sense of
unforeseen breaking fresh grounds.

---

[7]For a literary-historical discussion on the Decalogue, cf.: F. Crüsemann, *Die Tora: Theologie
und Sozialgeschichte des alttestamentlichen Gesetzes* (München: Chr. Kaiser, 1992), passim.
English: *The Torah. Theology and Social History of Old Testament Law* (Minneapolis:
Fortress Press, 1996), passim; Schmidt, et al., *Die Zehn Gebote im Rahmen alttestamentlicher
Ethik*; Otto, *Dekalog. I. Altes Testament*, pp. 709–12; A. Graupner, Die zehn Gebote im
Rahmen alttestamentlicher Ethik, in H. G. Reventlow (ed.), *Weisheit, Ethos und Gebot:
Weisheits- und Dekalogtraditionen in der Bibel und im frühen Judentum* (BThSt 43;
Neukirchen-Vluyn: Neukirchener, 2001), pp. 61–95; E. Aurelius, 'Der Ursprung des ersten
Gebots', in: *ZThK* 100 (2003), pp. 1–21; Dohmen, *Exodus*, pp. 82–137; Veijola, *Das fünfte
Buch Mose. Deuteronomium*, pp. 125–73; C. Frevel, et al. (eds.), *Die Zehn Worte: der Dekalog
als Testfall der Pentateuchkritik* (QD 212; Freiburg im Breisgau: Herder, 2005); A. Diesel, '*Ich
bin Jahwe': der Aufstieg der Ich-bin-Jahwe-Aussage zum Schlüsselwort des alttestamentlichen
Monotheismus* (WMANT 110; Neukirchen-Vluyn: Neukirchener, 2006), pp. 224–38;
Köckert, *Die Zehn Gebote*.
[8]The use of quotation marks indicates that the prohibition of imagery had not always existed
and was not uniform as the Decalogue suggests. We may expect a historical development of
the prohibition of imagery, too, which can be reconstructed by historical analytical work on
Old Testament texts. The Old Testament is the result of and witness to a development of the
Israelite faith over centuries. Certain experiences took place in ever differing historical, social,
cultural and religious situations so that the pertinent texts had to be revisited, considered as to
their relevance, and changed accordingly. The understanding of the prohibition of imagery
changed in the course of history.
[9]Gerhard von Rad emphasized the differential function. Regarding the prohibition of imagery
in the Old Testament 'we shall be on the right track if, with Israels' religious environment in
mind, we understand the commandment as the expression of an utterly different view of the
world'. G. von Rad, *Theologie des Alten Testaments, Vol. 1* (EETh 1; München: Chr. Kaiser,
1987). English: *Old Testament Theology. Vol. 1* (trans. by D. M. G. Stalker; London: S. C. M.
Press, 1975), pp. 217–18. A. Wagner, Alttestamentlicher Monotheismus und seine Bindung an
das Wort, in Wagner, *Gott im Wort - Gott im Bild*, pp. 1–22.

The prohibition of imagery in the Decalogue

To begin with we must clarify which 'images' are affected by the prohibition. The central texts here are the versions of the Decalogue found in Exod. 20 and Deut. 5.[10]

Exod. 20.4–6, Deut. 5.8–10

> v.3 *You shall have no other Gods before me.* v.4 **You shall not make any** **pæsæl (idol)** *and (no) likeness of things in heaven above, on earth below or what is in the water under the earth.* v.5 *Do not bow down to* **them** *(to worship them) and do not serve* **them**!

Them can refer to *pæsæl* + likeness and must not necessarily refer to the *other Gods* (v.3).

> v.7 *You shall have no other Gods before me.* v.8 **You shall not make any** **pæsæl (idol)** *of any form as it is in heaven above, on earth below and in the water under the earth.* v.9 *Do not bow down to* **them** *(to worship them) and do not serve them!*

Them can only refer here to the *other Gods* (v.7)

> *For I am Yhwh, your God, (am) a jealous God who visits the sins of the fathers on the children to the third and fourth generation of those who hate me,* v.6/v.10 *but who is faithful to thousands who love me and keep my commandments.*

Legal texts like the Decalogue state God's will in directive precepts for mankind, in a condensed form. They tend to stand at the end of the reflective process on justice and the behaviour of mankind rather than at the beginning. The Decalogue in Exod. 20 and Deut. 5, as we know it today, is a late legal text which, however, contains older components.[11]

---

[10]The prohibition of imagery is not limited to both versions of the Decalogue. 'The Hebrew Bible does not record a unitary prohibition of images; it is formulated in several ways, which cannot be traced to a single original. The functional relationship of the various texts is shown by the appearance of the prohibition in one form or another in a prominent position in each of the major legal corpora'. C. Uehlinger, '*Bilderverbot*', *RGG*[4] 1 (1998) pp. 1574–77. English: '*Prohibition of Images*', RPP 10 (2011), pp. 420–2, here: 420. Cf. e.g.: Exod. 34.14.17, Lev. 19.4, Exod. 20.23, Deut. 27.15. For a discussion of the relevant texts, C. Dohmen, *Das Bilderverbot: seine Entstehung und seine Entwicklung im Alten Testament* (BBB 62; Frankfurt: Athenäum, 1987).
[11]Cf.: Crüsemann, *Die Tora*, Schmidt, *Die Zehn Gebote im Rahmen alttestamentlicher Ethik*; Otto: *Dekalog. I. Altes Testament*, pp. 709–12; Graupner, *Die zehn Gebote im Rahmen alttestamentlicher Ethik*, pp. 61–95; Aurelius, Der Ursprung des ersten Gebots, pp. 1–21;

We can recognize additions to the Decalogue text, such as the clarifications added to the scant formulations (in **bold** type in the previous translation) at the beginning of the prohibitions. The differing developments of the core of the commandment illustrate the diverging paths taken by Exod. 20 and Deut. 5.

The prohibition of imagery forbids idols (pæsæl)

The Hebrew word *pæsæl* is crucial to both versions of the Decalogue's prohibition of imagery (pronounced päsäl, stressing the first ä, like the "a" in "man"). It means the handmade idol. The verb *psl* from which the noun is formed, is used for handmade production, mostly hewing wood and stone (letter-spaced in the following).

1 Kgs 5.18

And Solomon's craftsmen and Hiram's craftsmen hewed/and trimmed them (large stones); they prepared timber and stone in this way to build the house.

A *pæsæl* can be understood, therefore, as something that can be hewn, a sculptural, three-dimensional 'image'. On a few occasions, *pæsæl* is found in combination with *massekāh/finished product in precious metal, in particular in goldsmithing*. It then means 'a sculptural portrayal (*psl*) together with the necessary paraphernalia – for a cult idol – of the art of goldsmithing (*massekāh*)'.[12]

Idols from Israel's vicinity are made in this way, as texts and archaeological finds show. Most of the idols dating from the late Bronze Age through to the Iron Age in Palestine are not larger than 15 cm; a few surviving fragments suggest larger statues (up to life-sized). A. Berlejung describes the appearance of such idols (independent of size) as follows:

1. The *head* of the image is wrought with the most details: most of the gods have a crown, some have chin-length hair and a beard. Eyes, eyebrows, mouth, ears and nose are clearly recognisable. ...

   The *eyes* of the bronze and composite statues are usually inlayed, so that they look human. The arched eyebrows, (generally) unconnected over the bridge of the nose, are fashioned out of coloured material and mounted on the statue. ...

Dohmen, *Exodus*, pp. 82–137; Köckert, *Die Zehn Gebote*. Christoph Dohmen, Decalogue, in: T. B. Dozeman, C. A. Evans and J. N. Nohr (eds.), *The Book of Exodus: Composition, Reception, and Interpretation* (VT.S 164; Leiden and Boston: Brill, 2014), pp. 193–219; Markl (ed.), *The Decalogue and its Cultural Influence*.
[12]C. Dohmen, 'פסל *psl*', ThWAT 6 (1989), pp. 688-97, here 692.

The *hair* on the bronzes, if it was thought of at all, was cast with the figure. The *beard* could be inserted expressly, and was of a naturalistic black colour. ...

The *skin* was ideally made of gold or silver, with which they were entirely coated. ...

The accentuated *faces* and *hands* of the figures show that in Palestine, too, the faces and hands of the gods received particular attention. Establishing contact with the gods was concentrated here [as in Mesopotamia] on these points. ...

2. *Posture, feet* and *arms*: in straight frontal posture the gods were shown sitting upright as well as standing on a small pedestal, whereby the left foot was more or less placed to the fore. The soles always stand firmly on the ground. ...

Since *gestures* are also acts of communication, the body language of the statues allows us to see how the gods were perceived, or were intended to be perceived by their worshippers.

If the armed right arm was raised to strike, the left forearm bent and thrust out or pointed down (the left foot placed to the fore), then the usual intention of this posture was to signalise sovereignty and predominance.

We often find sitting deities who raise their right hand in greeting or benediction, signaling positive contact with the supplicant. ...

Since the LBA [late Bronze Age] female deities are equipped with clothing and accompanying attributes. Their gestures indicate (standing) benedictive, martial figures and accord to corresponding male role models. ...

3. *Clothing and jewellery*: the figures show that the gods were dressed in short or long clothes, belts and crowns and sometimes wore shoes. Jewellery can rarely be substantiated but we often find earlobe piercing to which earrings could be attached. Jewellery and clothing accentuate the neck and hips. The statues were mounted on their pedestals with a gudgeon so that they appeared to be even larger.[13]

Figures 2.1 and 2.2 should at least allow an impression of such cult objects.[14]

We also have pictorial representations of gods on stele, such as the god Melkart. Research suggests that only the statuesque figures or idols were dressed and fed and so on. The similarity of the statues to humans suggests that it is possible to treat divine bodies like human ones, while devotion to the gods is expressed by caring for the figures.

---

[13]Berlejung, *Die Theologie der Bilder*, pp. 296–99.
[14]Cf. further pictures: ANEP; Keel and Uehlinger, *Gods, Goddesses, and Images of God in Ancient Israel*; H. E. F. W. Gressmann (ed.), Altorientalische Bilder zum Alten Testament (Berlin/Leipzig: deGruyter, ²1927)

FIGURE 2.1 *God from Minet el-Beida (close to Ugarit, Ancient Syria).* 'Figure of
*a god wearing a high crown (similar to white crown of Upper Egypt). A gold ring is
around his right arm, which is extended upwards as he brandishes a weapon (now
lost). The left hand extended forward, perhaps to grasp a lance or staff. Louvre,
Minet el-Beida. Bronze; headdress and head covered with gold, body with silver.
Height: 0.179 m. Fifteenth-fourteenth century ...' ANEP,* p. 305, fig. 481, p. 166.

The prohibition of imagery in the Decalogue prohibits idols (*pæsæl*) –
but which idols are forbidden, idols of Yhwh or idols of foreign gods? The
answer depends on our view of the history of the prohibition of imagery.
Two possible explanations have gained traction in the current discussion:

1. If something is forbidden, then some issue must have provoked
    the prohibition. One possibility is that the lack of depictions is
    a primeval element of the Yhwh religixon (an idol-less form of
    religion[15]). Violations then led to increasingly severe formulations

---

[15]Dohmen, *Das Bilderverbot*, pp. 276–7, cf. pp. 237–44. Dohmen attempted to trace the path
the prohibition took. In his opinion, it belonged to the origin of the Yhwh religion as an idol-
less form of religion, influenced to begin with by the first commandment which determined the
Yhwh religion increasingly from the ninth/eighth century onwards, drawing new contours and
finally becoming one of the main characteristics of the Yhwh religion: 'The intent to draw
boundaries before foreign gods and cultures [first commandment] could only be effective when
everything indicated in this direction. Pictures and symbols were most affected. The command-

FIGURE 2.2 *God from Megiddo: 'Bronze. Height: about 0,13 m. Late Bronze II (1350–1200).' ANEP, p. 307, fig. 496, p. 169.*

of the prohibition. It should be pointed out that although we do not have human depictions of Yhwh, we do find animal depictions (Exod. 32 'the golden calf') 'even if the ways in which these were understood remains obscure'.[16] In addition, the prohibition of imagery is related to the prohibition of foreign gods: The latter was the 'driving force' behind the increasingly severe formulations of the prohibition of imagery (C. Dohmen).[17]

2. The second possibility is that the prohibition of imagery only came into existence later; that is, the absence of images had not always been part of the Yhwh religion. C. Uehlinger sums it up when he writes that 'given the recent recognition that it [the prohibition of imagery] does not appear in any pre-exilic texts …', 'the prohibition

---

ment, you shall have no other gods before me, is the actual motor (for the rise of the main characteristic) and its concretion and led to the emergence (or rather the restructuring) of the prohibition of imagery (as found in the Decalogue)'.

[16]Schmidt, *Die Zehn Gebote im Rahmen alttestamentlicher Ethik*, p. 68.

[17]Cf.: Dohmen, *Exodus*, pp. 106–13. Also: 'The [second] commandment originally referred to pictures of Yhwh. Otherwise it would only repeat the prohibition of foreign gods. Later the two commandments were connected … . When later foreign gods became irrelevant for Israel and their existence was disclaimed, the increasingly strict understanding of the prohibition of imagery as the differential criteria came more and more to the fore'. Schmidt, *Die Zehn Gebote im Rahmen alttestamentlicher Ethik*, pp. 67–8.

FIGURE 2.3 *The god Milqart: 'Basalt. Height: 1.15 m.* 9th century BCE.' *ANEP,* p. 308, fig. 499, p. 170.

must be considered a problem related to the Judahite and early Jewish cult during the exilic and postexilic period'. Uehlinger points to the fact that in exile (that away from the Temple to which the idol was connected)' 'it was not (or no longer) possible to venerate a cultic image'. 'The exile quite likely contributed substantially to psychological emancipation from the image cult'; the Israelites had to develop 'new "mental" images' which 'did not need the material focus of a cultic object'. According to Uehlinger, the prohibition of foreign gods was decisive for the formulation or indeed the emergence of the prohibition of imagery. However, the assumption that a pre-exile cult image of Yhwh existed 'has been conjectured as an explanation, but is undocumented'.[18]

However we deduce the origin of the prohibition of imagery, it seems certain that through the intensification and the apodictic nature of the formulation in exilic/post-exilic texts (such as the Decalogue), it became an integral, enduring element of the Yhwh religion. Since then, it has remained a strong differential criterion to all other religions with which Israel and ancient Judaism came into contact.[19]

---

[18]Uehlinger, *Bilderverbot,* pp. 1574–77, Englisch: '*Prohibition of Images*', RPP 10 (2011), pp. 420–2, here: 421. Also: Uehlinger, *Exodus, Stierbild und biblisches Kultbildverbot,* pp. 42–77; O. Keel, Warum im Jerusalemer Tempel kein anthropomorphes Kultbild gestanden haben dürfte, in G. Boehm (ed.), *Homo pictor* (Colloquium Rauricum 7, München: K. G. Saur, 2001), pp. 244–81.
[19]Wagner, *Alttestamentlicher Monotheismus und seine Bindung an das Wort.*

The prohibition of imagery opens up new possibilities

Prohibitions not only create distinctions, they also open up new possibilities. The prohibition of material images of Yhwh opened the way for *verbal images* and for material images independent of idols. Verbal images are depicted in section 2.2. Thousands of material non-cult images existed in Ancient Israelite culture, as we now know from archaeological finds (cf. section 2.3). The prohibition of imagery only forbid images of Yhwh, but not pictorial depictions altogether. Since this work concentrates on the human or divine body, I will not discuss these depictions. Images of humans will be treated in section 2.3.

I should point out, however, that verbal–mental depictions can be refined into visual depictions in the imagination so that there is a fundamental relationship between verbal and material images.

2.2 The corporeal depiction of Yhwh and the corporeal depiction of man

Before we take a closer look at the peculiar characteristics of verbal images of God, we need to take an initial look at the verbal 'image' of God's external appearance itself. In the following survey, I have collected statements from the Old Testament which give an impression of the corporeal concept of God, restricted to external appearance. I will concentrate on the external appearance, for it is this which can be compared with the types of graphic or sculptural depictions that were the intended targets of image prohibition. To emphasize the analogy with the human external form, so striking in verbal 'depictions' of God, I have placed statements on the concept of the human body alongside those of God.

The 'depiction' of God only emerges as a depiction of the whole form when we reconstruct the whole figure, as it existed in the mind of the recipients of the texts. For these people many texts and images from various texts were present in the mind simultaneously. In time, things heard and read in the past can come together to build a whole 'image' of God. Although this reconstruction can make it easier to understand the following overview, it cannot replace consistent and prolonged contact with Old Testament texts.

The following examples give a first impression of the uninhibited manner in which Old Testament texts talk of God's corporeal form, the concept of the body of God. The equivalents of the human and the divine body are emphasized in Table 2.1, which is organized according to specific parts of the body. The reader should keep in mind that the number of texts is huge and only a few are mentioned here! Table 2.1 covers all forms of Old Testament literature from various eras. For the choice of body parts, and the frequency and distribution of the images, please see Chapter 5.

TABLE 2.1 *Matching of exemplary biblical references for the comparison of bodily forms of God and man, respectively*

Body part	Bodily form – external verbal 'image' of God	Bodily form – external verbal 'image' of man
roʾš head	Isa. 59.17 *He [Yhwh] put on righteousness as his breastplate and set the helmet of salvation on his head and put on the garments of revenge and attired himself with zeal as with a cloak.*	Num. 6.5 *As long as his vow lasts no razor shall be used on his head. He is holy until the time he has vowed himself to Yhwh has passed and he must allow the hair on his head to grow long.*
	Ps. 60.9 *[God has spoken in his sanctuary: ...] Gilead is mine, Manasseh is mine, Ephraim is the safeguard on my head, Judah is my sceptre* (par. Ps. 108.9).	Zech. 6.11 *Take silver and gold from them and make crowns and crown the head of Joshua, the high priest, the son of Jehozadak,*
	Dan. 7.9 *I saw how thrones were set in place, and one who was ancient sat down. His clothing was white as snow and the hair on his head pure as wool ...*	
pānîm face, countenance	Gen. 33.10 *Jacob answered: No, please! If I have found favour in your eyes, accept the gift from my hands; for I saw your face as if I saw God's countenance, and you were gracious to me.*	Gen. 43.31 *And after he [Joseph] had cried, had washed his face, he went out and controlled himself and said: Serve the food!*
	Job 2.7 *So Satan went out from the countenance of the Lord and afflicted Job with painful sores from the soles of his feet to the top of his head.*	2. Sam. 19.5 *But the King covered his face and cried aloud: O my son Absalom! Absalom, my son, my son!*
ʿayin eye	Amos 9.3 *And though they hide themselves on the Mount of Carmel, I will search for them and bring them down; and though they conceal themselves before my eyes at the bottom of the sea I will command the serpent to bite them there.*	Deut. 19.21 *Life for life, eye for eye, tooth for tooth, hand for hand, foot for foot.*
	Gen. 6.8 *But Noah found favour in the eyes of Yhwh.*	Ps. 6.8 *My eyes grow weak with sorrow and fail because I have so many foes.*

(Continued)

TABLE 2.1 *(Continued)*

Body part	Bodily form – external verbal 'image' of God	Bodily form – external verbal 'image' of man
ʾōzæn ear	2. Kgs 19.16 [Hezekiah says] *Yhwh,* **give ear** *and hear, open your eyes, and see and hear the words Sennacherib has sent to insult the living God.*	Exod. 32.2 *Aaron spoke to them: Take off the golden ear-rings on the* **ears** *of your wives, your sons and your daughters, and bring them to me.*
	2. Chron. 7.15 [the speaker is Yhwh] *Now my eyes will be open and* **my ears** *attentive to the prayer offered in this place.*	Ezek. 23.25 *I will direct my jealousy against you [Oholiba], and they will deal furiously with you. They will cut off your nose and your* **ears***, and what is left shall fall by the sword. They shall take your sons and your daughters and what remains of you shall be consumed by fire.*
ʾap nose	2. Sam. 22.9 *Smoke rose from his* **nostrils/nose** *and consuming fire from his mouth, flames came from him.*	Gen. 2.7 *And Yhwh God formed man out of earth from the field and blew the breath of life into his* **nostrils/nose***. And man became a living soul.*
	Isa. 65.5 [Yhwh talks about the disobedient] *They are smoke in* **my nostrils/nose***, a fire that burns the whole day.*	Prov. 30.33 *For when one churns milk it produces butter, and when one blows his* **nose** *hard, he forces out blood, and when one stirs up anger he produces strife.*
pæh mouth	Lev. 24.12 *And took him [a blaspheming Israelite] prisoner, until they received a clear answer from the* **mouth of Yhwh.**	Judg. 7.6 *The number of men who lapped was three hundred. All the rest of the people drank kneeling, from the hand to the* **mouth.**
	Ps. 33.6 *The heavens were made by the word of Yhwh and his host by the breath* **of his mouth.**	Song 1.2 *He kissed me with the kisses of his* **mouth***; for your love is more delightful than wine.*
næpæš throat, neck	Jer. 6.8 *Mend your ways, Jerusalem, before I turn my* **næpæš** *(neck?) from you and make you a desolate country, in which no-one lives!*	Ps. 69.2 *God, help me! For the water has come up to my* **neck.**
	Ezek. 23.18 *When she carried out her prostitution openly and exposed her nakedness, I turned my* **næpæš** *(neck?) ....*	Prov. 25.25 *Good news from a distant land is like cool water for a parched* **throat.**

(Continued)

TABLE 2.1 *(Continued)*

Body part	Bodily form – external verbal 'image' of God	Bodily form – external verbal 'image' of man
$z^e r\hat{o}^{ac}$ arm	Exod. 15.16 *Terror and dread fell upon them; they froze like stones in the face of* **your powerful arm,** *until your people, Yhwh, passed by, until the people passed by who you purchased.*	Ps. 18.35 *He teaches my hands to fight and* **my arm** *to bend the bronze bow.*
	Ps. 89.11 *You beat Rahab to death and scattered your enemies with* **your strong arm.**	Song 8.6 *Place me like a seal over your heart, like a seal over your* **arm** *...*
$y\bar{a}m\hat{i}n$ right hand	Isa. 62.8 *Yhwh has sworn by his* **right hand** *and by his mighty arm ...*	Gen. 48.13 *Then Joseph took them both, Ephraim on his* **right hand** *towards Israel's left hand and Manasseh by his left hand towards Israel's right hand, and brought them to him.*
	Ps. 48.11 *Like your name, O God, your glory reaches to the ends of the earth.* **Your right hand** *is filled with righteousness.*	Judg. 16.29 *And he [Samson] encompassed the two central pillars on which the house stood, one with his* **right** *and the other with his left* **hand,** *and braced himself against them.*
$y\bar{a}d$ hand	Jer. 18.6 *Can I not treat you, you from the house if Israel, as this potter does? Yhwh declares. Look, like clay in the hand of the potter, so are you in my* **hand,** *O house of Israel.*	Prov. 26.15 *The sluggard buries his* **hand** *in the dish, and he is too lazy to bring it to his mouth.*
	Ps. 75.9 *For Yhwh has a cup in his* **hand,** *filled to the brim with spiced wine.*	Song 5.4 *My friend thrust his* **hand** *through the latch hole, and my heart began to pound for him.*
$r\ae g\ae l$ foot (leg)	2. Sam. 22.10 *He [Yhwh] bowed the heavens and came down, and darkness was under* **his feet.**	Gen. 18.4 *Let a little water be brought to wash your* **feet,** *and take a seat under this tree.*
	Isa. 66.1 *This is what Yhwh says: Heaven is my throne and the earth is the footstool under* **my feet!** *...*	Jos. 5.15 *And the commander of Yhwh's army said to Joshua: Take your shoes off your* **feet;** *for the place where you are standing is holy. And Joshua did so.*

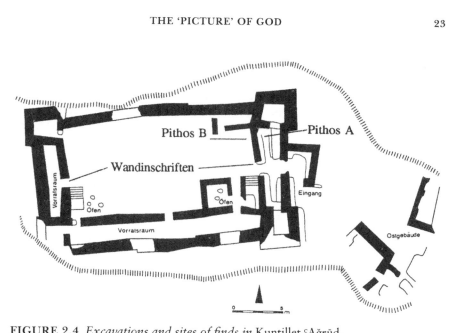

FIGURE 2.4 *Excavations and sites of finds in* Kuntillet ᶜAğrūd.

Source: Keel and Uehlinger, *Gods, Goddesses, and Images of God in Ancient Israel*, p. 211, fig. 218.

FIGURE 2.5 *The drawings on pithos B.*

Source: Keel and Uehlinger, *Gods, Goddesses, and Images of God in Ancient Israel*, p. 214, fig. 221.

It is not difficult, therefore, to reconstruct an idea of the body of God or the body of man from the various individual depictions found in the previously mentioned texts. The parallels between the corporeal images are just as clear.

Before we can analyse this verbal image further, we must consider the material images that were present in Ancient Israel. This will enable a new approach to the verbal image of man and the verbal image of God.

2.3 Israelite drawings/graphic depictions of man

Contrary to the widespread assumption that there were no pictures in Israel,[20] newer research has discovered a large number of various types of depiction. These have widened our knowledge of pictures in Ancient Israel and modified our understanding of the issue. A few years ago, a work entitled *In Israel gab es Bilder* (*Pictures existed in Israel*) caused a sensation.[21] Today research on pictures from Ancient Israel in the Syrian–Palestinian and the Ancient Oriental cultural context have become a fascinating and fertile discipline within Old Testament studies. The conviction that the prohibition of imagery extended to all types of images still has to be overcome in some, particularly protestant, minds.[22]

A more detailed examination of Israelite pictures with representations of the body/person will follow but for the moment I intend to cite just one very vivid example.

In the 1970s Israeli archaeologists led an excavation in the Jordan desert, around 50 kilometres South of Qadesch Barnea, in the ruins of *Kuntillet ʿAǧrūd*.[23] There they found the remains of a caravanserai.[24] Despite the location in the South of Israel, *Kuntillet ʿAǧrūd* does not belong to the

---

[20]Israel means Ancient Israel here and in the following, which builds the historical background of the texts of the Old Testament. It not only refers to the Northern Kingdom which was named Israel, but also to the whole geographical sphere which in more modern times is called 'Palestine/Israel', cf. Schroer and Keel, *IPIAO*; chronologically, we are referring to the timespan from the beginning of the Old Testament tradition to its completion.

[21]Schroer, *In Israel gab es Bilder*.

[22]Cf.: Keel and Uehlinger, *Gods, Goddesses, and Images of God in Ancient Israel*; Keel and Uehlinger, *Altorientalische Miniaturkunst*, pp. 9–23.

[23]Cf.: H. Weippert, *Palästina in vorhellenistischer Zeit* (Handbuch der Archäologie: Vorderasien 2, Vol. 1, München: Beck, 1988); Keel and Uehlinger, *Gods, Goddesses, and Images of God in Ancient Israel*; B. B. Schmidt, 'The iron age pithoi drawings from Horvat Teman or Kuntillet ʿAjrud: Some New Proposals', in: *JANER* 2 (2002), pp. 91–125; Z. Meshel, *Kuntillet ʿAjrud (Ḥorvat Teman): An Iron Age II religious site on the Judah-Sinai border* (Jerusalem: Israel Exploration Society, 2012).

[24]Cf.: Weippert, *Palästina in vorhellenistischer Zeit*, pp. 626–7. Other explanations for *Kuntillet ʿAǧrūd*, cf.; W. Zwickel, 'Überlegungen zur wirtschaftlichen und historischen Funktion von *Kuntillet ʿAǧrūd*', in: *ZDPV* 116.2 (2000), pp. 139–42; Meshel, *Kuntillet ʿAǧrūd (Ḥorvat Teman)*.

FIGURE 2.6 *Human representation from the drawing on pithos B from* Kuntillet ᶜAǧrūd.

Source: Keel and Uehlinger, *Gods, Goddesses, and Images of God in Ancient Israel*, p. 214, fig. 221

Judean sphere of influence: 'The mention of "Yahweh of Samaria" … the fact that the theophoric personal names found at *Kuntillet ᶜAǧrūd* are formed without exception using the element *-yw* (not *-yhw*)… the paleographic commonalities that link the pithos inscriptions [pithos see below] and the ostraca from Samaria … as well as the iconographically and epigraphically demonstrable combination of elements of (Syro-) Phoenician and Israelite culture all demonstrate clearly that the caravanserai at *Kuntillet ᶜAǧrūd* was not Judahite. It was set up using Phoenician "know-how" but was controlled by *Israelites* and had no local roots. It was probably in use no longer than one generation'.[25]

Archaeologists found two large storage pots, pithoi, close to the gates. They are named pithos A and pithos B. Both display drawings and Hebrew inscriptions, pointing to a Hebrew recipient group. The drawings on pithos B:

Even a quick glance at [the drawings] shows that the various paintings on each side of the jars do not form a coherent composition, but are rather made up largely of a set of motifs that are positioned paratactically either next to one another or above one another.[26]

---

[25]Keel and Uehlinger, *Gods, Goddesses, and Images of God in Ancient Israel*, p. 247.
[26]Ibid., p. 212; also Schmidt, *The iron age pithoi drawings from Horvat Teman or Kuntillet ᶜAǧrūd.*

The group of figures at the top right is of the most interest for the depiction of persons and human bodies. O. Keel/C. Uehlinger describe them in the following manner:

> The representations are stylistically quite different from the rest of the painting on the vessel ... so that one can identify them readily as a group. These figures, the only human figures on the pithoi that are arranged facing left, were done by a very unpracticed hand. The details on each of these five individuals are rendered quite differently (hair, arm position, clothing), so that it seems that these were painted 'spontaneously,' unlike the other images that adhere clearly to a (Syro-Phoenician) artistic 'canon'.
>
> In light of this relative 'spontaneity,' it is probably justified to speak of this as a procession of worshipers, in spite of the irregular arrangement and the fact that they do not all seem to be standing on the same level.[27]

If we select one figure from the group, then we see a drawing which shows a human figure, the 'picture of a Hebrew'.

To begin with, we can ascertain from this that depictions of the human form existed in the Hebrew-Ancient Israelite culture. Therefore, analogous to the verbal image, a depiction of God in human form is absolutely conceivable. However, an unambiguous depiction which clearly only refers to Yhwh has not yet been found. Considering the Old Testament prohibition on imagery, such a find is unlikely, at least for the later exilic–post-exilic period.

This chapter has covered a number of themes which can best be summarized as follows in Table 2.2.

TABLE 2.2 *Conclusion*

Verbal image (depiction) of a figure	of man	of God
	documented in the Old Testament	documented in the Old Testament
	(cf. section 2.2 external form verbal 'image' of man)	(cf. section 2.2 external form verbal 'image' of God)
drawn/painted/ plastic/material image (depiction) of the form	**of man**	**of God**
	documented for Ancient Israel	Ø not documented for Ancient Israel
	(cf. section 2.3 depiction from *Kuntillet ʿAǧrūd*)	(cf. section 2.1 prohibition of imagery)

[27]Ibid., p. 225.

A verbal depiction of the human body and of God's body is evident in the Old Testament, as this short overview has intimated, a view which will be confirmed in the exposition that follows. We have also known of material depictions of human persons and bodies from the region of Ancient Israel for some decades as has been observed. However, material images of God from Old Testament times, in particular three-dimensional ones, do not exist. A principal explanation for this phenomenon is most probably the prohibition of images and of idols.

3

God in human form – Anthropomorphism[1] as a theological problem

Generally, the criticism, condemnation and prohibition of images – mostly[2] anthropomorphic images – in the Old Testament are directed against *material* images of God and deities. We must be careful to differentiate exactly: Old Testament criticism of images is aimed at the use of images as idols (see Chapter 2). The concept of an anthropomorphic God in human form is not called into question[3] (nor is it in the Ancient Orient[4])!

---

[1]Cf.: For the history of the term anthropomorphism from its origins to the eighteenth century, see Christ, *Menschlich von Gott reden*, pp. 16–76.

[2]Cf.: This criticism is also directed against theriomorphic idols (Ezek. 8.10); within the Old Testament we hardly find any decidedly theriomorphic linguistic concepts for Yhwh; cf: J. Hempel, '*Jahwegleichnisse der israelitischen Propheten*', in: ZAW 42 (Berlin: deGruyter, 1924), pp. 74–104; J. Hempel, '*Die Grenzen des Anthropomorphismus Jahwes im Alten Testament*', in: ZAW 57 (Berlin: deGruyter, 1939), pp. 75–85. The calves in Dan/Bet-El and so on are not representational depictions of Yhwh, but rather pedestals, see J. Jeremias, *Der Prophet Hosea* (Göttingen: Vandenhoeck & Ruprecht, 1983), pp. 106–7; cf. for this discussion: H. Pfeiffer, *Das Heiligtum von Bethel im Spiegel des Hoseabuches* (Göttingen: Vandenhoeck & Ruprecht, 1999), pp. 42–64. For theriomorphic representations cf: 'Theriomorphic representations [from Palestine] are common from the Bronze and late Iron Age. The animals were symbols or attributes of the respective cultic god. They were either an adjunct to the anthropomorphic figure or represented the god. A symbolic animal generally represents emblematically an important characteristic of the deity, which is also a characteristic of the animal in question (e.g. bull – wild strength, aggression). For individual animals, apotropaic coherence must be assumed.' Berlejung, *Die Theologie der Bilder*, pp. 288–9; Uehlinger assumes theriomorphic Yhwh-cult images in Bet-El; for the Persian era he assumes that theriomorphic representations of Yhwh no longer existed, without explaining this further, cf.: Uehlinger, *Exodus, Stierbild und biblisches Kultbildverbot*, p. 72.

[3]It still applies, 'The Old Testament does not know of any anti-anthropomorphic tendencies'. Kuitert, *Gott in Menschengestalt*, p. 37; E. J. Hamori, *When Gods Were Men: The Embodied God in Biblical and Near Eastern Literature* (Berlin: deGruyter, 2008); B. D. Sommer, *The Bodies of God and the World of Ancient Israel* (Cambridge: Cambridge University Press, 2009), pp. 1–4.

[4]K. Oberhuber, *Die Kultur des Alten Orients* (Frankfurt: Athenaion, 1972), pp. 115–53; E. Otto, '*Art. Anthropomorphismus*', LÄ 1 (1975), col. 311–18; Berlejung, *Die Theologie der Bilder*,

In line with the focus of this work, we will consider anthropomorphism in the *external human form of God*, as it is found in the Old Testament. This narrows the field. The phenomenon of anthropomorphism itself naturally includes all forms of 'divine' emotions (anthropopathism), and all forms of anthropomorphic *action*.[5] Anthropomorphism can also be understood in a much wider sense: the term anthropomorphism 'originally comprises an enquiry into the language of faith, ultimately into language itself. Martin Heidegger expressed this original meaning when, at the end of his lecture on Schelling's Philosophical Inquiries into the Essence of Human Freedom, he said 'only humans can take action, and the highest determinants are discovered in correlation with man. Therefore we are continually haunted by the question which we can call "anthropomorphistic"'.[6] This fundamental hermeneutic, anthropomorphistic problem will not be given priority here.[7]

An anthropomorphic concept of God (of Yhwh), as shown previously for the verbal image, is used consistently in the Old Testament itself. As Ludwig Köhler said, 'The hominid perception of God is expressed in great detail, unconcernedly and drastically on every page of the Old Testament.'[8] The New Testament treats anthropomorphism just as naturally.

It is only in the post-biblical era that biblical anthropomorphic statements begin to become a theological problem. Within Christianity in particular, the question of depiction and anthropomorphism causes great tension. The figure of Jesus Christ, the incarnation of God in human, graphic form, inevitably brings about a change in the problem of imagery and anthropomorphism. As far as Christology is concerned 'anthropomorphism is not only to be seen as permissible but also as a proper form of speaking about God'.[9] Images

---

pp. 35–61; B. N. Porter, *What is a God? Anthropomorphic and Non-anthropomorphic Aspects of Deity in Ancient Mesopotamia* (The Casco Bay Assyriological Institute 2; Winona Lake, Indiana: Eisenbrauns, 2009); Machinist, *Anthropomorphism in Mesopotamian Religion*; M. S. Smith, *Ugaritic Anthropomorphism, Theomorphism, Theriomorphism*, in: A. Wagner: *Göttliche Körper – Göttliche Gefühle*, (OBO 270; Fribourg: Academic Press; Göttingen: Vandenhoeck & Ruprecht, 2014).
[5]Cf.: Kuitert, *Gott in Menschengestalt*, pp. 12–13; Christ, *Menschlich von Gott reden*, pp. 16–76.
[6]Christ, *Menschlich von Gott reden*, p. 16.
[7]Cf. For anthropomorphism as a theological hermeneutical problem, D. Michel, *Israels Glaube im Wandel: Einführungen in die Forschung am Alten Testament* (Berlin: Verlag Die Spur, 1971), pp. 11–19; E. Jüngel, *Gott als Geheimnis der Welt: zur Begründung der Theologie des Gekreuzigten im Streit zwischen Theismus und Atheismus* (Tübingen: Mohr Siebeck, 1977), p. 353; Christ, *Menschlich von Gott reden*, pp. 27–49. The question of anthropomorphism in general is tellingly discussed by Heidegger as well as by Camus: 'The cat's universe is not the universe of the anthill. The truism "All thought is anthropomorphic" has no other meaning.' A. Camus, *The Myth of Sisyphus* (trans. [from French] J. O'Brien; UK: Hamish Hamilton, 1955).
[8]L. Köhler, *Theologie des Alten Testaments* (Tübingen: Mohr Siebeck, 1953), p. 4. Cf.: Sommer, *The Bodies of God and the World of Ancient Israel*, pp. 1–4.
[9]U. B. Körtner, 'Art. Anthropomorphismus VI. Dogmatisch', RGG⁴ 1 (1998). English: 'Anthropomorphism VI. Dogmatics', RPP 1 (2007), p. 262.

of Jesus Christ in human form are therefore beyond suspicion. On the other hand, the prohibition of imagery from the Old Testament remains and is applied to Hellenistic concepts of God.[10] Influenced by the Logos concept, God is conceived without spatial and temporal existence, without human properties and affects. This was true for Justin or Clemens, as it was true for Philo of Alexandria ('God is free from irrational passions of the soul, the limbs and parts of the body'[11]).[12] This ties in with the Logos-orientated understanding of God and raises a theological question: how can we recognize God? An appropriate answer can be found in Philo: 'Since God is featureless and sublimely superior, it is impossible that we can recognise him. We must be content to know that he is, without understanding what he is like.'[13] One avenue of escape from this problem is to trace God's *ministry* along the lines of his *power*: 'Because God's goodness bestows us with so many gifts and is untiring we can compare it, according to Philo and Clemens, with a well which refreshes the thirsty soul with its water but never dries out.'[14] Because we are 'creatures' made in his image, we can perceive that the gifts are from God. We can recognize revelations because God adapts himself and condescends to reveal himself: 'The spiritual God adapts himself to a great extent to the materiality of his creation in his revelation.'[15]

Under the influence of Logos theology, anti-anthropomorphism initially remains predominant. 'In the Christian context the concept of anthropomorphism appears first in Augustine who described the Audians [a sect named after Audios in the fourth/fifth century CE] as "anthropomorphites", accusing them of a sensuous conception of God in keeping with the image of a mortal human. This influenced discussion of the concept of anthropomorphism for a considerable time.'[16] It was possible for Christian authors to fall back on the Greek tradition (at all times, from the ancient church until today) in order to strengthen their polemic against the human form of the gods.[17] One of the best examples from this Greek tradition

---

[10]The question of representation and the question of anthropomorphism must be differentiated even if they have a tendency to intertwine. For the history of the contemporary theological question cf.: Nordhofen (ed.), *Bilderverbot*; Janowski and Zchomelidse (eds.), *Die Sichtbarkeit des Unsichtbaren*; Jacobi, et al. (eds.), *Im Zwischenreich der Bilder*; Wagner, et al. (eds.), *Gott im Wort - Gott im Bild*.

[11]Quoted according to P. Heinisch, *Der Einfluss Philos auf die älteste christliche Exegese (Barnabas, Justin und Clemens von Alexandria): ein Beitrag zur Geschichte der allegorisch-mystischen Schriftauslegung im christlichen Altertum* (Münster: Aschendorff, 1908), p. 126.

[12]Cf.: Ibid., p. 126; Kuitert, *Gott in Menschengestalt*, pp. 56–77.

[13]Heinisch, *Der Einfluss Philos auf die älteste christliche Exegese*, p. 129.

[14]Ibid., p. 135.

[15]Kuitert, *Gott in Menschengestalt*, p. 84.

[16]Körtner, 'Art. *Anthropomorphismus VI. Dogmatisch*'. English: '*Anthropomorphism VI. Dogmatics*', p. 262.

[17]Cf.: F. Graf, *Der Eigensinn der Götterbilder in antiken religiösen Diskursen*, in: G. Boehm (ed.), *Homo pictor* (München: K. G. Saur, 2001), pp. 232–3.

is found in Xenophanes of Colophon (b. about 580 BC in Colophon in Asia Minor, d. after 478 BC). He points out with great irony that the gods cannot be compared in their bodily form to man or to earthly creatures:

> If oxen and horses and lions could draw and make tools like man, the horses would draw the gods with the form and body of horses, oxen would draw oxen.[18]

We cannot unfold the discussion in the ancient church any further here, but these short comments reveal the overriding structure, which is also evident in later criticism of anthropomorphism. In the phenomenon of anthropomorphism, biblical facts clash, through the ages, with basic theological positions which, similar to the Logos concepts and ancient church theology in general, are not only fed by biblical tradition – in other words: In anthropomorphism, biblical statements come into conflict with fundamental theological, or even general 'human', positions. The ancient church criticized the Logos theology from an anthropomorphic point of view, since it made 'the limbs and parts of the body' and the 'irrational passions of the soul' a subject of discussion. Later, anthropomorphic phenomena in biblical language are refuted from a rational position because they contradict reasonable concepts of God.[19] Or, as in Rudolf Bultmann, they are accorded a place in the mythical language/world of the Old Testament, and must be overcome in modern times.[20]

Objections raised against anthropomorphism must be taken seriously. Above all, anthropomorphism harbours the danger of losing sight of God's divinity and its aseity. 'If man is made in God's image, then God looks like man. He walks in paradise in the evening, he talks or is silent, he is angry and jealous, he takes revenge, but he can also be solicited and persuaded, he changes his mind.'[21] If God is like this, is 'he' a God at all? Is this merely an 'abuse of our human concept of God'?[22] Does man create God in his own image?

In Old Testament exegetical discussion, we find many of the queries and objections to anthropomorphism, which are also found in general theological discussion. However, we also see an endeavour to understand Old Testament anthropomorphism in an adequate manner.

I shall start with the statement made by Friedrich Delitzsch in the context of the Babel-Bible dispute. Pre-biblical Akkadian texts from

---

[18]Xenophanes, B 15, FVS, Nr. 21; cf. H. Diels and W. Kranz (ed.), *Die Fragmente der Vorsokratiker* (Hamburg: Rowohlt, 1957). For the Stoics, cf.: Chrysippos, Frg. 1076 (SVF, II, 315); Diogenes von Babylon, Frg. 33 (SVF, III, 217).
[19]Cf.: Kuitert, *Gott in Menschengestalt*, pp. 143–6.
[20]Ibid., pp. 146–54.
[21]W. Trillhaas, *Dogmatik* (Berlin: deGruyter, [4]1980), p. 100.
[22]Trillhaas, *Dogmatik*, p. 101.

Babel found in the nineteenth century questioned the authority of the Bible. The catalyst for this widely publicized dispute was a lecture held by Delitzsch with the title *Babel and the Bible* (Leipzig 1902). Since the dispute was ultimately about basic questions of Old Testament exegesis and Christian theology, Delitzsch also addressed the problem of Old Testament anthropomorphism: 'The Yhwh-faith too ... remained tainted with sundry human weaknesses over many centuries [in comparison with Babylonian religion]: with those naïve anthropomorphic opinions unique to the adolescence of humanity, with Israeli particularism, heathen sacrificial cults and outward legalism.'[23]

Delitzsch's opinion holds that anthropomorphisms are naïve. This is a common prejudice. Like sacrificial cults, legalism and particularism, anthropomorphisms should be overcome by a higher religion if possible. The evolutionary concept, characteristic of the nineteenth century, can be heard clearly here. The more highly developed a phenomenon was, the more advanced it was considered to be. Evaluations were quick off the mark. Feuerbach's arguments are even more radical; one of the main statements of his work *Das Wesen des Christentums* (1841; English: *The Essence of Christianity*) was 'Religion, at least the Christian, is the relation of man to himself, or more correctly to his own nature. ... The divine being is nothing else than the human being, or, rather, the human nature purified, freed from the limits of the individual man. ... All the attributes of the divine nature are, therefore, attributes of the human nature.'[24] This also applies to the human figure, the figure of man respectively.

E. Sellin (1933) attempted to solve reservations against anthropomorphism by calling anthropomorphic statements an 'early' form of revelation, later overcome within the Old Testament itself by the 'proper' faith in God: 'The most primitive form [of revelation] is, of course, that God himself appears corporeally and talks with mankind. It has been shown sufficiently that this form contradicts the proper Mosaic faith in God.'[25]

In order to describe Old Testament facts, Sellin takes up a strategy which had been used for quite some time in the anthropomorphism problem – accommodation. God adjusts to the stage of development which man – or in the Old Testament, Israel – has reached. Older stages in Israel's development, for which anthropomorphism was typical or necessary, are overcome through later developments (the 'actual Mosaic faith') and so

[23]Quoted according to the commentary edition in R. G. Lehmann, *Friedrich Delitzsch und der Babel-Bibel-Streit* (OBO 133; Fribourg: Academic Press; Göttingen: Vandenhoeck & Ruprecht, 1994), p. 90.
[24]L. Feuerbach, *Das Wesen des Christentums* (Leipzig, 1841) (Ludwig Feuerbach. Werke in sechs Bänden, hg. v. E. Thies; Frankfurt: Suhrkamp, 1976). English: *The Essence of Christianity* (trans. George Eliot; New York, Evanston and London: Harper & Row, 1957), p. 14.
[25]E. Sellin, *Theologie des Alten Testaments* (Leipzig: Quelle & Meyer, 1933), p. 44.

appear to be 'inconsistent'.[26] This line of argument is problematic. A decline in anthropomorphism in later Old Testament texts, or a clear assignment to earlier texts alone, cannot be proved (cf. section 5.4). We must also ask whether a depreciation of earlier stages of development in light of later ones is acceptable. Does not every age experience God immediately?

The arguments brought forward by W. Eichrodt (1935) are similar to those of Sellin. He emphasizes that 'the force of such [anthropomorphic] passages' cannot be dismissed.[27] As far as the prophets are concerned, he says: 'It will be better to revert to an observation made earlier, namely that the immediate proximity and reality of God, which for us are all too easily obscured by spiritualizing concepts, are outstanding features of the Old Testament revelation, and compel men to clothe the divine presence in human form.'[28]

Eichrodt then refers to a further development: 'Alongside these naïve conceptions, however, there existed from the very first a sense that it is impossible to speak of actually seeing God.'[29] In his chapter on the spiritualization of the theophany' he describes means, from various levels of spiritualization, which overcome 'naïve' anthropomorphism: Yhwh's messenger, Yhwh's kābôd (splendour), God's countenance (in a figurative sense) and the name of Yhwh. What follows is a description of God's worldly powers (word, spirit, wisdom of God), by which he can be recognized – to the present day. These arguments, too, are familiar to us from the theological attempts undertaken by the ancient church to overcome anthropomorphism (see the previous).

Sellin and Eichrodt are both in danger of assuming a concept of God strongly influenced by post-biblical, Logos-orientated, rational concepts, and present over long stretches of the history of theology.[30]

P. Heinisch (1940) sees the 'reason why biblical authors used such expressions … in the human inability to describe God adequately'.[31]

---

[26]Accommodation was crucial for the Ancient Church (see the beginning of this chapter) and it remains an important interpretation to the present day. It can be used further if it is accepted that following generations must do their best to interpret revelation historically as taking place in a particular time under prevailing conditions, cf.: Michel, *Israels Glaube im Wandel*, pp. 11–19.

[27]W. Eichrodt, *Theologie des Alten Testaments, Teil 2* (Leipzig: J.C. Hinrichs, 1935). English: *Theology of the Old Testament Vol. II* (trans. J. A. Baker; The Old Testament Library; Bloomsbury Street London: S. C. M. Press, 1967), p. 21.

[28]Eichrodt, *Theologie des Alten Testaments, Teil 2*, p. 21.

[29]Ibid., p. 23.

[30]Vriezen is also against denigrating anthropomorphism: 'It is not true that, on the ground of anthropomorphisms, certain parts of the Old Testament may be considered as standing on a particularly low level.' Th. C. Vriezen, *Theologie des Alten Testaments in Grundzügen* (Wageningen: Veenman & Zonen, 1956). English: *An Outline of Old Testament Theology* (Oxford: Basil Blackwell 21970), p. 321.

[31]P. Heinisch, *Theologie des Alten Testaments: Die Heilige Schrift des Alten Testaments Ergänzungsband 1* (Bonn: Hanstein, 1940), p. 33; cf: Hempel, '*Die Grenzen des Anthropomorphismus Jahwes im Alten Testament*', p. 79.

Gerhard von Rad (1957 first ed./1987 ninth ed.) is awestruck by anthropomorphism, for example the Genesis texts which he ascribes to the 'Yahwist':

> Yahweh walks in the garden in the cool of the evening; he himself closes the ark; he descends to inspect the Tower of Babel, etc. This is anything but the bluntness and naïveté of an archaic narrator. It is, rather, the candor and lack of hesitation which is only the mark of a lofty and mature way of thinking. This glasslike, transparent, and fragile way of thinking in the Yahwistic narratives makes of every exposition, which inevitably coarsens the original text, a difficult and almost insoluble task.[32]

Is there no alternative to standing awestruck before the 'transparent fragile spirituality' of anthropomorphism? von Rad grapples with this phenomenon and denies himself any interpretation at this point. In his theology he chooses a different expedient:

> Actually, Israel conceived even Jahweh himself as having human form. But the way of putting it which we use runs in precisely the wrong direction according to Old Testament ideas, for, according to the ideas of Jahwism, it cannot be said that Israel regarded God anthropomorphically, but the reverse, that she considered man as theomorphic.[33]

He points out the distance between God and man which the Old Testament had also emphasized.[34] No further interpretation of anthropomorphism is attempted here either.

Horst Dietrich Preuss (1991) approaches the problem in his discussion of Old Testament anthropomorphism, from the aspect of accommodation: 'He [God] desires a relationship between himself and us, us and himself. He agrees to our conditions through his chosen action, and yet there is nothing with which we could compare him.'[35]

Otto Kaiser (1998) takes up the broad (hermeneutic) understanding of anthropomorphism: 'All positive statements about God's relation with the world are ultimately anthropomorphisms; as the absolute transcendental being, mankind can only really make negative statements about him. *Theologia negativa* ends in silent worship of the secret. In comparison to

---

[32]G. von Rad, *Das erste Buch Mose* (Göttingen: Vandenhoeck & Ruprecht, 1987). English: *Genesis. A Commentary* (trans. J. H. Marks; The Old Testament Library; Bloomsbury Street London: SCM Press Ltd, 1963), p. 24–5.

[33]G. von Rad, Old Testament Theology. Vol. 1, (1962), p. 145.

[34]Similarly to von Rad, so does Zimmerli, 'Hier [in Gen 1] wird nicht von einer Menschengestaltigkeit Gottes, sondern von einer Gottesgestaltigkeit des Menschen geredet.' W. Zimmerli, *Grundriß der alttestamentlichen Theologie* (Stuttgart: Kohlhammer, [7]1999 ([1]1972), Sp. 28.

[35]H. D. Preuss, *Theologie des Alten Testaments Vol. I* (Stuttgart: Kohlhammer, 1991), p. 281.

the *via negativa* of theology as philosophy of religion, religion resorts to envisaging thought. Its instrument is not terminology, but the metaphor.'[36]

O. Kaiser sees anthropomorphisms 'not as statements about the aseity of God', but as 'relational and functional understanding': 'their task is to express God's relationship at a certain instant of time in a certain mundane situation.'[37] Anthropomorphisms are 'metaphors, necessary in order to talk conceivably of his ministry in the world and mankind.'[38] 'God is simply inaccessible to mankind in his aseity.'[39]

Rolf Rendtorff (2001) ascribes anthropomorphic descriptions to God's perceivable ministry. 'No one can know what God is really like. [But] people can experience God in different ways.'[40] Above all one experiences God's ministry, which is not described 'in non-graphic terms' in the Old Testament. 'On the contrary, a large proportion of the statements about God are highly graphic, "anthropomorphic," one might say.'[41] In Rendtorff's opinion, criticism of anthropomorphism should not take place in the context of Old Testament theology; it belongs in the realm of discussion on religious criticism. 'Criticism of the anthropomorphism of biblical language is an element of the criticism of biblical religion as a whole; so in the context of representation of biblical statements it has no meaningful function, cf. EKL³, 1559.'[42]

Reflections on anthropomorphism touch on a further issue, which I will consider in more detail at the end of this book. Suffice it to say that if we think of God as a person – what he looks like, how he acts and feels – then we have to ask what kind of personality God has. 'Ywhw's personality is particularly deeply engraved in Israel through the adoption of two "codes", significant in revelatory language: Ywhw has a "countenance" and a "heart". Since Hebrew has no terminology for "person" and for "personality" these two terms offer a more than adequate alternative. ... The attempt to imagine God as a person has repeatedly caused trouble in the history of mankind. Eastern thought in particular, sees a threat to divine infinity and limitlessness.'[43] H. D. Preuss is of a similar opinion: 'Anthropomorphisms

---

[36] O. Kaiser, *Der Gott des Alten Testaments. Wesen und Wirken. Theologie des Alten Testaments 2: Jahwe, der Gott Israels, Schöpfer der Welt und des Menschen* (Göttingen: Vandenhoeck & Ruprecht, 1998), p. 313.

[37] Kaiser, *Der Gott des Alten Testaments*, p. 315.

[38] Ibid., p. 316.

[39] Ibid.

[40] R. Rendtorff, *Theologie des Alten Testaments: Ein kanonischer Entwurf.* Vol. 2 (Neukirchen-Vluyn: Neukirchener-Verlag 2001). English: *The Canonical Hebrew Bible: A Theology of the Old Testament* (trans. D. E. Orton; Tools for Biblical Study, 7; Leiden: Deo Publishing, 2005), p. 609.

[41] Rendtorff, *Theologie des Alten Testaments*, p. 610.

[42] Ibid.

[43] A. Deissler, *Die Grundbotschaft des Alte Testaments* (Freiburg im Breisgau: Herder, 1995), pp. 56–7.

underline the personal character of the Old Testament God, making God accessible to humans, and this indeed is their function.'[44]

These various approaches to anthropomorphism show that all this is still a matter of debate to the present day. Our brief excursion through several theological positions – I make no claim to have presented the whole range – shows how varied approaches to the human form of God can be.

More recent discussions of single aspects of anthropomorphism will be included in our ongoing discussion. One further aspect enables a new approach to Old Testament anthropomorphism from an Old Testament perspective – the 'new' understanding (see Chapter 1) of the Old Testament/ Ancient Oriental perceptions of 'corporeality' and 'image'. Following the attempt (Chapters 4–6) to describe Old Testament anthropomorphism with its own 'metaphors' (see previous discussion on Kaiser), the theological positions and queries raised by anthropomorphism will be reconsidered and further modern approaches will be explored (Chapter 7).

---

[44]Preuss, *Theologie des Alten Testaments Vol. I*, p. 281.

4

Deciphering the language of images and of corporeal depictions

4.1 The 'language' of images and verbal depictions

Language is capable of presenting objects vividly, descriptively and graphically. Sometimes one word alone can call an object to mind. For example, if I say the word *tree* then I can see a 'tree' in 'my mind's eye'. Yet when described in this way, by just one word, this imagined object remains blurred.

If I describe the object more closely, then I have a more detailed graphical (optical) conception:

> *A tree with a trunk which an adult can just encompass with both arms, beaten by a continual west wind to one side so that it grows at a 45° eternal tilt, highly branched, the annual budding shooting straight upwards.*

A picture of this specific tree develops in our mind's eye when we read this text; each statement substantiates it and adds more detail. This only occurs if I can understand the language spoken. Further, the more knowledge I have of the object in question, the easier it is. If I have never seen a tree so beaten by the wind before, then it would be harder to imagine such a tree than if I were familiar with the phenomenon. Therefore, I need linguistic and factual knowledge of the issue, if I hope to understand a verbal image.

The composition induced by a verbal description, however, requires more details: Is there movement in the depiction or not? Did the branches sway in the wind? Or do I see it like a painting which preserves momentary motion? Do I only see a solitary tree or does it stand in a landscape? Is the picture like an exact photograph or does it possess expressionist quality? Colour or black and white? – How I fill in all these details of a picture depends on how I have learnt to see with my mind's eye. The culture in which I grew up delivers most of the prerequisites; the amount of practice I have in translating verbal pictures into inner pictures delivers more; and the situation in each case is crucial, where I am and how I feel. There are bound to be other factors. The translation of a verbal image into an inner picture will never be the same twice, just as our understanding of the same text in is never identical.

We should not despair at this basic hermeneutic experience. To contemplate a text, a verbal image, a second time in a different situation – and perhaps to understand it even better – to see and understand other new aspects, does not mean that we give up hope of understanding it fully. It only means various degrees of understanding, under varying situational circumstances: each and every understanding is comprised of repetition and recognition, but also of new insight. The more a phenomenon challenges us to contemplate it anew, demanding new insight, the more appealing it becomes. Goethe called such phenomena 'incommensurable' (e.g. the Bible), inconstruable in the sense that there is no end to interpretation. Yet even if we continually discover new things in an object, much remains the same. Since our starting point for a given object is generally constant – whether it is a word or a text – our understanding is never completely *random*, but *guided* by the purport of the word or text itself.[1]

Much of what we have elicited for our general and situational understanding of a verbal image is also true for material images. They, too, develop in the beholder's consciousness. However, the sensual source material is not the same as in the verbal image. Paintings are viewed in a different way and the method of reproduction is different – colours are reproduced with colours and not with the names of colours, and body and form can be depicted graphically and so on.[2]

The fascinating question is whether (within one culture) the principles behind understanding are the same in verbal images as for material images

---

[1]All modern hermeneutic approaches emphasize this, cf.: H. G. Gadamer, *Wahrheit und Methode Hermeneutik I* (5th edn, Tübingen: J.C.B. Mohr, 1986). English: *Truth and Method* (trans. W. Glen-Doepel; London: Sheed and Ward, 1979). Cf.: also recent textbooks on hermeneutics: M. Oeming, *Biblische Hermeneutik: Eine Einführung* (Darmstadt: Wissenschaftliche Buchgesellschaft, 1998). English: *Contemporary Biblical Hermeneutics: An Introduction* (trans. J. F. Vette, Aldershot, England/Burlington, VT: Ashgate, 2006); A. Behrens, *Verstehen des Glaubens: Eine Einführung in Fragestellungen evangelischer Hermeneutik* (Neukirchen-Vluyn: Neukirchener Verl. 2005); P. Müller, H. Dierk and A. Müller-Friese, *Verstehen lernen: Ein Arbeitsbuch zur Hermeneutik* (Stuttgart: Calwer, 2005), pp. 20–41.
[2]Cf.: O. Bätschmann, *Einführung in die kunstgeschichtliche Hermeneutik: die Auslegung von Bildern* (5th edn, Darmstadt: Wissenschaftliche Buchgesellschaft, 2001), pp. 36–45.

(i.e. paintings, sculptures, reliefs and so on, excluding 'standing' images which are of particular interest to us in terms of the Old Testament and the Ancient Orient).

I advocate the following hypothesis in this matter: in one respect, verbal and non-verbal images are subject to the same laws and conditions. To understand these laws and conditions we can, and indeed must, also analyse non-verbal images (in one culture), so that we can see how pictures (both material and verbal) function.

As far as the Old Testament is concerned I add a second hypothesis: since the Old Testament does not differ fundamentally from the Ancient Orient as far as understanding and generating images is concerned (with the exception of the prohibition of images), it is legitimate to consult images found outside of Israel and the Old Testament to further our comprehension.

The scope of this book does not allow us to discuss all the principles which lie behind understanding, effect and statement for verbal and non-verbal images (e.g. types of pictures, content and motives, questions of style, form and development). To further our understanding of the image of the body of God, it is enough to concentrate on one aspect of the problem. This encompasses two areas, first, the basic 'rules' underlying the images, which are fundamental to all Ancient Oriental cultures including those of the Old Testament (see section 4.2), and secondly we will observe that pictorial statements in the Ancient Orient are aimed less at the form of an object than at its function (see section 4.3).

For both of these areas a further fundamental observation applies, contained here in a third hypothesis: our observations concerning the fundamental 'pictorial rules' for the representation of images in the Ancient Orient suggest that basic rules of depiction are slow to change.[3] They survive for centuries and millennia, they are beyond individual expressions and transcend the limits of all genre. It was only the influence of Greek art and its pictorial principles which brought about their downfall. Therefore, the fundamental rules for the representation of images can be seen as a longue durée[4] phenomena, thus justifying the use of pictorial data from various

---

[3]Cf: E. H. Gombrich, *Die Geschichte der Kunst* (16th edn, Berlin: Phaidon Press, 1996). English: *The Story of Art* (16th edn, London: Phaidon Press, 1995), pp. 65–8.
[4]The term 'longue durée' (long duration) was created by the Annales school and is often associated with Fernand Braudel in particular. According to this approach, various chronological strata, which play a role in our consideration of history, are differentiated: (a) the longue durée points to social, political and economic structures or geographical conditions which change very slowly or not at all; we must dissociate (b) economic booms, meaning economic fluctuations and economic cycles which take place over many years or even decades, and (c) the 'classical' history of events which has recourse to (generally) political events, wars and so on with a time frame of years, weeks or days and sometimes only hours, cf.: F. Braudel, Geschichte und Sozialwissenschaften. Die longue durée, in M. Bloch and F. Braudel (eds.), *Schrift und Materie in der Geschichte: Vorschläge zur systematischen Aneignung historischer Prozesse* (edition Suhrkamp, 814 Berlin: Suhrkamp, 1977), pp. 47–85.

ages (and cultures) for our investigation. That is not to say that we intend to negate historical developments or to refrain from consulting the historical dimensions of individual pictorial 'data'.

Therefore, we shall attempt to grasp the language of the images, their 'grammar', and to work out what verbal and non-verbal images have in common.

4.2 The basic framework of pictorial language: The concept of body and depiction in Ancient Israelite and Ancient Oriental images

4.2.1 Bas-relief depictions

4.2.1.1 Israelite depictions – images in Israel

Whether (historically authentic) texts belong to the Ancient Israelite-Hebrew tradition is relatively easy to establish: if a text is in the Hebrew language and (the ancient Hebrew) script, then there is every indication that it is an Israelite text (i.e. from the Northern Kingdom of Israel, the Southern Kingdom of Judah or to the post-national religious body of 'Israel').[5]

The classification of *images* is much more difficult. A purely theoretical iconographic classification of a given image as 'Israelite' is not (yet) possible since the nature of the depictions, the techniques employed and the iconographic programme have not yet been systematically researched. Therefore, we do not possess a generally acceptable 'pictorial history' for the whole cultural period in Israel. For this reason, it is difficult to classify individual pictures culturally and chronologically according to their message.

In order to be classified as 'Israelite', they need to have been found in an 'Israelite' locality or context. The locality is central for an *archaeological classification*. The combination of context and a detailed archaeological analysis of the locality usually make a temporal and cultural allocation possible.[6] However, even an Israelite locality does not automatically indicate that it is an Israelite picture. The picture might be imported or originate from

---

[5]The Ancient Hebrew language and script do not always coincide. As the finds from *Kuntillet ʿAǧrūd* show, the Ancient Hebrew language can be written in Phoenician script, cf.: J. Renz and W. Röllig, *Handbuch der althebräischen Epigraphik, Vol. I* (Darmstadt: Wissenschaftliche Buchgesellschaft, 1995), pp. 57–9.

[6]Cf.: V. Fritz, *Einführung in die biblische Archäologie* (Darmstadt: Wissenschaftliche Buchgesellschaft, 1985). English: *An Introduction to Biblical Archaeology* (JSOT.S 172; trans. B. Mänz-Davies; Sheffield: Sheffield Academic Press, 1994), pp. 52–69; U. Hübner, 'Archäologie. II. Biblische Archäologie', RGG⁴ 1 (1998) pp. 709–11. English: 'Archaeology. II. Biblical Archaeology', RPP 1 (2007), pp. 354–6.

non-Israelites. In my opinion, even this sort of picture can afford information about the understanding of images in the culture within which they were found, in which Israel should certainly be included. I will go one step further in order to make myself clear.

My investigation will begin with images which are combined with Hebrew text. The texts make the recipients clear: a Hebrew text is aimed at Israelites. Due to the combination of text and picture, the associated images are clearly assigned to Israelite recipients. The observations which can be made about non-verbal images will, therefore, first be demonstrated in these pictures. We can then go on to include further images which, as we will see, follow the same basic principles but offer further details, thus making a classification of the concept of the body easier. Important information on their cultural affiliation is provided by the locality of the find, as well as by the current iconographic classification.

Section 2.3 introduced the depiction of a human figure from the eighth century BCE *Kuntillet ʿAǧrūd*. This representation from pithos B combines Hebrew text and pictorial representation on one and the same object, suggesting Israelite recipients.[7] I shall begin with this (Figure 4.1), to be

FIGURE 4.1 *Human representation from the drawing on pithos B from* Kuntillet ʿAǧrūd.

Source: Keel and Uehlinger, *Gods, Goddesses, and Images of God in Ancient Israel*, p. 214, fig. 221.

---

[7]For the interconnection of pictorial representation and inscription, cf.: Schmidt, *Proposals*, pp. 91–125.

more exact with the portrayal of one figure out of the group, in order to explain the principles of corporeal depiction.

What are we familiar with in these pictures, what is unfamiliar?[8] How do we make sense of such pictures? Let us begin by collecting observations. The 'spontaneous' character of these graffiti sketches is apparent.[9] The execution is part of the individual characteristic of this work, but we can hardly call it a 'work of art'. The spontaneity is in complete contrast to the technically and artistically polished representations of highest quality found in Egypt, Mesopotamia, Assyria and so on. Despite this, we find features in the corporeal representation that are completely identical with those found in much more elaborate Egyptian and Ancient Oriental works. These features are what interest me particularly, and not so much the type of representation (spontaneous, etc.), the technique or the material (clay, rock relief, seal, drawing, etc.) employed, nor even the cultural peculiarities of style (the depiction from Kuntillet ʿAǧrūd does not appear to be Egyptian at first glance because it lacks the typical stylistic features, just as it does not appear to be Assyrian for the same reasons).

Similarly, the function of each work of art, what it states, and means, is not the first priority, even if this initially surprises the reader. Of course, these are important questions for the interpretation of pictures. As far as this study is concerned, which is aimed at the depiction of human bodies and human forms, I shall concentrate on corporeal representations. For the picture from Kuntillet ʿAǧrūd, this means it is of no great importance whether it shows a procession or some other kind of group of worshippers.

This example from Kuntillet ʿAǧrūd is sketchy and spontaneous, but it provides telling insights for the concept of the body. Spontaneous drawings draw on basic accepted principles without much forethought.

Let us start with the head. We see hair, a face, a mouth, a nose, eyes and eyebrows. The depiction, therefore, is limited to the essential elements. As far as we are concerned, details are completely lacking: there are no hints as to the individual physiognomy, nor to age, the head form shows no individuality, the picture does not reveal what the skin was like, muscles and bones (e.g. cheeks) are not visible.

The general view of the head is determined by the nose and the mouth which are clearly drawn in profile, sideways. Therefore, the whole head appears to be depicted in side view, in profile. The hair seems to follow this

---

[8]Perhaps we could go even further, assuming a vague fundamental view of Egyptian/Ancient Oriental art based on Egyptian representations and ask what is typical as far as human representation is concerned? A similar question is posed at the beginning of another discussion of Egyptian art, cf.: H. Schäfer, Von Ägyptischer Kunst: Eine Grundlage (4th edn, Wiesbaden: Harrassowitz, 1963). English: Principles of Egyptian Art (3rd edn, trans. J. Baines; ed. E. Brunner-Traut; Oxford: Griffith Institute, 1986), p. 14.
[9]Cf.: Keel and Uehlinger, Gods, p. 225.

principle. The eyes, however, are seen from the front. A profile of a head never has a front view of the eyes, not for a human!

The neck can be seen clearly (in my opinion slightly too long in this figure, as in all of the figures in the group discussed previously, see section 2.3). The torso is seen from the front – an unusual contrast to the head in profile to our way of thinking! The arms are seen in profile, so that they are parallel, and the crook of the arm is shown to full advantage. This is important since the position of the arms probably indicate worship or prayer. Hands (and fingers) are completely lacking. As the movement and the posture of legs and feet clearly show, they are depicted in side view. Here, too, there are no details.

The patterns on legs and torso are also conspicuous. In my opinion, the theory broached by Keel and Uehlinger, that the dots against a grid background 'show which portions of the body ... were to be thought of as clothed',[10] is very plausible. However, this pattern is one of the peculiarities of the *Kuntillet ʿAǧrūd* depiction and as such it is not relevant to our discussion of corporeal concept.

As far as our normal manner of viewing things is concerned, the unusual combination of various viewpoints within one composition is odd. How can you put a head in profile on a torso in front view, the legs again in profile and the eyes in front view? This principle of composition is not, however, unique to *Kuntillet ʿAǧrūd*, as further pictorial representations will demonstrate – depictions of humans taken from written compositions which were most probably addressed to a Hebrew audience.

To begin with, we have a seal which Keel and Uehlinger allocate to the 'Iron Age IIB specialty items produced by Phoenicia and Israel' (Figure 4.2).[11]

The four-winged god in the second register from the top is generally the main focus of discussion on the seal from the eighth century BCE. We, however, are far more interested in the two *human worshippers* in the same register (Figure 4.3). The inscription names an unknown Menachem as the owner of the seal. Although the exact origin is unclear 'the owners' names [of the pertinent group of seals to which this belongs] and the iconography' certainly make it at least possible that they are Israelite'.[12]

Here we find the mannerisms already known to us from *Kuntillet ʿAǧrūd*: The head in profile, the torso in front view, arms in profile, feet and legs in profile striding out. There are no details, not even any eyes, but it seems possible to discern hands. The arm gesture is the same as in *Kuntillet ʿAǧrūd*.

A bull from the so-called 'Burnt Archive' displays similarities; it 'may have come from Jerusalem. In any case, [255 bullae from the "Burnt Archive"] list such famous citizens of Jerusalem from the time of Jeremiah as his secretary

---

[10]Ibid., p. 222, Footnote 59, see also p. 225.
[11]Ibid., p. 195.
[12]Ibid., p. 197.

FIGURE 4.2 *Seal, Phoenician-Israelite artisan craft work from the Iron Age IIB.*
Source: Keel and Uehlinger, *Gods, Goddesses, and Images of God in Ancient Israel*, p. 196, fig. 211b.

FIGURE 4.3 *Detail from seal, see figure 4.2.*

Berechyahu ben Neriyahu ... and perhaps also the high priest Azarya ben Hilqiyahu (1 Chron. 5.39 ...). ... The most interesting [iconographic motif] among them has a scenic composition [cf. Figure 4.4], that being the bulla of *šr h°r*, the "city commandant", that includes a figurative design. It portrays an official, with hand raised in greeting, in front of a man armed with sword, arrow, and bow, who might be identified as the Judahite king, even though this man interestingly wears neither diadem nor crown. ... Bow and arrow are attributes of royal rule. ...The image emphasizes ... that legitimate power is in the hands of the king. By contrast, the official (identified most likely from the inscription as the city commandant) functions loyally and uses only the power that has been delegated to him by the king.'[13]

The human representation we encounter here is by now familiar: head in profile, this time with a superb head of hair and a beard (also in profile),

---

[13]Ibid., p. 357.

FIGURE 4.4 *Bulla from the so-called 'Burnt Archive'.*

Source: Keel and Uehlinger, *Gods, Goddesses, and Images of God in Ancient Israel*, p. 411, fig. 346.

FIGURE 4.5 *Seal from the Persian(?) era.*

Source: Keel and Uehlinger, *Gods, Goddesses, and Images of God in Ancient Israel*, p. 375, fig. 358c.

nose and mouth in profile, eye in front view, legs and feet in profile when they are not concealed by clothing. The clothing is distinct and the figures of high standing personalities have patterned vestments. The arms are in profile revealing the stance and the gesture (greeting) clearly. Details are missing in the corporeal depiction (physiognomy, muscles, joints in fingers and feet, etc.), but the insinuated thumb on the hand of the figure to the right, raised in greeting, is striking.

The next picture (Figure 4.5) is found on a seal from the Persian era (end of sixth century/beginning of fifth century BCE); the inscription names a (Persian?) 'Inspector of Judah/Yehud', who is portrayed as a devotee of the moon god.[14] The head in profile and the eye in front view correspond to the other cases discussed here, but the torso is incomprehensible (are Assyrian-Babylonian influences responsible for omitting the torso in front view, cf. section 4.2.1.3?). The gesture of the arms held in prayer is familiar. What is noticeable though is the splayed out thumb on the hand.

Corporeal depictions in Israelite pictures – a first résumé

The basic principles of corporeal depiction in the pictures discussed thus far do not differ. What they have in common is the combination of body parts in varying, but typical aspect (head in profile, eye in front view). This is contrary to our customary manner of looking at things, which usually demands a coherent aspect within a two-dimensional picture (see below). The corporeal representations are still restricted to the essential parts of the body. The following emerge: head, face, eye, nose, mouth (lips), neck, torso, arm/hand, foot/leg. Individual features of physiognomy and details are completely lacking.[15]

The absence of details in the corporeal depiction is striking. Perhaps, in light of the spontaneous character of *Kuntillet ʿAǧrūd* and the character of the carrier (i.e. the miniature size of the seals and bulls), it is the result of limited options. A comparison with further portrayals of humans is helpful here, in particular with those where the facilities were not so limited (e.g. in bas-reliefs or reliefs from Egypt, Assyria etc., for more see below).

4.2.1.2 Pictures from Syria-Palestine[16]

The representations discussed so far were, as script and language indicate, directed towards Ancient Israelite (Northern Israelite or Jewish) recipients. The next step is to widen our discussion to Syria-Palestine and to include periods of time other than Iron Age II (III). As is well-known to experts on Ancient Oriental representations, the basic principles of human

---

[14]Ibid., p. 376, cf. p. 375, fig. 358c; cf.: P. Bordreuil, 'Charges et fonction en Syrie-Palestine d'après quelques sceaux ouest-sémitiques du second et du premier millénaire', in: *CRAI* 130 (1986), pp. 290–307. Esp. see pp. 305–7; G. I. Davies, *Ancient Hebrew Inscriptions: Corpus and Concordance* (Cambridge: Cambridge University Press, 1991), p. 252.
[15]Ears are evidently not of such importance in many glyptic pictures.
[16]'Syria-Palestine' means the region to which Ancient Israel and the neighbouring cultures belonged, that is the Near Eastern region bordered to the West by the Mediterranean, to the South by the Sinai peninsula, to the Southeast by the Arabian Desert, to the East by Mesopotamia and to the North by Asia Minor.

representation do not differ greatly within this broader category from those of solely Israelite depictions. Therefore, discussion of this well-known phenomenon can be kept brief.

While emphasizing that the basic principles of representation are the same, I do not mean to deny that there are manifold differences in the iconographic programme, in style, symbolism or other relevant iconographic factors. Pictures from Syria-Palestine were exposed to many varied cultural influences. We must observe and discuss these carefully when we attempt a chronological and more detailed iconographic classification. A simple example illustrates this well: generally, the 'Egyptian' element can be recognized easily (cf. 4.2.1.3) in works from Egypt, or works strongly influenced by Egypt, even by the untrained eye. Stylistic features can be identified as relevant iconographic factors (image motifs, symbols, type of representation, etc.) which together produce the 'Egyptian' impression. However, the basic principles of corporeal representation (and of images in general) are not particularly affected by this, since they are on quite a different level see for example below 4.2.1.4.

Egyptian influence is evident in the next two pictures:

This scarab (Figure 4.6) shows the Pharaoh on the left; on the right 'the royal god Amun presents the sword of victory to the pharaoh. ... The pharaoh then either consecrates or kills a prisoner with this sword in front of the god who has given him the victory.'[17] The find comes from the Egyptian centre Bet-Schean[18] in the late Bronze Age II and is allocated by Keel/Uehlinger to the time of Ramses II.

By now we are familiar with the essential features which are also present in this figure of the Pharaoh: head in profile, torso in front view, arms right and left alongside the torso but in profile (the gesture, the raised arm with a sword, is important for the message conveyed by the picture), legs in profile and striding. The enemy who is being slain is much smaller than the Pharaoh. This is not because the enemy was physically smaller than the Pharaoh but to emphasize the Pharaoh's importance, using size to make the point. There are no further details in the corporeal depiction.

A similar motif originates from Megiddo in Iron Age I. Here (Figure 4.7), too, we see the triumphal Pharaoh; description of the body as for Figure 4.6.

The focus of the next picture (Figure 4.8) is the crescent moon standard which is flanked by two worshippers. The find comes from Hazor, and according to

---

[17]Keel and Uehlinger, *Gods,* p. 92.

[18]'Beth-Shean ... controls the eastern entrance of the great central valley that separates the central hill country from the Galilee. It is at the crossroads where the east–west route from the Mediterranean to Transjordan meets the north–south route that runs along the Jordan valley. This important strategic location was probably what made Beth-Shean an important Egyptian center from the fifteenth century on and especially so during the thirteenth century'. Keel and Uehlinger, *Gods,* p. 82.

FIGURE 4.6 *Scarab.*

Source: Keel and Uehlinger, *Gods, Goddesses, and Images of God in Ancient Israel*, p. 91, fig. 114a.

FIGURE 4.7 *Scarab.*

Source: Keel and Uehlinger, *Gods, Goddesses, and Images of God in Ancient Israel*, p. 121, fig. 144a.

FIGURE 4.8 *Seal impression from Hazor (10th century BCE).*

Source: Keel and Uehlinger, *Gods, Goddesses, and Images of God in Ancient Israel*, p. 148, fig. 171a.

Keel/Uehlinger it is from the tenth century BCE. The imagery shows northern Syrian influence, since the standard was the symbol of the moon god Haran.[19]

In this image, the corporeal representation of both worshippers has nothing unusual on offer: the head in profile, torso in front view, legs in profile and the stride position all correspond to the multi-perspective corporeal depictions discussed so far.

The next picture (Figure 4.9) also shows worshippers on a scarab from Samaria, seventh century BCE. We find 'two *worshippers* facing each other', turned towards the revered god in 'an astral manifestation as a crescent moon'.[20]

The corporeal depiction here adheres to the principles discussed so far. It seems as if the two worshippers were intended to be complementary: one worships optically (left, worshipper with eye and no ear) and one acoustically (right, worshipper with ear but no eye). Or is the 'eye' on the right figure only badly executed? (For the eye/ear issue see sections 5.2.8 and 5.2.9.)

In the next two pictures (Figure 4.10), both from the Persian era, there are again no great deviations from the principles of corporeal representation found previously: bodies in front view, head in profile, eyes in front view, complete absence of details.

The seals from the Syrian–Palestine region which we have investigated so far, therefore display the same basic principles for human depiction as those

[19]Ibid., p. 146.
[20]Ibid., p. 319.

FIGURE 4.9 *Scarab from Samaria (7th century BCE).*

Source: Keel and Uehlinger, *Gods, Goddesses, and Images of God in Ancient Israel*, p. 321, fig. 311a.

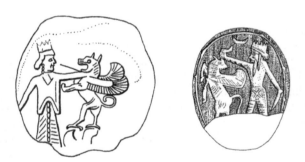

FIGURE 4.10 *Bulla and scarab with motifs of a royal hero (6th century BCE).*

Source: Keel and Uehlinger, *Gods, Goddesses, and Images of God in Ancient Israel*, p. 375, fig. 360a and b.

discussed in the previous section on Israelite representations. The pictures discussed here are, of course, only a small selection but it is clear that the depictions of humans or of hominid figures/bodies do not differ in terms of the basic principles from those shown here. We may therefore assume a relatively uniform basic concept of human representation in the Syria-Palestine region, including Ancient Israel, through the Late Bronze and Iron Ages (mid second millennium–mid first millennium BCE).

A clear deviation from the basic principles of Syrian–Palestinian (or Ancient Oriental) human representation is first seen under Greek influence,

FIGURE 4.11 *Seal from* ᶜAtlīt.

Source: Keel and Uehlinger, *Gods, Goddesses, and Images of God in Ancient Israel*, p. 379, fig. 367c.

beginning in the Phoenician region.[21] We not only find different motifs, as in the next picture from the town of ᶜAtlīt, north of Dor (featuring Hercules as a martial hero, a motif from the Greek world), but also a very different concept of the body. The corporeal perspective in the next picture (Figure 4.11) can be recognized immediately – the body with contoured muscles, that is, a modelled body, is clearly seen. Many of the features from the 'old' corporeal representation are still present (torso in front view, head in profile, eye in front view, absence of ears) but an orientation along Greek lines cannot be denied.

4.2.1.3 Pictures from Egypt, pictures of the Assyrians, Babylonians and Persians

We will consider several pictures from Egypt and Mesopotamia here, to show that the principles of corporeal representation discovered so far in

---

[21]Cf.: For Phoenician art: A. Parrot, A. Chehab, H. Maurice and S. Moscati, *Die Phoenizier: Die Entwicklung der phönizischen Kunst von den Anfängen bis zum Ende des dritten punischen Krieges* (Universum der Kunst 23, München: C.H. Beck, 1977). English: S. Moscati, et al., *The Phoenicians* (London: I. B. Tauris, 2000). For Greek influence, cf.: A. Nunn, Die Phönizier und ihre südlichen Nachbarn in der achämenidischen und frühhellenistischen Zeit – Ein Bildervergleich, in M. Witte et al. (eds.), *Israeliten und Phönizier: Ihre Beziehungen im Spiegel der Archäologie und der Literatur des Alten Testaments und seiner Umwelt* (OBO 235; Göttingen: Vandenhoeck & Ruprecht, 2008), pp. 95–123. See esp. pp. 109–23.

the Israelite and Syria-Palestinian depictions are the same as those which determine pictorial conceptualization in other Ancient Oriental cultures such as Egypt and Mesopotamia. In terms of the basic principles of human representation, the greater cultural region, from Egypt through Syria-Palestine to Mesopotamia, displays uniformity, at least until the Hellenistic period. This pictorial concept was not inherited from the pre-historical era, as developments within Egyptian art[22] and the very different nature of pre-historical pictorial representations in Neolithic times show.[23] Under Greek-Hellenistic influence, as I indicated previously, corporeal depictions then began to change fundamentally.[24]

Egypt (Figures 4.12–4.14)
In a colourful picture full of objects, the Pharaoh is depicted hunting (Figure 4.12). The size of the figures makes very clear that the Pharaoh, as the largest

FIGURE 4.12 *Pharaoh on a chariot.*

Source: Brunner-Traut, *Frühformen des Erkennens: am Beispiel Altägyptens,* p. 14.

---

[22]Schäfer, *Principles of Egyptian Art,* pp. 9–68 and 277–309.
[23]E. Anati, *Höhlenmalerei. Die Bilderwelt der prähistorischen Felskunst* (trans. Dorette Deutsch; Düsseldorf: Albatros Verlag, 1997).
[24]Naturally, development within Greek culture from an 'archaic' human depiction without any perspective to a 'classical' one with perspective took place, cf.: J. Boardman (ed.), *Greek Art* (4th edn, London: Thames & Hudson, 1996); T. Hölscher, *Die griechische Kunst* (Beck'sche Reihe 2551, München: Verlag C.H. Beck, 2007).

FIGURE 4.13 *Scribe.*
Source: Schäfer, *Principles of Egyptian Art*, Plate 14.

FIGURE 4.14 *A master of the household with his wife and son.*
Source: Schäfer, *Principles of Egyptian Art*, Plate 12.

figure, is the most important. However, the representation of the body follows familiar principles: the torso is in front view, the head in profile, eyes in front view and so on. 'Multi-perspectivity' characterizes this picture, as it does in the two following pictures, the first of a scribe (Figure 4.13) and the second of the head of a household with his wife and son (Figure 4.14).

All of these three pictures are highly skilled works of art, certainly not executed in haste or under pressure, nor are they restricted by the carrier as depictions on seals are. It is important to make these observations, for the absence of certain features thus cannot be ascribed to the circumstances surrounding their creation. What is absent is not the result of poor care but (unconsciously) omitted for conceptual reasons. Almost no individual features can be perceived in these depictions, which is typical for almost all depictions of persons in the Ancient Orient.[25] This is true of the faces and of the physiognomy.

Although the carefully executed depictions from Egypt show more details than the representations on seals and so on (finger nails and muscles are occasionally indicated), others are missing (body hair, visible individual skin features, features of age/condition, etc.). These pictures are a far cry from naturalistic representations.

The same principles of human representation are found in Assyrian, Babylonian and Persian art, despite the evident cultural differences.

Assyria (Figures 4.15–17)

In the first picture (Figure 4.15) we see King Asarhaddon with his two sons Assurbanipal and Assurschumukin. The respective size of the figures allows us to recognize immediately which figure is the most important. The King is large, his adult sons smaller, but bigger than the conquered rulers who the King holds captive at the end of a rope.

In all three depictions, we immediately recognize that the principles of body depiction are identical to representations from the Egyptian and Syria-Palestinian region: legs in profile and stride movement, head in profile, the eye in front view, the addition of perspective, absence of individual features, no depiction of sight, typical or ideal gestures and so on. However, Assyrian human representations seem to be more interested in some details of the body – even in seals we find representations of muscles on the arms and calves, indications of knees and ankles – so that the whole impression is more natural than in Egyptian depictions. This is endorsed by a different approach to the depiction of the torso, which is often shown in profile, as here, and not in front view. With that said, individuality and an 'optical' impression of sight are just as absent in the Assyrian representations as they are in the images investigated so far. In fact, this is true even when the

---

[25] As far as Egypt is concerned, exceptions do exist in the Amarna era and are seen in a few other trends.

FIGURE 4.15 *King Asarhaddon and both his sons, Asssurbanipal and Assurschumukin. Stele from Dolerith, 3.18 m high, Zincirli (7th century BCE).*

Source: Matthiae, *Geschichte der Kunst im Alten Orient*, p. 73.

FIGURE 4.16 *Asarhaddon kills a lion, royal cylinder seal rolled in clay, 8.8 cm high, Nimrud.*

Source: Matthiae, *Geschichte der Kunst im Alten Orient*, p. 103.

FIGURE 4.17 *Assurnasirpal III's troops cross the river, alabaster relief from Nimrud-Kalach (9th century BCE).*

Source: Schäfer and Andrae, *Die Kunst des Alten Orients*, pp. 506 and 651.

FIGURE 4.18 *Marble document from King Mardukbaliddin II (Babylonia), 46 cm high (715 BCE).*

Source: Schäfer and Andrae, *Die Kunst des Alten Orients*, pp. 487 and 645.

FIGURE 4.19 *Stele of Nabonid, Trachyt, 52 cm high (6th century BCE).*
Source: Schäfer and Andrae, *Die Kunst des Alten Orients*, pp. 492 and 646.

FIGURE 4.20 *Procession of Persian and Median sentries, relief (detail), limestone, Persepolis, Apadana, Northern entrance (6th–5th century BCE).*
Source: Matthiae, *Geschichte der Kunst im Alten Orient*, p. 213.

FIGURE 4.21 *Persian, scored gold plate, 15 cm high, from the Oxus treasure, Bactria (6th–5th century BCE).*
Source: Matthiae, *Geschichte der Kunst im Alten Orient*, p. 219.

situation depicted necessitates details which would otherwise be unseen, as in the picture of the river crossing (Figure 4.17); here the backs of naked soldiers can be seen.

Babylon and Persia (Figures 4.18–21)
This does not change in Babylonian or Persian human representations, which close our short journey through the Ancient Oriental pictorial world.[26]

4.2.1.4 Features of corporeal representation common to both Ancient Oriental and Israelite depictions which transcend culture and time

The representation of the human body cannot be separated from the representation of other objects and motifs. The coincidental multi-perspectivity

---

[26]Hittite, Phoenician and other pre-Greek art and depictions from the Syria-Palestine region do not differ greatly. Cf.: A. Nunn, *Der figürliche Motivschatz Phöniziens, Syriens und Transjordaniens vom 6. bis zum 4. Jahrhundert v. Chr.* (OBO.A 18; Fribourg: Universitätsverlag, 2000). For Hittite and Aramean, see Schäfer and Andrae, *Die Kunst des Alten Orients*, pp. 551–70. For Urartian, see Matthiae, *Geschichte der Kunst im Alten Orient*, pp. 105–39. For Elamite, Mannaean and Median, see Matthiae, *Geschichte der Kunst im Alten Orient*, pp. 179–207.

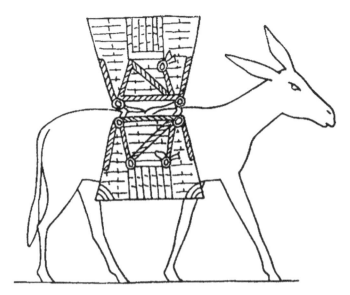

FIGURE 4.22 *Donkey with saddle-bags.*
Source: Schäfer, *Principles of Egyptian Art*, p. 119.

investigated previously emerges as a joint band, independent of culture and era. Indeed it distinguishes this type of rendering in these cultures, quite independent of the depicted objects. I shall introduce only a few proven and significant examples based on H. Schäfer[27] and E. Gombrich.[28] Since I can only look at a few examples and only in so far as it helps our investigation, further information on the principles of representation can be found in the literature cited.

> A painter had to show a donkey with pack-bags hanging down on both sides and tied to each other over its back. In the picture ... [see Figure 4.22] the pack-bag next to the viewer is hanging in its correct place; the other appears to be standing upright on the donkey's back like a basket. The whole picture can easily be confused with ones showing donkeys carrying burdens on their backs as well as others slung over their sides. ... The artist who drew the double bag was concerned only to show that a second equivalent bag corresponded to the first one. Anyone who looked at the picture would know where the second bag hung.[29]

---

[27]Schäfer, *Principles of Egyptian Art*; A. Wagner, 'Heinrich Schäfer', *BBKL* 8 (1994), col. 1518–31; A. Wagner, 'Heinrich Schäfer', *NDB* (2005), pp. 507–08.
[28]Cf.: Gombrich, *The Story of Art*.
[29]Schäfer, *Principles of Egyptian Art*, p. 112.

FIGURE 4.23 *Bed.*

Source: Schäfer, *Principles of Egyptian Art*, p. 112, fig. 69.

Unlike most portrayals from the European tradition (in particular in modern times), pictures from Ancient Oriental tradition do not display what the artist sees but what is essential to the object he depicts. The picture does not reflect an optical impression, but rather information about the object depicted. Objects depicted are therefore reduced to the typical and essential elements. Not all that could be seen of an object and its context is depicted, but only what is essential to the object. The following picture (Figure 4.23) depicts a bedside scene. Essential and typical for a bed is the frame and the side-boards. We see a group of women on the bed, 'and above them the heavens as a symbol of a religious act (birth of the King)'.[30]

The principle of representation could therefore be phrased in the following manner: 'As many aspects of an object as are necessary to distinguish it are placed next to each other.'[31]

The aspects of the object are displayed in their typical view, in this case the bed-frame from above, the side-boards in profile. We find the same combination of perspectives, the same multi-perspectivity, which we have observed in human representations. Straight aspects are almost exclusively chosen (front view, profile, overview) while oblique views are avoided completely. H. Schäfer therefore names this art *geradansichtig*, that is, 'viewed from the front'.[32]

---

[30]Brunner-Traut, *Frühformen des Erkennens*, p. 19.
[31]Ibid.
[32]Schäfer, *Principles of Egyptian Art*, p. 91.

All these observations presuppose that we do not depict a body as it is seen but as it is thought, independent of the image we see. Therefore, we can justifiably talk of 'conceived images'. In H. Schäfer's opinion, concepts are at work here; hence, he calls these kinds of pictures '*geradansichtig-"vorstellig"*', which means 'based on an image viewed from the front'.[33]

Since 'single figures' are central to human representation, too, I will add two further examples which demonstrate the, for us unfamiliar, multi-perspective approach. Given that we are familiar with the pictorial 'logic' from the previously mentioned, I can be brief.

In Figure 4.24, we see a stool. The representation is determined by the understanding of a stool as a piece of furniture for sitting on, which is defined

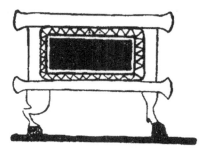

FIGURE 4.24 *Stool.*

Source: Schäfer, *Principles of Egyptian Art*, p. 140, fig. 122.

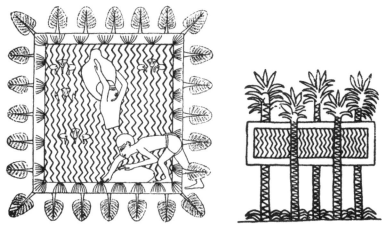

FIGURE 4.25 *Depictions of a pool.*

Source: Brunner-Traut, *Frühformen des Erkennens*, p. 20.

[33]Ibid.

in the main by two things; legs (best seen in profile) and the seat (best seen from above). The depiction of the whole stool, therefore, combines these two aspects, retaining the best view of each part.

What is depicted here (Figure 4.25), as the easily recognizable sheet of water shows, is a pool. The pictures adopt varied means of displaying a pool surrounded by trees and bushes. The principle behind both pictures is the composition as a whole (pool surrounded by trees/bushes) through the summation of the typical parts (pool as a square seen from above, trees/bushes in profile). Both manners of representation make clear that the pool is between the trees/bushes.

In all the pictures mentioned so far, other means of depiction are used than those customarily chosen for pictures which are 'seen'. They do not use perspective to portray space; bodies are not modelled with shadows; the use of colour is singular; the differences in size do not show depth but rather the importance of the objects/persons displayed (gauge of significance); the composition of a picture is determined by the addition of parts and not by a perspective representation of what is seen, which aims at a visual entity and so on. The essential differences between these modes of representation are summarized in the following table:

Characteristics of Ancient Oriental representation:	Characteristics of perspective representation:
• Straight view-conceived representation (H. Schäfer); artists do not follow seen image but their conception of an object; generally, in straight view (front/side view)	• The picture forces the viewer to adopt his perspective; recognition of the whole can only succeed if we not only look two-dimensionally but also survey the whole (three-dimensional) space and the objects within it
• See previous	• Mostly oblique view and rotation of objects
• Single elements, aspects, are in the foreground, not the general view, the perspective overview, therefore E. Brunner-Traut named this type of representation aspective (E. Gombrich)	• Considers the whole picture as an optical unit; organic-uniform understanding of the whole picture where all parts relate to each other functionally
	• Attached and cast shadow clarifies curvature and space
	• Portrayal of physiognomy and individuality

(Continued)

Characteristics of Ancient Oriental representation:	Characteristics of perspective representation:
	• Elements of a representation are subordinated to the whole, single parts may be foreshortened (with increasing distance) or not visible, for example, if they are concealed by other objects
• Knowledge of object determines type of representation, intellectual realism (conceptual representation)	• Visual realism (seen images)
	• Corporeal perspective representations from the end of the sixth century BCE in Greek art, central perspective from Renaissance onwards

In the light of this knowledge, we can now take another look at human representations (Figures 4.26 and 4.27).[34]

The profile is not universal, rather eye and shoulder are depicted frontally, because this is how these parts of the body can be seen best. ... The Egyptian artist [can] place several aspects next to each other in one picture to emphasise each of them. Each is captured singly, and all parts assembled to a whole. The single parts relate to their neighbours, but not necessarily to the whole. Therefore, eye and shoulder are unhesitatingly placed in full front view within a picture of a man otherwise in profile.[35]

What is said here about Egyptian representations is equally true for Hebrew portrayals and for human representation in general in pre-Greek Ancient Oriental art.[36]

The stride movement of the legs is typical for persons portrayed in profile and indicates that living persons are concerned. In Egyptian depictions the

---

[34]We should emphasize again that all the representations, from various Ancient Oriental eras and cultures, shown previously, are determined by the same principles. It is therefore not surprising that I consider that these principles deserve the epithet longue durée. Since Israel is determined by these principles, as are other Ancient Oriental cultures, it is legitimate to discuss Israelite depictions as part of the Ancient Oriental circle and to use Ancient Oriental analogies. This in no way negates historical development, nor cultural differentiation. H. Schäfer's work offers many observations on the historical change which Egyptian art underwent. The few depictions from various cultures shown here allow us to recognize the differences immediately. We should not, however, lose sight of their common characteristics.

[35]Brunner-Traut, *Frühformen des Erkennens*, pp. 34–5.

[36]For the commencement and its limitations, cf.: Schäfer, *Principles of Egyptian Art*.

FIGURE 4.26 *Egyptian married couple.*

Source: Schäfer, *Principles of Egyptian Art*, p. 174, fig. 166.

FIGURE 4.27 *Human representation from the drawing on pithos B from* Kuntillet ᶜАǧrūd.

Source: Keel and Uehlinger, *Gods, Goddesses, and Images of God in Ancient Israel*, p. 214, fig. 221.

feet are striking: in the Old Kingdom of Egypt (ca. 2655–2155 BCE), feet are seen from the inside so that the arch is visible – on both feet! Hands are usually both shown in the same aspect, if they are participating in the same deed.

In corporeal depiction, therefore, the single elements are shown in their plainest, most typical aspect; a person is depicted as the addition of a head in profile, an eye in front view, torso in profile and chest in front view. It is not essential in corporeal depiction what a figure looks like, but rather how it is conceived.

These principles explain in great part why the representations are so conventional. E. Gombrich highlighted this feature:

> What mattered most was not prettiness but completeness. It was the artists' task to preserve everything as clearly and permanently as possible. So they did *not* set out to sketch nature as it appeared to them from any fortuitous angle [*this includes individual physiognomy!*]. They drew from memory, according to strict rules [*without models, no individual portraits*] which ensured that everything that had to go into the picture would stand out in perfect clarity. ... Every artist ... once he had mastered all these rules ... had finished his apprenticeship. No one wanted anything different, no one asked him to be 'original'. On the contrary, he was probably considered the best artist who could make his statues most like the admired monuments of the past. So it happened that in the course of three thousand years or more, Egyptian art changed very little.[37]

This explains why in our eyes most human representations appear to be so lacking in individuality and so idealized. What is depicted is not the natural likeness, what we see, but that which makes a human 'human', and which is typical for the type of person portrayed, whoever they may be, King, hero and so on. It is this human/typical, idealized form that is displayed, and each depicted person is viewed from this human/typical perspective.

The concept of mankind displayed by these principles of pictorial representation

What is expressed in this form of representation reflects certain basic understandings of the world and of mankind.

Compared to a natural manner of depiction, this portrayal of mankind is characterized by reduction, typecast and idealization. This is equally true for the representation of persons of high standing and for elaborate and

---

[37] Cf: Gombrich, *The Story of Art*, pp. 60–5. Emphases in cursive type and comments by A. W. in square brackets.

meticulous works of art.[38] Depictions from Egypt, Mesopotamia and Persia in particular demonstrate this. Essential and typical parts of a person are depicted and added up to a whole. Since the conception does not begin with a model sitting to be portrayed, the basic concept of mankind is expressed particularly clearly. The strongest indicator of this is the complete absence of corporeal individuality. Individuality was of no great importance in the cultures which produced this art form. Therefore, individuals are not identified by external personal characteristics but, if at all necessary (e.g. Kings, Pharaohs or important officials), by particular attributes or the addition of inscriptions. In general, any details which could indicate a particular body form (fat, thin, big, small), age or bodily state (healthy, ill, exhausted, relaxed) are omitted. In a few select cases, we can find a more detailed depiction of the body if it enhances the message to be conveyed. This can be seen in Figure 4.17, the image from Nimrud, which shows soldiers swimming naked through water. The thigh muscles, the buttocks, the naked back and so on are not usually seen in hominid depictions since they are only visible in this particular situation (swimming across a river). The swimming soldiers are not further identified; there is no differentiation of size, and their physiognomy is identical.

In general, therefore, Ancient Oriental depictions of humans display the 'conceived' image of a person; it indicates how a person – in view of his typical and ideal exterior – is conceptualized.

What is important here is that all the body parts depicted are considered important in themselves, and further, that everything which is absent is missing for conceptual reasons; that is, the reduction to the typical is made on conceptual grounds. What is lacking in the depictions thus is not a deficit; it is neither an accident nor the result of inability. It is done for conceptual reasons, even if unwittingly. The choice of elements is therefore crucial for a representation constructed according to this concept.

The choice of parts can only be attributed in a certain respect to the carrier or the motif to be depicted. The more sketchy a depiction is or the rougher the carrier, the stronger the element of reduction becomes. However, the comparison for a depiction such as the one from *Kuntillet ʿAǧrūd* is not a naturalistic representation as we know them from photographs. It is a representation like those found in good works of art from Egypt or Mesopotamia; that is, one that is a depiction according to the ideal, typical concept of a human described previously.

Given the phenomena of reduction, typecast and idealization, which criteria determine the choice of elements in a human representation and what lies behind the combination of these elements?

---

[38]Cf: A. Nunn, Körperkonzeption in der altorientalischen Kunst, in: Wagner (ed.), *Anthropologische Aufbrüche*, pp. 119–50. See p. 140: 'Language and pictures (as far as their corporeal concept is concerned) clearly show that neither form nor appearance interested the Ancient Orientals; only the impact which it should have.' Comments by A.W.

4.2.2 The corporeal concept of statues

The basic principles of corporeal representation in three-dimensional representations (tondo, sculpture, statue, etc.) and in reliefs do not differ from those for bas-reliefs. Since this work will not focus on statues, we shall only touch on this briefly (Figures 4.28–4.32).

In three-dimensional objects, the human form is also depicted in such a manner that the front, back and side aspects are always connected. As far as the single elements are concerned, the figure indeed appears as a naturalistic replica. Oblique prospect, movement, torsion, distension and so on are, however, avoided completely. This gives the statues a static character: 'The observation of nature, and the regularity of the whole, are so evenly balanced that they impress us as being lifelike and yet remote and enduring.'[39]

If we add what H. Schäfer called of pictures, among others, *geradansichtig-vorstellig*, that is 'based on frontal images', as explored previously for reliefs, then we can characterize Ancient Oriental statues as follows: the representation starts with the surface of the body to be reproduced; front, back and side view are at angles to each other in three-dimensional space, in contrast to two-dimensional pictures where all the body surfaces are on one level. This explains why in two-dimensional pictures various aspects are combined (front and side view, etc.) on one level. Sculptures, especially those with human form, are different.

> Their main aspects are ... determined by the main aspects of the face, the feet and the legs which stand peacefully at right angles to the shoulder and the torso. The concept is ruled by the right angled encounter between the side and the front aspects, so much so that the levels in which the artist embodies his concept of the limbs is determined. And so the head, torso, upper arms and thighs are composed to a great extent as a unit, aligned as a right angled intersection, both still and in movement.[40]

The whole, therefore, of a sculpture in human form is the result of the reproduction of parts of the body, each in their typical aspect. Sculptures in human form appear at first sight to be more naturalistic, but they follow the same basic 'construction principles' as representations in relief do.

Sculptural representations, with their strong tendency towards a right-angled intersection of levels, come to fulfilment in the depiction of standing or sitting (kneeling, squatting, etc.) figures. Therefore, the repertoire of positions for sculptures is generally restricted to these two.

---

[39]Gombrich, *The Story of Art*, p. 58.
[40]H. Schäfer, Die Kunst Ägyptens, in: Schäfer and Andrae, *Die Kunst des Alten Orients*, pp. 9–122. See p. 16.

FIGURE 4.28 *Granite statue of a King, 12th dynasty.*
Source: Hamann, *Ägyptische Kunst: Wesen und Geschichte*, p. 12, fig. 3.

FIGURE 4.29 *Scribe.*
Source: Cf. Schroer and Keel, *IPIAO*, Vol. 1, p. 255, fig. 150.

FIGURE 4.30 *Statuette Thutmosis III.*
Source: Hamann, *Ägyptische Kunst*, p. 214, fig. 225.

FIGURE 4.31 *Copper statue of Prince Merenre.*
Source: Hamann, *Ägyptische Kunst*, p. 136, fig. 139.

While reclining figures are seldom found (Figure 4.32), they also fulfil the pictorial principles described so far.

As far as the content of the depictions is concerned, that is the rendering of corporeal details (hair, muscles, and so on are symptoms of age and health) and individual physiognomy (stature, face) and so on, sculptural representations also do not generally differ from reliefs. They, too, tend strongly towards a rendition of the 'ideal' human body, as it was 'conceived'; they, too, are conceptual images.

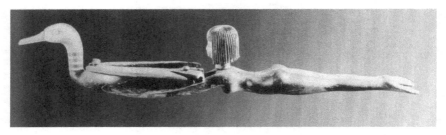

FIGURE 4.32 *Unguent spoon, swimming type, 18th dynasty.*
Source: Michalowski, *Die ägyptische Kunst*, p. 431, fig. 837.

FIGURE 4.33 *The Discobolus Lancelotti (marble replica).*
Source: Boardman, *Greek Art*, p. 175, fig. 202.

How great the variance to Greek sculptures was, can be seen in the following representation (Figure 4.33).

4.3 Function rather than form in depictions of the body or of parts of the body

Verbal images, comparisons, metaphors and so on – I shall use the widest semantic form 'verbal images' – are one of the most fascinating phenomena of language. Verbal images are found in all variations from everyday speech to poetry. They not only convey statements graphically, but they also impart further information en passant in the way they are constituted, where they come from and how the riddle of the picture is to be solved.

Images and comparisons always depend on comparative phenomena from distinct domains. Sometimes this allows us to recognize a speaker's predisposition: for example, if an Old Testament prophet uses agricultural images, then we may assume that he and his audience knew the agricultural world.[41]

As I indicated in section 4.1, we need to have knowledge of the 'things' addressed in verbal images in order to understand their import. It is clear that they develop culturally and historically. The understanding of a house varies considerably between Europe and Polynesia. A couple of examples

FIGURE 4.34 *Tower in a vineyard.*

Source: Morawe, *Turm,* col. 2032.

---

[41]Cf.: H. Weippert, K. Seybold and M. Weippert, *Beiträge zur prophetischen Bildsprache in Israel und Assyrien* (OBO 64; Göttingen: Vandenhoeck & Ruprecht, 1985).

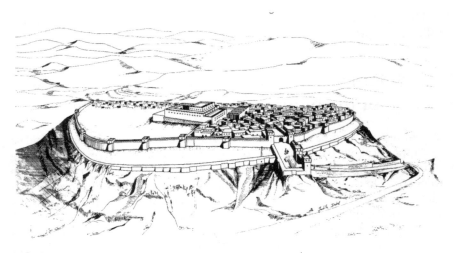

FIGURE 4.35 *Towers on the town wall in Lachisch.*
Source: Fritz, *Die Stadt im alten Israel*, p. 88.

from the Old Testament context will illustrate how historical developments influence our understanding of depictions.

How comparisons are drawn is a central issue. What is the point of a comparison? Cultural characteristics play a role here and they must be understood if we hope to interpret a depiction adequately. Let us now take a closer look at this aspect, which is so decisive for our understanding of anthropomorphism as such. Later it will become clear that this is not relevant for verbal images only.

In a descriptive hymn about a woman in the Song of Songs (Canticum) we find the following metaphorical comparison:

Cant. 4.4 (description of the woman)

4a: *your neck is like the tower of David*

4b: *built as a fortification (in layers)*

The woman's neck is compared with a tower (*David's* tower is a superlative here). A part of the body is compared here to an object present in the real, physical world. If we resolve this comparison clumsily, then we might say that the woman's neck looks like a tower, meaning slim and/ or soaring like a tower. However, we have conveyed two common modern assumptions into the interpretation of the comparison, thereby distorting the biblical statement.

To begin with, we must try to reconstruct our understanding of a 'tower'. Towers in the Old Testament were not slim (round) minarets. In general, they were stocky, square or round, and usually part of a fortification. Towers were also built in vineyards as protective watchtowers (Isa. 5.2), as in the two following depictions (Figures 4.34 and 4.35).

Therefore, the comparison of neck and tower can hardly have had to do with its *form*. Our interpretation of this representation must go in a different direction.

In some texts, not only the neck, but also the nose, is compared to a tower:

Cant. 7.4

5d: *your nose is like the tower of Lebanon,*

5e: *looking towards Damascus.*

Could it mean, as Würthwein suggests, that the nose is *clear-cut, and not flattened*?[42] Rudolph explains the comparison as follows: 'The comparison of a nose with the tower of Lebanon is overly grotesque if we think of it as a building on Lebanon; a rock formation or a mountain ledge named the 'tower of Lebanon' is much more likely. Unfortunately, this comparison does not allow any conclusion as to the form of the nose'.[43] The comparison here does not seem to be aimed at the form. The fact that both neck and nose are compared with a tower should provide food for thought and prevent us from associating it all too quickly with the form. A third part of the body is also compared with a tower, which underlines this thought: the breasts! The form can hardly be the point of comparison for neck, nose and breasts!

Cant. 8.10

10a: *I am a wall*

10b: *and my breasts are like towers*

In his commentary on Cant. 8.10 Rudolph hints at another possibility: breasts are depicted here 'as large as towers and as *powerful to resist* as towers' (author's emphasis).[44] Rudolph clearly senses that this is not about the form of the breasts but about their accessibility or the woman's defensive attitude. This is the right track.

The hymn's context appears to support this interpretation. The hymn is about a sister who, according to her brothers (or perhaps her older sisters?), is inaccessible ('like a wall') or too accessible ('like the leaf of a door') during the search for a bride. The sister answers in v.10 and commits herself to be like a wall towards all suitors and to have breasts defensive as towers, except for her lover to whom she surrenders:

---

[42]Cf. E. Würthwein, Das Hohelied, in: E. Würthwein, K. Galling and O. Plöger (eds.), *Die fünf Megilloth* (2nd edn, HAT I718, Tübingen: Mohr, 1969), p. 63.

[43]W. Rudolph, *Das Buch Ruth; Das Hohe Lied; Die Klagelieder* (3rd edn, KAT XVII 1–3, Gütersloh: Mohn, 1962), p. 173.

[44]Rudolph, *Das Buch Ruth; Das Hohe Lied; Die Klagelieder*, p. 184.

Cant. 8.8–10

> 8: *We have a little sister; and she does not yet have breasts. What shall we do with our sister on the day she is spoken for?*
>
> 9: *If she is a wall, we will build a silver crest on her. And if she is the leaf of a door we will strengthen it with a board of cedar.*
>
> 10: *I am a wall and my breasts are like towers, in his eyes I am like one who has found schalom* (one who has capitulated?).

The point, therefore, is not the form of the towers or the breasts, but the function (defence). The comparison is made not along the lines of form but of function! This cannot be explained in my opinion with 'our' concept of the body, which is so concerned with form. However, we should not jump to conclusions too quickly. O. Keel has opened up many new perspectives in his work on the images and their comparisons in the Song of Songs.[45] Keel summarized: 'The function of the tower is defense and protection, its characteristics are strength, height and inaccessibility. It expresses pride. The comparison of the neck, the nose, the breasts, with towers signals the presence of these forces and properties and this attitude in the ... [person represented].'[46]

The comparison of the tower had been explained in a similar manner by T. Boman:

> We express the same maidenly bearing verbally. When we think of a young lady who wants to resist a young man, she does today precisely what the tower images describe; she holds her nose high (thy nose is a tower), her neck is straightened, and she holds her head high (thy neck is a tower), and she holds herself proudly aloof (Ger. '*sie brüstet sich*') (my breasts are towers). Obviously the Song of Songs aims to express by means of the tower image the same three feminine reactions and motions.[47]

Boman's observation shows clearly that the functional meaning (generally) grows out of the gestural-mimic meaning (including body stance, etc.).

Parts of the body such as neck, nose and breasts can, as I have tried to show so far, have a functional meaning alongside their specific one. In a second step, we must acknowledge that this functional meaning is not bound to a statement in a comparison (your neck is like a tower) which illustrates the defensive attitude of the woman very graphically. This becomes clear when the word (and therefore the representation) *ṣawwā'r*/neck stands on its own for 'pride'.

---

[45]Cf.: O. Keel, *Deine Blicke sind Tauben: Zur Metaphorik des Hohen Liedes* (SBS 114/115; Stuttgart: Verl. Katholisches Bibelwerk, 1984).

[46]Cf.: Keel, *Deine Blicke sind Tauben*, p. 34.

[47]T. Boman, *Hebrew Thought Compared with Greek* (trans. J. L. Moreau; New York: W. W. Norton & Company, 1970), p. 78.

Job 15.25–26

For he has shaken his hand against God, and vaunts himself against the Almighty/Schaddai. He runs against him beṣawwāʾr.

(beʿ = in/with/through, ṣawwāʾr = neck)

Ṣawwāʾr cannot possibly be translated with neck here, no one can run against God 'with the neck'. The only sensible translation of neck is the functional meaning, 'pride'.
He runs against him with pride.

In Ps. 75.6 *beṣawwāʾr* must be understood in a similar way.

Ps. 75.6

(The evildoers are warned:)

Do not lift up your horn to the heights, do not speak with the neck (better: *pride, beṣawwāʾr, arrogance.*

To further demonstrate the functional approach to parts of the body, a second example is helpful, this time concerning our understanding of 'eyes' or the expression 'eyes are like doves/pigeons'.

Cant. 1.15

(See), you are beautiful, my friend, (see) you are beautiful. Your eyes are doves.

Cant. 4.1

See, you are beautiful, my friend, see you are beautiful. Your eyes behind your veil are doves.

Cant. 5.12

(See) his eyes are like doves on streams of water, washed/bathed in milk, which sit above a filled (basin?)

How should we understand this verbal expression 'your/his eyes, which are (like) doves'?[48] Since it is used several times we must assume it is an accepted expression.

Various attempts have been made to explain this verbal expression. H. P. Müller assumes that this is a 'logical ellipse', chosen deliberately by the text so that 'thoughts might float'. 'How the hearer understands the doves is left to his fantasy. No word specifies the comparison of eyes and doves'.[49] This

---

[48]These considerations are based on: Keel, *Deine Blicke sind Tauben*, pp. 53–62.
[49]H. -P. Müller, O. Kaiser and J. A. Loader, *Das Hohelied; Klagelieder; Das Buch Ester* (4th edn, ATD 16.2; Göttingen: Vandenhoeck und Ruprecht, 1992), p. 21.

statement is not quite satisfying. We must ask what was not said but could have been meant. It cannot refer to the shape of a dove's eyes: they are like buttons and have little expression! In Palestine, doves such as the *columba livia* (rock dove or rock pigeon) among others are common, but the colour of their eyes affords little room for comparison, nor do their contours.[50]

Older commentaries suggest that the dove is a symbol for innocence and naivety (cf. the disciples are taught in Mt. 10.16: *Be as harmless as doves!*).[51] However the texts from the Song of Songs are certainly not about innocence and naivety.

A comparison of form or of symbolical meaning does not help us here. A comparison of function is far more revealing:

Prov. 23.31

Do not gaze at wine when it is so red, and shows its eyes in the cup: it goes down smoothly (32 but then it bites like a snake and stings like a viper.)

'Shows its eyes' means the gleam of the wine, its sparkle. The use of *ᶜayin* (eye) in Ezek. 1.7 (cf. Dan. 10.6) is similar:

Ezek. 1.7

… the feet of the visionary figures were like the feet of bulls… and sparkled like the eyes of burnished copper.

In this case, 'sparkled like the eyes of burnished copper' means sparkled like the gleam/lustre/sparkle of burnished copper. These texts imply a strong dynamic component in *ᶜayin* (eye). The following text from Cant. 4.9 should be contemplated with the same dynamic:

Cant. 4.9

You drive me out of my mind, my sister, my bride, you drive me out of my mind with one of your eyes …

Does this really mean *ᶜajin* in the sense of eye (form), eye as part of the body? It would be better to say something like 'with one of your sparkling organs', or even better, 'with one of your glances'. 'Glance' expresses the dynamic-functional quality of *ᶜajin* (eye) best of all. Cant. 6.5 should be understood in this sense:

Cant. 6.5

Turn your eyes/glance from me, for they dazzle me/confuse me/madden me

---

[50]The contours are particularly well emphasized in: G. Gerleman, *Ruth: Das Hohelied* (BK 18, Neukirchen/Neukirchen-Vluyn: Neukirchener Verlag, 1965), p. 114.
[51] Cf.: F. Delitzsch, Hoheslied und Kohelet (BC.AT 4.2; Leipzig: Dörffling und Franke, 1875), p. 37.

Of course 'eyes' or 'glance' in combination with doves have further meanings, too. Keel points out other meanings as for example in Cant. 5.12. Here we find 'refreshed' doves by the water, 'white' doves bathed in milk, doves on the edge of a vessel[52] – 'glances' of the beloved also have all these 'refreshing' effects. We should also not forget that the (white) dove was the attribute of the goddess of love; 'where it appeared and indicated its own sphere, it was understood as the messenger of the goddess of love and of love itself' (wo sie auftauchte, ihre Sphäre signalisierte und ... als Bote der Liebesgöttin und der Liebe verstanden wurde).[53] Keel suggests that the translation should be 'your glances are messengers of love!'[54] What is of importance here is that it is not the form of the eyes, nor their quality as part of the body, that is of consequence for the comparison with a dove; instead, it is their function as an active organ of communication which is the focus, to glance/look. This understanding also applies in Cant. 1.15, 4.1 and 5.12.

We must *always take into account* the functional meaning of parts of the body in the Old Testament. There is no lack of examples for this. I will discuss the parts of the body which are important for understanding anthropomorphism in Chapter 5. Here, we are interested in the general phenomenon of the functional meaning of parts of the body in language (including verbal images). The functional interpretation is also of importance, as the next section will show, for many material depictions of parts of the body (see section 4.4, this chapter).

The words for parts of the body can take on various shades of meaning. The functional meaning does not appear in every case. Sometimes the actual part of the body is meant (cf. the overview of parts of the body in section 2.2).[55]

---

[52]Cf.: Keel, *Deine Blicke sind Tauben*, pp. 56–8.
[53]Ibid., p. 62.
[54]Ibid.
[55]It could be that Schroer and Staubli go too far here, when they emphasize the functional meaning so exclusively: 'Semitic thought, as shown both in its language and its plastic arts, is *never* oriented to forms, appearances and perspectives, but always to the *dynamis*, the activity of something. When the lovers say to one another in the Song of Songs "your eyes are doves," this is not about the shape of the eyes but about the quality of the beloved, loving glance. ... So also in the case of hand, foot, nose, etc., Israelites did *not* think *primarily* of their external form, but of their activity, the power exercised by a strong hand, the foot standing on the neck of the enemy as a gesture of subjugation, the wrathful snorting of the nose ...' (Schroer and Staubli, *Body Symbolism in the Bible*, pp. 24–6, author's emphasis in italic, except 'dynamis'). What matters here is that nuances are possible; the change from one area of meaning to another can be observed in other fields too, for example in the transition from abstract to specific, cf.: Keel, *The Symbolism of the Biblical World*, pp. 8–11. Schroer and Staubli themselves point this out: 'Every concrete thing, for example the hand, that is, points beyond itself. On the other hand it is simply impossible to think of or name an abstract concept like power or strength without a concrete expression', see Schroer and Staubli, *Body*

H. W. Wolff explains this[56] in his anthropology in great detail:

(Stereometric) Thinking thus simultaneously presupposes a synopsis of
the members and organs of the human body with their capacities and
functions. It is *synthetic* thinking, which in naming the part of the body
refers to its function. When the Prophet cries (Isa. 52.7):
   How beautiful upon the mountains are the feet of him who brings
good tidings, it is not the graceful form of the feet that he means, but their
swift movement: 'How beautiful it is that the messenger is hurrying over
the mountains!' Feet, says the Hebrew, but he is thinking of the approach
by leaps and bounds. In Judg. 7.2 Israel's dreaded self-praise is expressed
in the sentence: 'My own hand has helped me.' What is meant of course
is Israel's own efforts – its own strength. The member and its efficacious
action are synthesized. With a relatively small vocabulary, through which
he names things and particularly the parts of the human body, the Hebrew
can and must express a multiplicity of fine nuances by extracting from the
context of the sentence the possibilities, activities, qualities or experiences
of what is named. ... We shall see that the stereotyped translation of a
Hebrew term by the same word inevitably leads the understanding astray
in most cases; it misses all too often the real statement that is being made
about man.[57]

The functional meaning of the parts of the body is determined by history. We
cannot unravel the meaning immediately in every case. In order to unravel
the functional meaning, we must consult both the linguistic transmission
and the transmission of material images. The parts of the body as a whole
build a 'language', a cultural code, and every single part is associated with
a specific meaning. This language must be learnt if we intend to understand
Old Testament statements in which parts of the body play a role. It goes
without saying that this insight is essential to an understanding of the
(linguistic) depiction of the body of God.

Symbolism in the Bible, p. 26. Or put another way, this amounts to the 'openness of the
world toward the supernatural and infernal', cf. B. Janowski, *Konfliktgespräche mit Gott:
eine Anthropologie der Psalmen* (2nd edn, Neukirchen-Vluyn: Neukirchener Verlag, 2006).
English: *Arguing with God: A Theological Anthropology of the Psalms* (trans. A. Siedlecki;
Louisville, KY: Westminster John Knox Press, 2013), p. 28, after Keel, *The Symbolism of
the Biblical World*, p. 56. At the very least, it is asking for misunderstanding to consider this
characteristic 'Semitic; for in the O.T. Egyptians (Hamito-Semites) and Hittites (Indogermans)
also follow this paradigm, and probably there were many other premodern cultures which
thought in similar ways. Whether this was the case in all Semitic languages, at all times,
is unclear.
[56]J. Horst, 'οὖς' *ThWNT* V (1954), col. 543–58.
[57]Wolff, *Anthropologie des Alten Testaments*.

4.4 What is common to material and verbal corporeal depictions?

The accessory knowledge acquired in section 4.1–3 for the phenomena of anthropomorphism can be summarized in four sections.

Verbal depictions of humans function similarly to material depictions of humans

The theory formulated in section 4.1, that verbal and material depictions follow the same pictorial principles in a particular culture, can be described in detail. Thus, let us compare a material image of man with a typical verbal one. A good example here is the Song of Songs since it drafts 'complete' verbal images of beloved persons in the descriptive hymns. The descriptive hymns may be considered representative of the portrayal of humans.[58]

Cant. 7.2–6

2a: How beautiful are your *feet* in their sandals,

2b: O prince's daughter.

2c: The curves of your *thighs* are like jewels,

2d: the work of the hands of a craftsman.

3a: Your *navel* is a rounded goblet,

3b: which never lacks blended wine.

3c: Your *belly* is like a mound of wheat

3d: encircled by lilies.

4a: Your two *breasts* are like two fauns,

4b: twins of a gazelle.

5a: Your *neck* is like an ivory tower (...)

5b: Your *eyes/glances* are the pools of Heshbon

5c: at the gate 'daughter of many'.

5d: Your *nose* is like the tower of Lebanon,

5e: looking towards Damascus.

6a: Your *head* upon you is like Carmel,

6b: the *hair* of your head like purple,

6c: a King is captive in its tresses.

---

[58]For further types of Egyptian and Akkadian texts which express corporeal concepts linguistically, see Brunner-Traut, *Frühformen des Erkennens*, pp. 71–81.

Cant. 5.9–16

9a: What is your beloved more than another beloved

9b: most beautiful of women,

9c: what is your beloved more than another beloved

9d: that you charge us so?

10a: My beloved is radiant and red/ruddy

10b: outstanding amongst ten thousand.

11a: His *head* is pure gold,

11b: his *curls* are date panicles,

11c: black as a raven

12a: His *eyes* are like doves

12b: by the water streams,

12c: washed/bathed in milk

12d: which sit over the filled (basin?).

13a: His *cheeks* are like the beds of balsam,

13b: towers of spices.

13c: His *lips* are like lotus flowers,

13d: dripping with myrrh.

14a: His *hands* are rods of gold,

14b: strewn with tarschisch/chrysolite/beryl

14c: His *belly* is like a work of art made of ivory

14d: overlaid with lapis lazuli

15a: His *thighs* are pillars of marble,

15b: set on bases of gold

15c: His *appearance* is like Lebanon,

15d: choice as its cedars.

16a: His *mouth* is sweet,

16b: he is altogether lovely.

16c: This is my love and this is my friend,

16d: daughters of Jerusalem.

The immediate feeling is that these texts function like the pictures described previously:

- The choice of components, which are like a glance sweeping up and down the body, does not appear to be fixed, either in number or selection. Whether there are more or less elements seems not to play a great role. These hymns are not concerned with a figure described in great detail, which would possess many more parts.

- Although the components are arranged according to the line of vision, the principle adhered to is that of addition and not organic cohesion.[59]

- Individual physical characteristics, individual facial or body physiognomy is not evident; there are no indications of age, condition (tired/relaxed) and so on.

- It is easily possible to talk of 'conceptual images' in the light of the idealized, conceptual representations drafted here, analogue to the material depictions. These are not visual depictions, neither in their rendition (for example steering the beholder's view to visible or concealed parts of the body) nor is a particular person depicted.

Reduction to just a few (typical) parts of the body

We have seen that a verbal human image, as in the previous descriptive hymns, drafts the human figure by assembling the parts into a whole. The choice of body parts is crucial, as in the material depictions. Some body parts are never named, others are rarely missing. In verbal images, too, reduction to the ideal concept, and the parts typical of this concept, is found. We will see that the parts of the body typical to language are generally the same as those used in pictures, a further clear indication that the same concept of the body is present.

Functional meaning of the parts of the body

In section 4.3 verbal examples show that in the concept and representation of the body in the Ancient Oriental-Old Testament region, the functional meaning of the parts of the body is important. What we can say about verbal images is also true for material images. A few examples must suffice to illustrate this point.

In many sources we find depictions of single parts of the body, in both the Palestinian–Israelite context and in the whole of the Ancient Oriental context. Generally, these are not fragments, but representations of single parts from the outset. This phenomenon can be seen very clearly in the depiction of a hand from *Chirbet el-Qôm* (Figure 4.36).

Various interpretations for this depiction of a hand exist: Schroer pleads an apotropaic function, Mittmann considers the hand to be God's protective hand.[60] At least the protective function is consensus. The hand

---

[59]Brunner-Traut, *Frühformen des Erkennens*, pp. 71–81.
[60]Cf.: S. Schroer, 'Zur Deutung der Hand unter der Grabinschrifft von Chirbet el Qôm', in: *UF* 15 (1983), pp. 191–9; S. Mittmann, Das Symbol der Hand in der altorientalischen Ikonographie, in: R. Kieffer and J. Bergman (eds.) *La main de Dieu. Die Hand Gottes* (WUNT 94; Tübingen: Mohr Siebeck, 1997), pp. 19–48.

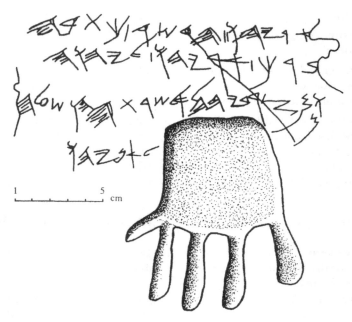

FIGURE 4.36 *Portrayal of a hand from* Chirbet el-Qôm.
Source: Schroer and Staubli, *Body Symbolism in the Bible*, p. 154, fig. 65.

is not an individual portrait, nor is the form important. It symbolizes the requested/desired protection. As was true for verbal images, the function is what matters: Also, with material images, one communicates with the body, the body parts are a sort of language and have certain functions.

Therefore, in order to understand this kind of imagery communication, like the hand in Figure 4.36, for instance, one has to focus on the context. The protective function of the hand manifests itself from the moment when it is contemplated and begins to operate.

Analogous to a speech act,[61] we must conceive a 'pictorial act'[62] here. Since it is there to induce the function and is not primarily representative, nor an emotional expression, we could talk explicitly of a performative or declarative situation.

---

[61]Cf.: A. Wagner, *Sprechakte und Sprechaktanalyse im Alten Testament: Untersuchungen im biblischen Hebräisch an der Nahtstelle zwischen Handlungsebene und Grammatik* (BZAW 253; Berlin/New York: deGruyter, 1997).
[62]Bredekamp, Horst. Bild – Akt – Geschichte, in: GeschichtsBilder 46. Deutscher Historikertag vom 19.-22. September 2007 in Konstanz. Berichtsband, herausgegeben von Clemens Wischermann, Armin Müller, Rudolf Schlögl und Jürgen Leipold, Konstanz, 2007, S. 289–309.

Conventionalism

Conceivably, there is a common ancient tendency that imagery is merely mind-oriented, which also provokes a focus on representing the ideal, rather than reality. This, consequently, leads to a rather conservative sort of reproducing images, verbal ones as well as material. Conventionalism exists in both areas than we find in modern imagery. Indeed, the goal is to be conventional, whether in verbal images or in material ones. It is a positive quality. There is no question that 'pictorial language' in the Ancient Orient is a longue durée phenomenon.

Individuality and conventionalism

As O. Keel exemplarily showed in the Song of Songs the addressees of the biblical texts and the conventionalized types (in the language of imagery) are complementing each other in a positive way.[63] In fact, we often find this in the Old Testament. Only recently did B. Janowski find this in the Psalms,[64] since these texts are meant to be relatable to every individual person. Therefore, verbal repeatability for individual prayers and the like as well as standardized texts or contents are a hallmark of the Psalms.

In these processes of communication, the motion is from the (highly esteemed) conventional to the individual. Individual expression is not in the foreground for the artist, but rather the supra-individual. For the recipient, the individual links in with the conventional and benefits from it by appropriating the content, which opens up new, verbally mediated, horizons of experience.

The same applies in all probability to portrayals. If we look at the devotees from section 2.3 portrayed in *Kuntillet ʿAǧrūd*, then we do not see individuals practising their religion on a particular date in a specific place, recording their event 'historically'. Instead, we see devotees as a type, to whom everyone can relate.

Significance for anthropomorphism

The characteristics named (functionality, conventionalism, etc.) are also found in verbal 'comprehensive pictures', such as the portrayal of God's body as it is found in the entirety of the Old Testament. This image of God is never condensed, as is the image of mankind in descriptive hymns. There are no texts in the Old Testament about the body of God in its entirety.

---

[63]Cf., for instance: Keel, *Deine Blicke sind Tauben*, pp. 15–16.
[64]Janowski, *Konfliktgespräche mit Gott.*, especially, pp. 1–52, and 347–374.

Instead, this comprehensive picture of God's body is formed over the whole of the Old Testament, through smaller references in single texts in which several parts of God's body are mentioned, and through successive perusal and tradition. All in all, however, the form of God's body is not subject to pictorial principles which differ greatly from those already described for verbal and material depictions. Let us now turn to this comprehensive picture of God in more detail.[65]

---

[65]An interesting but not decisive question is whether pictures are understood as being static or animated. If a culture has tuned its recipients to animated pictures (film, television, video, etc.), then this will influence their understanding of verbal pictures. Perhaps this is enough to influence our understanding of a simple word like 'tree' (cf. section 4.1): A tree can be understood as a conceived picture or as a visible picture; as an animated picture or a static one and so on. This influences our understanding of pictures made for quite different recipients; distortion is a real danger and a reflective approach must be sought, which differentiates temporal and cultural influences in interpretation. Independent of modern animated pictorial communication, language allows us to create animated pictures with the help of verbs, nouns which indicate movement and other mediums. The question of movement in material pictures opens another field of discussion; even (nominally) static pictures preserve movement; the observer resolves and augments the depiction of movement, in, before and after.

5

God's body (the external figure) – Its theological message

5.1 The significance of the choice of which parts of the body are depicted

5.1.1 Observations derived from pictures

Our analysis of the depiction of the body will start with a comparison of the material depictions of the body, as seen in Chapter 4. Which parts of the body are fundamental components and are never absent? These fundamental components are the basis of the corporeal conceptual image. The choice of certain body parts, and not others, as fundamental components is in itself a statement on the concept of the body.

Although our comparison is based on a relatively narrow selection of pictures, as far as their number and distribution is concerned, it still affords a helpful approach. The results can be cross-checked with further material at any time.

Table 5.1 lists the characteristics derived from the comparison made in section 4.2.1.4 regarding the Hebrew from *Kuntillet ʿAğrūd* and an Egyptian couple. The left column lists the Hebrew terms for the parts of the body. The first two columns in grey show the invariables (head, hand, foot, etc.) which are found in all cultures. The other columns list phenomena which are associated with single cultures and are changeable (clothes, hair, jewellery).

It is immediately apparent that there is more variance in terms of cultural characteristics than in terms of parts of the body. Since the body remains the same, this is hardly surprising. As far as the number of components depicted is concerned, we must refer to the summary of body depictions made in section 4.2.1.4. In all depictions, we can observe reduction and typecast/idealism. Photographic-naturalistic representations with an abundance of detail are not present. Within these basic observations, however, we find

TABLE 5.1 *Comparison between general and specific cultural depictions*

	Corporeal characteristics: (specific to culture/picture)		Clothing: (specific to culture/picture)		Hair: (specific to culture/picture)		Jewellery:	
	Egyptians	Hebrews	Egyptians	Hebrews	Egyptians	Hebrews	Egyptians	Hebrews
head	x	x			x	x		
face	x	x						
eye	x	x						
ear	x							
nose	x	x						
mouth	x	x						
lips	x	x						
throat, neck	x	x					x	
trunk (!)	x	x						
arm	x	x		(x)			x	
right hand	x							
hand	x							
palm	x							
finger(-nails)	x							
leg/foot	x	x	(x)	(x)				
Sexual characteristics/ differentiation male/female (!)	x	(x)			x			

variations in the grade of reduction, caused by the type of the carrier, the grade of artificiality and so on. Reduction, therefore, has a certain spectrum. The smallest number of body components is found in sketches, such as those from *Kuntillet ʿAǧrūd*, or on seals such as those discussed previously. These are limited by the space available, while the 'stroke' is determined by the material and by skill. If we take all these factors into account, then the results, from the 18[1] depictions investigated (the numbers given in brackets () refer to the number of occurrences – that is, 18x means that the body part is seen in all 18 depictions) are as follows in Table 5.2.

We must take into account that individual physiognomy is not portrayed. It is impossible to extrapolate a real person (e.g. the model) or their body parts (a particular person's face) from a depiction. In these Ancient Oriental corporeal depictions, most of which are taken from pictures of high technical and artistic quality, further parts of the body, or characteristics, are added (see Table 5.3).

Despite this greater variety of details, it remains true for Egyptian/ Ancient Oriental pictures that there are no naturalistic depictions of humans (many details are absent in general: Body hair, skin, etc.) and individual physiognomy is almost completely lacking. Indications of condition are also omitted (tiredness, exhaustion, illness, etc.) unless they are the object of the depiction, for example pictures of Egyptian everyday life, which are rare. The figure is only of interest as far as it is necessary for the perception of humanity.

We are interested in the parts of the body which are chosen to express humanity. The core elements of the body occur consistently throughout the material images. We must interpret this selection in order to develop a clear conception of the 'whole human'. The selection is characteristic for the conceptual image of man; it can be considered as the 'draft' for man,

TABLE 5.2 *Parts of the body*

Head/face	Body below the head
head (18x)	*throat*, neck (18x)
face (18x)	*trunk* (18x)
nose (16x)	*arm* (18x)
eye (14x)	*leg (foot)* (18x)
mouth (lips) (11x)	*hand (right palm)* (7x)
ear (1x?)	

[1]Cf. the group from *Kuntillet ʿAǧrūd* and further representations from section 4.2.1.1.

TABLE 5.3 *Further parts of the body*

Head/face	Body below the head
eyebrows	*tendons*
eyelids	*muscles*
cheek bones	*joints*
jaw	*finger(nails)*
	toe(nails)
	arch of the foot
	sexual characteristics, differentiation male/female

the basic anthropological statement. This does not mean that there were no further concepts, no further knowledge, nor further consciousness of elements of the body. Yet a selection was made, and we need to ask what the criteria were if we want to understand the concept of man. The awareness of further characteristics and properties is demonstrated above all in language, as we shall see in the next section.

5.1.2 Observations on language and texts in the Old Testament (verbal images)

We can regard verbal representations of parts of the body from various points of view. For one thing the verbal ascertainment of parts of the body is an explicit recognition that these parts of the body exist. Naming and recognizing belong together. For another, the verbal context also offers further understanding of the parts of the body, for example gesture and functional meaning. The parts of the body named in language and text form a 'comprehensive picture' which is related to corporeal depictions in material images. In all these aspects, the catalogue of body terms, and their frequency, play a great role. Let us now consider these elements.

Catalogue of body terms

A catalogue of the Hebrew terms for body parts (initially only the nouns) follows (Table 5.4): this could be augmented with adjectives and verbs, but the list is already highly informative as it is. I have concentrated on terms which name, or refer to, external parts of the body since these are decisive for the anthropomorphism of the external form. They are also our reference

TABLE 5.4 *Catalogue of external body terms*

ʾaṣṣîl armpit	ʿerwāh bareness/nakedness	ræḡæl foot/leg	toʾar figure
kātēp armpit/shoulder	ʿeryāh nakedness	kap ræḡæl sole of the foot	temûnāh figure
ʾezrôaʿ arm	qālôn shame (?)	ḥēk roof of the mouth	qārḥāb baldness
zerôaʿ arm	šad breast/chest	malqôaḥ roof of the mouth/part of the pharyngeal cavity	qāraḥat baldness
bat ʿayin eyeball	baṭen breast		[bad], bāśār penis
bābat ʿayin eyeball	gab back/hunch(back)	ræsæn bit/teeth	yeṣurîm limbs/extremities
ʿayin eye	ḥēq bosom (in the sense of 'grasping sb. in someone's arms')	ʾaṣṣîl [ʾārbāb] joint	gargerôt throat
ʿapʿappayim eyes (poet.)		mapræqæt neck/nape	śēʿār hair
gab eyebrow	ḥob bosom	qēbāb genitals	śaʿarāb hair
ḥor cavity of the eye	ḥoṣæn bosom	šēt bottom	śêbāb hair, grey
šemurāh eyelid	beḥôn thumb	ʿopæl growth/tumour	qādqod śēʿār parting/vertex (in the hair)
ʿapʿappayim eyelashes/-lids	bohæn yād thumb	teḥorîm tumours	gargerôt neck/nape/cervix
marʾeh look	ʾammāh ell	māzôr festering/purulent wound	gārôn neck/throat
leḥi cheek	ʿerwāh nakedness		ṣauwaʾr neck
yāḥēp barefoot	ʿāqēb heel	šeḥîn pox- or leprosy-related growth/wound	yād hand
zāqān beard	lāšād fat/(bone) marrow	śeʾēh growth	ʾeṣbaʿôt hand
baṭen belly	pîmāh fat	ʾabaʿbuʿot pox-related growth/wound	kap hand
ḥomæš belly	ḥēlæb fat (especially of the omentum)		ḥopæn hollow of the hand
kārēš belly	šemæn fat	pānîm face	šoʿal hollow of the hand
qēbāb belly	temûnāh figure	hôd complexion, fresh	ʾaṣṣîlê yādayim wrists
qeræb abdominal cavity (bowels)	ʾeṣbaʿ finger	gizrāh frame/figure/form	rôʾš head
śēʿār hairiness	qoṭæn little finger	marʾeb figure	dallāh hair
šôq leg/thigh	ṣiporæn fingernail	ʿayin figure	pæraʿ hair
ʿopæl boil	bāśār flesh	ṣîr figure	bāśār skin
yabælæt blister	šeʾēr flesh	qeṣæb figure	gælæd skin
yērāqôn paleness			ʿôr skin
maʿar bareness/nakedness			

(Continued)

bohaq skin eruption
baherœt fleck (on the skin)
ᵓešek testicle
yārēk hip/loin
ḥᵃlāsayim hips/loins
mātnayim hips/loins
nāšeb pelvis
gibēᵃḥ baldhead
qērēᵃḥ baldhead
nœpœš throat
lᵉḥî jaw
bœrœk knee
sᵉᶜîpîm kneepit
qarsol ankle
ᵓapsayim ankles
gœrœm bone
ᶜœṣœm bone
ᶜoṣœm bone
roᵓš head
bāśar body
gap gᵘwiyāh body
ᶜœṣœm body
mātnayim lower back
bœṭœn body
bāśar body
gᵘwiyāh body
hālāṣ loin
yārēk loin/hip
kœsœl loin

śᵉmoᵓl left (side)
śāpāh lip(s)
śāpām mustache
qᵉwuṣṣōt curls
pānîm mien/expression
pœh mouth
ḥēk mouth
midbār mouth
śāpāh mouth
šad breast (mother's)
ᶜorœp nape
ṣauwāᵓr cervix
sᵉḥœm neck
ṣārœbœt scar
ᵓap nose
ᵓapsayim nasal orifices/ nostrils/nares
ᵓozœn ear
bᵉdal ᵓozœn earlobe
tᵉnûk ᵓozœn earlobe
ᵓîšôn pupil
mᵉqôr dāmîn source of blood from monthly period
yāmîn right side/right hand/arm
ṣēlāᶜ rib/costa
gᵘdûdah incision/wound (due to trauma)
gab back
gaw back

gēw back
gap back
ᵓāḥôr hinder part
gulgolœt skull
bāśār pudendum virile (penis)
nablût pudenda muliebria/ pudendum (vulva)
pot pudenda muliebria/ pudendum (vulva)
mᵉbûšîm pudenda muliebria/ pudendum (vulva)
māᶜôr pudenda
qādqod top of the head
šôq leg/thigh
raqqāh temple
pᵉᵓāh temples
ḥœrœs slough/crust/slab/ eschar
mispaḥat slough/crust/slab/ eschar
sapaḥat slough/crust/slab/ eschar
mipśāᶜāh crutch
kātēp shoulder
šᵉkœm shoulder
kātēp shoulder blade/ bladebone/scapula

qāneh the higher bone of the arm/shoulder joint
gîd tendon
ᵓēṣœl side
ṣad side
mēṣaḥ forehead
ṣiṣit forelock
gizrāh waist
ḥomœš lower abdomen (?)
mēᶜeb lower abdomen (?)
zᵉrôᵃᶜ forearm
ᶜārlāh foreskin/prepuce
ḥabûrāh bruise
māzôr wound
maḥaṣ wound
makāh contusion
ᶜaṣṣœbœt wound
pœṣaᶜ wound
šēn tooth
mᵉtallᶜᵊôt teeth
maltāᶜôt teeth
ᶜôr šinnayim gums
ᵓœṣbaᶜ raglayim toe
bohœn rœgœl big toe
ᵓœṣbaᶜ forefinger
maḥlāpôt plaits of hair
lāšôn tongue

TABLE 5.5 *Body terms which appear more than 100 times*

	Number	THAT-Rang	Tora (26,82% of Old Testament)	Nebiim (47,07% of Old Testament)	Ketubim (26,12% of Old Testament)
01 *pānîm* face	2127	25	627	925	575
02 *yād* hand	1618	30	382	800	436
+ *kap* palm	192	235			
+ *yāmîn* right hand	139	306			
03 *ᶜayin* eye	866	51	217	394	255
04 *næpæš* throat, neck	754	63	205	272	277
05 *roʾš* head	596	84	ca. 144	ca. 224	ca. 207
06 *pæh* mouth	500	102			
07 *ʾap* nose	277	178			
08 *ræg<æl* foot	247	192			
09 *ʾozæn* ear	187	239			
10 *śāpāh* lips	176	252			
11 *zᵉrôᵃᶜ* arm	93*	–			

*sole exception, just below 100 times

point for comparisons with pictorial representations. As far as I am aware, there are no representations with inner organs in Ancient Israelite pictures.

This list makes us aware of the concept of the body as a basic principle. It also supplies information on the explicit names for parts of the body. You may well be astonished to find such a diversity of terms, considering that the verbal corpus of the Old Testament is not so vast.

In our context, this catalogue has two particular functions:

- For one thing it becomes clear that many more parts of the body are available and named in the Hebrew language than are revealed by pictorial representations. Thus, it can be said that the body parts not depicted are marginalized from the reality of perception. This emphasizes the reduction and selection present in pictorial representation, due not to poor perception but to a particular representational intention.

- The collection supplies the background for a list of those body features most often used; the demarcation between terms used frequently and those seldom used is very clear.

TABLE 5.6 *Comparison of importance of body parts in written and pictorial sources*

Rating (according to frequency)	The eleven most frequent corporeal elements *linguistically*		Rating (according to frequency)	The eleven central parts of the body in Hebrew pictorial *representation* (as far as they have been discussed here, numbers in brackets)	
	head/face	body below the head		head/face	body below the head
01	*pānîm* face		01 (6x)	head (18x)	
02		*yād* hand + *kap* palm of the hand + *yāmîn* right hand	—	face (18x)	
03	*ʿayin* eye		—		throat, neck (18x)
04		*næpæš* throat, neck	—		arm (18x)
05	*roʾš* head		—		leg (foot) (18x)
06	*pæh* mouth		—		trunk (18x)
07	*ʾap* nose		07	nose (16x)	
08		*rægel* leg/foot	08	eye (14x)	
09	*ʾozæn* ear		09	mouth (11x) (lip)	
10	*śāpāh* lips		10		hand (7x) (right hand, palm of the hand)
11		*zᵉrôaʿ* arm	11	ear (1x?)	

The frequency of body terms

The terms used frequently are clearly evident in the complete catalogue of body terms. High frequency underlines the importance accorded to these parts of the body. Less important parts were mentioned less often.

Let us now compare those parts of the body most commonly found in Old Testament language with those found in pictures (see Table 5.6).

The more or less complete concurrence is very striking. The eleven verbal terms used most frequently are all present as core parts of the body in pictorial representations.

The emphasis varies slightly: This is seen most clearly in the 'arm' which is a constitutive part of pictures but is most infrequent on the verbal list.

There are two further striking observations:

- There is no verbal equivalent for the 'trunk' of the body which is always portrayed in the pictures. It is unlikely that the absence of this word in Old Testament Hebrew texts is coincidental, considering the high number of body terms on record. It is far more plausible that Hebrew does not possess this term.

- Disinterest in the ear in pictorial representations is also conspicuous. In material representations, the ear appears to be superfluous, but in texts the ear belongs to the 'top ten' body terms mentioned. This contradiction will be discussed subsequently.

5.2 The functions of the integral (external) parts of the body

5.2.1 Synthetic spectrum of meaning

Beginning with specific corporeal concepts and before proceeding via functions of gesture and facial expression to further functional aspects, we will investigate the functions of those parts of the body used most frequently in language and picture. These three aspects are not sharply separated and generally one predominates over the others. As far as language is concerned, it is important to emphasize that all three aspects use one common Hebrew term which combines all these meanings. We cannot always translate Hebrew terms with the same meaning, as H. W. Wolff has pointed out.[2] The Hebrew terms are an important bracket holding together all aspects of

---

[2]Wolff, *Anthropologie des Alten Testaments*, pp. 7–9, esp. p. 8. Quotation can be found in section 4.3, p. 80.

meaning for a given part of the body. Oscillation between specific, gestural-mimic and functional aspects is possible, the joint term being the hinge. Current literature, in particular that of H. W. Wolff, and S. Schroer and T. Staubli, is full of ideas for the range of meanings.[3]

In order to make the various facets of meaning comprehensible, I will use specific texts. Generally speaking, the meaning is made evident by the context: therefore, if an explanation is not necessary I will let the text speak for itself. To illustrate the breadth of meanings and the inclusion, according to Wolff, of aspects beyond the specific, I will speak of the 'synthetic spectrum of meaning' of a part of the body.[4] Since this is particularly easy to see in the active organs (hand, arm, foot) I will start with these. Initially, the hand will be discussed in more detail; other parts of the body will only be discussed as far as is necessary to reveal their function within the entire picture of the human figure, that is, in anthropomorphism. Further explanations can be found in the literature indicated.

5.2.2 Synthetic spectrum of interpretation for *hand/right hand/(right) palm*[5]

Our first references point to the hand as a part of the body which performs corresponding actions:

a   Aspect: Corporeality of the hand

Judg. 16.29 *And he [Samson] took hold of the two middle pillars upon which the house stood, and he braced himself against them, his right hand on the one and his left hand on the other.*

Prov. 26.15 *The sluggard buries his hand in the dish, and he is too lazy/it grieves him to bring it back to his mouth.*

Gen. 48.13 *Then Joseph took them both, Ephraim on his right hand towards Israel's left hand and Manasseh on his left towards Israel's right hand, and brought them close to him.*

We encounter the combination of specific and gestural meaning, as found in Gen. 48.13, quite often. 'Taking ... by the hand' presupposes specific action in, and through, that part of the body.

---

[3]Cf.: Wolff, *Anthropologie des Alten Testaments*; Schroer and Staubli, *Body Symbolism in the Bible*.
[4]Wagner, *Das synthetische Bedeutungsspektrum hebräischer Körperteilbezeichnungen*, pp. 1–11.
[5]Cf.: A. Wagner, 'Hand', *WiBiLex* (2007), retrieved from Deutsche Bibelgesellschaft: https://www.bibelwissenschaft.de/stichwort/40970/.

The spectrum of meaning for the 'hand' includes several gestural aspects. It is important to recognize that gestures are not all, and not automatically, valid for all cultures and ages. Some of the gestures found in the Old Testament can be comprehended immediately; others cannot. The following short list does not claim to be complete but instead aims to give a brief overview:

b Aspect: Gestural meaning of the hand

- *gesture*: To shake hands (to seal an arrangement/validity):

2 Kgs 10.15 *After he [Jehu] left there, he met Jehonadab son of Recab, who came to meet him. He saluted him and said to him: Is your heart in accord as my heart is with your heart? Jehonadab said: Yes. If so, give me your hand! And he [Jehonadab] gave him his hand. And Jehu took him up to him into the chariot and said: Come with me and see my zeal for Yhwh! And he let him ride with him in his chariot.*

This gesture was probably used when an agreement was concluded. It can also be seen in a contemporary depiction found on a limestone relief from Salmanassar II's throne room (858–824 BCE) in Nimrod (Iraq). The Assyrian King seals an agreement with a fellow King by shaking hands (both give their right hand).

- *gesture*: to clap hands (gesture of joy)

Ezek. 25.6 *For this is what Adonaj Yhwh said: Because you have clapped your hands and stamped your feet and because you rejoiced with all the malice of your heart (beⁿnœpœš) against the land of Israel …*

FIGURE 5.1 *Limestone relief from the throne room of Salmanassar II. (858–824 BCE).*

Source: Keel, *The Symbolism of the Biblical World*, p. 96, fig. 123.

Isa. 55.12 *Verily, you shall go out in joy and be led forth in peace. Mountains and hills will burst into song and all the trees of the field will clap their hands* (The trees are personalized and anthropomorphized).

Ezek. 25.6 indicates that clapping hands were associated with joy in the Old Testament (it is combined with the verb *śmḥ rejoice*) – although in this case the fact that the Ammonites clap their hands for joy is a negative event from Yhwh's point of view. Clapping hands is equally connected with joy in Isa. 55.12. We can understand this gesture easily. Other explanations for clapping hands are more difficult for us to understand.

Depending on the context, however, clapping can express rejection rather than affirmation, or even expulsion. For example, in this apotropaic sense it was customary to clap in the presence of someone stricken by misfortune in order not to be drawn into the sphere of his or her accursedness (Job 27.23), or at sight of a ruined city (Lam. 2.15). Ezekiel is ordered to clap his hands over Israel and to stamp his feet because Israel has become a demonic horror to Yhwh (Ezek. 6.11) that must be driven out publicly, like wild beasts in the field. Or he is to clap his hands and raise the war cry like a warrior armed with the sword, and Yhwh will do the same (Ezek. 21.19, 22).[6]

• *gesture*: spread out hands in prayer

Ps. 44.20 *If we had forgotten the name of our God and spread out our hands to a foreign god: 21 would it not be so that God would discover it? Verily, he knows the hidden things/secrets of our hearts.*

Ps 44.20, of course, criticizes turning to a foreign god in prayer. The psalm does this with a gesture typical to the Old Testament and the Ancient Orient; the hands are spread out in prayer, and not clasped or folded. This gesture can be seen in the depiction from *Kuntillet ꜤAǧrūd* as discussed in Chapter 2.

Although the hands are not portrayed in this illustration (since details are completely lacking) the gesture can be recognized clearly – in physical terms the arm is part of the gesture, although it is not mentioned in the verbalized gesture.

• *gesture*: hands raised to swear an oath[7]

Gen. 14.22 *Abram said to the King of Sodom: 'I raise my hand to Yhwh, El Eljon, who created heaven and earth: [V.23 I will accept nothing which belongs to you, neither a thread nor a thong ...]'*

Deut. 32.40 *For I will lift my hand to heaven and declare: As sure as I live for ever: 41 when I sharpen my flashing sword and my hand grasps it in judgement, I will take vengeance on my adversaries and repay those who hate me.*

---

[6]Schroer and Staubli, *Body Symbolism in the Bible*, p. 153.
[7]Cf. Deut. 17.7; Ps. 106.25.

FIGURE 5.2 *Praying group (pithos B).*
Source: Keel and Uehlinger, *Gods, Goddesses and Images of God*, p. 214, fig. 221.

Ezek. 36.7 *Therefore, so says my Lord Yhwh: 'I raise my hand (to swear): (I swear with uplifted hand) Surely the nations that surround you will suffer humiliation.'*

Cf. Deut. 17.7, Ps. 106.25

- *gesture*: hands laid in oath on the partner's genitals

Gen. 24.1 *Abraham was old and well advanced in years, and Yhwh had blessed him in every way. 2 And Abraham said to his eldest servant in his house, who was in charge of all that he had: Put your hand under my thigh 3 and swear by Yhwh, the god of heaven and the God of earth, that you will not take a wife for my son from the daughters of Canaan among whom I am living, 4 but will go to my country and to my relatives and take a wife for my son Isaac (there).*

S. Schroer and T. Staubli rightly suggest that 'behind this archaic custom may lie the notion that the oathtaker swears by his manly strength, which will dry up if he breaks the oath'.[8] This gesture is also documented pictorially:

- *gesture*: to lay on hands in blessing

Gen. 48.14 *Israel reached out his right hand and put it on Ephraim's head, who was the younger, and crossing his arms, he put his left hand on Manasseh's head, though Manasseh was the firstborn. 15 And he blessed Joseph and said ...*

---

[8]Schroer and Staubli, *Body Symbolism in the Bible*, p. 156.

FIGURE 5.3 *Scarab (2nd millennium BCE?).*
Source: Keel, *Corpus der Stempelsiegel-Amulette aus Palästina/Israel*, p. 488, fig. 470.

The range of gestural meaning for the hand is indeed very wide. Many of these tend towards the abstract. Abstract and functional meanings are the focus of the next section.

   c aspect: functional meaning of the hand

- facets of functional meaning: to hold by the hand, in the positive sense of protecting, enclosing, and guiding: to have power over somebody.

Ps. 73.23 *Nevertheless I remain with you always; for you hold me by my right hand.*

The right hand/side is the side of honour; the emphasis on the right side expresses more than just being led by the hand. It expresses a 'friendly and trusting relationship'.[9]

- facet of functional meaning: to work:

Deut. 14.28 *At the end of three years, sort out the tenth of that year's produce and deposit it in your (gates=) living place/town. 29 And the Levite shall come, who has no part nor inheritance from you, and the*

---

[9]Ibid., p. 159.

stranger and the fatherless and the widow who lives in your town and
they shall eat and be satisfied so that Yhwh, your God, may bless you in
all the work of your hands.

- facet of functional meaning: to exercise power:

Ps. 22.16.20 *For dogs have surrounded me, a band of evil men encircle*
me ... 20 Deliver my life from the sword, my precious life from the hand
of the dog/from the power of the dog!

Deut. 2.24 *[Rise up! Set out! Cross the valley of Arnon!] I have given into*
your hand Sichon, the King of Heschbon, the Amorite and his country
[Begin to take possession of it and engage him in battle.][10]

2 Chron. 12.5 *[The prophet Shemaiah came ... and said to them:] 'This is*
what Yhwh says: You abandoned me and (now) I abandon you (and give
you) into the hands of Shishak'.

Job 1.12 *[Yhwh said to Satan] 'Everything he has is in your hands. But*
do not lay your hand on the man himself!' ...

Job 2.6 *[Yhwh said to Satan] 'He is in your hands. But spare his life'.*

The meaning of 'exercising power' can assume an independent existence free
of any reference to a part of the body, so that certain combinations of words
have a purely functional meaning. The expression 'the hand of the tongue'
Prov. 18.21 certainly does not mean a personalization or anthropomorphism
of the tongue, analogue to the personalization of the trees in Isa. 55.12;
rather it means the *'power of the tongue'* (*Death and life are in the power of*
the tongue ...). Josh. 8.20 is similar: *The men of Ai looked back and saw the*
smoke of the city rising against the sky and they had no 'hands' to flee this
way or that. ... It is quite clear that this does not mean the hand, as part of
the body, nor a gesture; rather the abstract-functional meaning 'possibility
to act' or 'power' is meant.[11]

These verbal examples of interpretations for the hand can be explained
relatively easily with the help of the contextual information available. Pictures
are more of a challenge. If a gesture is not the main focus of a picture, then
it is difficult to interpret the depiction of a hand, although solitary hands
are depicted, and with them the whole spectrum of possible meanings. We
saw the depiction of a hand in Chirbet el-Qôm previously (in section 4.4).
The interpretation is a matter of great debate: Just as a Hebrew term cannot
be translated with a stereotype, there is no stereotypical interpretation of a

---

[10]Wagner, *Sprechakte*, pp. 109–11.
[11]Cf.: Wolff, *Anthropology of the Old Testament*, pp. 67–8.

material or mental image of a hand. In the same way that we have to weigh up various possibilities in a picture puzzle, the intended meaning of a given picture must be sought.

As is true of pictures, verbal depictions have no interest in the individual form of a hand, not even when the intention is genuinely corporeal.

5.2.3 Synthetic spectrum of interpretation for *foot/leg*[12]

We have a few examples to begin with in which the corporeal aspect (without gesture or abstract meaning) determines the interpretation of the foot.

> Exod. 12.11 (from the regulations for the Passover): *This is how you are to eat it: with your loins girded and your shoes on your feet and your staff in your hand and you should eat it in haste. ...*

Feet are clothed with shoes to make it easier to walk; without doubt, the foot is designated here as the part of the body which 'bears' a man, with which he walks. Oddly enough, Hebrew does not differentiate between foot and leg.

> 1 Sam. 14.13 *And Jonathan climbed up with his hands and his feet and his armour bearer after him.*

Jonathan and his armour bearer climb up to a cliff fortification without any physical aids, other than those parts of their bodies, the hands and feet.

In the next example, the feet are an element in 'foot-washing'; here the actual part of the body, the foot, takes part in the ritual.

> Gen. 18.4 *Let a little water be brought, and wash your feet, and rest under the tree.*

In the Old Testament, foot-washing is a ritual: It was considered the lowest service of a slave. Thus, it was one of the daily activities that reflected social classes and structures of domination. Anyone who had to wash others' feet was counted among the losers. ... This is not altered by the fact that the action was understood as a loving gesture when a wife or children performed it for the *paterfamilias*, or as a sign of respect when disciples washed the feet of their teacher.'[13]

---

[12]Cf.: A. Wagner, 'Körperteile' (AT), *WiBiLex* (2013), retrieved from Deutsche Bibelgesellschaft: https://www.bibelwissenschaft.de/stichwort/64672/.
[13]Schroer and Staubli, *Body Symbolism in the Bible*, p. 197.

What is of particular interest in this ritual is that the foot-washing takes place in the context of power and hierarchy: we will encounter this relation between the foot and power repeatedly.

Josh. 5.15 touches on another relation: here the foot is that part of the body which also stands for a person's presence. The feet establish his contact with a particular place – the sanctity of the location where Joshua sojourns is only preserved if he has no shoes on his feet.

> Josh. 5.15 *And the commander of Yhwh's army said to Joshua: take off your shoes, for the place where you are standing is holy. And Joshua did so.*

Walking barefoot, as seen in Isa. 20.2, is a sign of poverty and helplessness, signalling the need for protection:

> Isa. 20.2 *Yhwh spoke though Isaiah, the son of Amoz, at that time and said: go, and take off the sackcloth from your body and take off your shoes. And he did so and went naked and barefoot. 3 And Yhwh said: Just as my servant Isaiah has gone naked and barefoot for three years as a sign and portent against Egypt and Cush, 4 so the King of Assyria will lead away naked and barefoot the Egyptian prisoners and those outcast from Cush, young and old, with buttocks bared, to Egypt's shame.*

Walking barefoot, one might say, touches on the negative aspect of the relation between the foot and power, on impotence. The boots of the warriors walking lockstep are the opposite of walking barefoot (Isa. 9.4).

The term foot is often resorted to in order to express the fullness of power, might and presence:

> Ps. 110.1 *Yhwh spoke to my Lord (the King): 'Sit at my right hand, until I make your enemies a footstool for your feet.'*

Whatever lies under our feet is subject to our power, whether these are our enemies as in Ps. 110 or creation as in Ps. 8.

> Ps. 8.4 *What is man that you are mindful of him, the son of man that you care for him? You have placed him a little lower than God and crowned him with honour and glory. 7 You have made him the ruler over the works of your hands, and placed everything under his feet. 8 sheep and cows, and the wild beasts, 9 the birds of the air and the fish in the sea and all that swims in the sea.*

Following this logic, we might think that those who desire to exercise power need 'feet'.

5.2.4 Synthetic spectrum of meaning for *arm*[14]

Many movements are accomplished with the arm. One of these, shooting with bow and arrow, is described in Ps. 18.35:

> Ps. 18.34 *He trains my hands for battle and my arms to bend a bow of bronze.*

As we saw for foot and hand, gestural meaning is clothed in language for the arm, too. One of these gestures, the outstretched arm as a sign of mightiness, was depicted in one of the illustrations in section 2.1. We find this motif above all in Egyptian depictions as a sign of the Pharaoh's power. Ezek. 30.21 assumes this knowledge and asserts Yhwh's supremacy over Pharaoh graphically, in that Yhwh breaks the Pharaoh's arm:

> Ezek. 30.21 *Son of man, I have broken the arm of Pharaoh, King of Egypt, and behold, it has not been bound so that it could heal, nor put in a splint so that it could become strong again. ...*

God's mighty arm is a motif often used in the Old Testament; in contrast to this, a king's mighty arm is not found in the Old Testament other than in contexts such as in Ezek. 30.21. 'At certain times the same motif was carved on amulets even in Palestine; these guaranteed the one who wore or carried them of the striking power of divine strength. Only in this way – but never as a symbol of human strength – the same motif entered the Bible.'[15]

> Jer. 32.21 *And [you, Yhwh] have brought your people Israel out of Egypt with signs and wonders, with a mighty hand and outstretched arm and with great terror.*

All the power of the (divine?) 'owner of the arm' is accessed via the arm amulet.

Several phrases and expressions which refer especially to the functional meaning develop from this connection between power, and the exercise of power, and the arm:

- a 'man of the arm' is a man with power, a magnate.

> Job 22.1 *Then Eliphaz of Teman replied and said: ... 8 the land belongs to the powerful man [ʾîš zᵉrôaᶜ/man of the arm] and his minion may live on it.*

---

[14]Cf.: A. Wagner, *Arm*.
[15]Schroer and Staubli, *Body Symbolism in the Bible*, p. 171.

- The following statement taken from Jer. 17.5 cannot be understood without knowledge of Old Testament anthropology. What kind of man counts 'flesh as his arm'?

Jer. 17.5 *This is what Yhwh says: cursed is the one who relies on man and deems flesh as his arm (considers flesh/bāśār mighty) and whose heart turns from Yhwh.*

In Hebrew, 'flesh' refers to man's transient nature; all living beings have 'flesh', but the term is never used in connection with God. God is not transient. We already know the meaning of the arm – the power which it can exercise. Therefore, it is the man who relies on the transience of mankind who is cursed in Jer. 17.5, the man who puts transient human power and strength before God's immortal power and strength. A free translation then reads as follows: *Cursed is the one who relies on man and considers himself strong, who relies on himself alone. ...*

Jer. 48.25 *Moab's horn is cut off and her arm is broken, says Yhwh.*

In Jer. 48.25, 'arm' is best translated with power/fighting strength (see the arm of Assur in Ps. 83.6); the arm motif cannot be understood literally here since a nation does not have a bodily arm, but the functional meaning is readily understood.

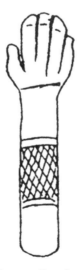

FIGURE 5.4 *Excavated in Tell Gemme (Southern Palestine), Iron Age II A–B.*
Source: Herrmann, *Ägyptische Amulette aus Palästina/Israel*, p. 775.

TABLE 5.7 *Hebrew words for hand, foot and arm and their functional meaning*

$z^e r \hat{o}^{ac}$ *arm*		exercise of power and presence execution of deeds
	yāmîn right hand	as for hand
	yād hand (also: kap hand/palm)	action (work), exercise of power
rægæl foot		exercise of power and presence

The functional meaning of the arm is graphically condensed in the depiction of a solitary arm which may even be carried as an amulet. All the might of the (divine?) 'owner of the arm' is accessed through the arm amulet.

Preliminary appraisal

Having considered the spectrum of meaning for arm, hand and foot we can now draw a preliminary balance: In Hebrew, the exercise of power, powerful deeds and so on is very often expressed verbally in phrases which in their essence concentrate on the specific or functional meanings of the arm, hand and foot (see Table 5.7). This personalizes the whole area of power and sovereignty, creating the impression that 'power' and 'powerful persons' are closely related, that power cannot exist without a powerful person.

We will now turn to the head and the face: head, face, eye, ear, nose, mouth (lips). I will not describe these parts of the body and their functions in great detail but only in as far as their performance is concerned.

5.2.5 Synthetic spectrum of meaning for *head*[16]

The head is one of the most important parts of the body named in the Old Testament. 'Head' differs from face in Hebrew as in English. While face/countenance describes the front of the head with eyes, nose, mouth and so on, head means the whole part of the body. This fact in itself can be the foundation for further meanings: Qoh. 2.14 *The wise man has (lit. his) eyes in his head.* The head is the highest part of the body in a man who walks upright.

The particular position of the head as the highest and foremost part of the body – the word for head in Hebrew, *roʾš*, also means *first* and *highest* – determines the method used to kill the head, above all in war. Chopping

---

[16]Cf.: A. Wagner, 'Kopf', WiBilex 2007, retrieved from Deutsche Bibelgesellschaft: www.wibilex.de/stichwort/

the head off destroys the highest part of the body irrevocably (2 Sam. 4.8); the person, the man, is more strongly hit and obliterated than for example through stabbing. The impact of this fearful method of killing is therefore particularly great. In the Old Testament (Ancient Oriental) world, the head was not connected with thought, or with intellectual–rational power. The heart was the location of the power of thought. Therefore, we must be wary when we consider whether the head is the 'centre of a person'.

The head can also signify the finiteness of human life. What goes beyond the head of man is often greater than mankind. In the narration of Elijah being taken up to heaven, his followers say to Elisha, Elijah's confident and successor: *Do you know that Yhwh is going to take your master [Elijah] over your head today?* (2 Kgs 2.3).

Gestural meanings, often found in verbal form in the Old Testament and in graphic form outside the Old Testament context, are closely related to specific and metaphorical meaning:

- To 'raise one's head' points to superiority: in the safe atmosphere of the temple the psalmist says, *And now my head will be exalted above the enemies who surround me* (Ps. 27.6); God lifts up the king's head (Ps. 110.7); enemies and haters also raise their heads (Ps. 83.4), so that a 'raised head' can also indicate 'arrogance'.

- The countermotion to 'raising the head' is 'lowering the head'. As far as this gesture originates in a person himself it expresses humiliation and self-debasement. Lowering one's head before superiors in social situations, for example at court, expresses hierarchy (proskynese). This gesture can also be used for other ends, cf. Lam. 2.10 (where the context is mourning the devastation of Judah and Jerusalem) *The elders of the Daughters of Zion sit on the ground in silence, they sprinkle dust on their heads and put on sackcloth. The maidens of Jerusalem bow their heads to the ground.*

- To 'raise someone else's bowed head' means ending humiliation; the person regains his or her honour: Gen. 40.13 *Within three days Pharaoh will lift up your head and restore you to your position*; Ps. 3.3 is similar: *But you, Yhwh, are a shield around me, you are my honour and lift up my head.*

- To 'shake one's head' has a different meaning in the Old Testament than nowadays: as Ps. 22.7 *All who see me mock me; they hurl insults, shaking their heads* and other verses show (cf. 2 Kgs 19.21, Ps. 109.25) this is not so much a gesture of astonishment or rejection, but rather connected with derision and expulsion.

- Alongside sinking one's head as a sign of mourning (see the previous) we find similar gestures and acts of mourning and humiliation which centre on the head: 'to cover one's head' (2 Sam. 15.30, Jer. 14.4); 'to strew sand and ashes on one's head' (Ezek. 27.30).

5.2.6 Synthetic spectrum of interpretation for *face*[17]

The Hebrew for face means the front side of an object; not only the face of man or of God. Buildings, too, have a face (Ezek. 41.14 the front of the temple) as does the surface of the earth (Gen. 7.3 *pānîm*).

The Hebrew language has, of course, a notion of the corporeal dimensions of a face:

> Gen. 43.31 *And after he [Joseph, after he had cried] had washed his face, he came out and controlling himself said, Serve the food!*

> 2 Sam. 19.4 *The king covered his face and cried aloud: O my son Absalom! Absalom, my son, my son!*

These passages show clearly how the face, as the front of the head, is treated – it is washed, and covered, completely in correspondence with our modern corporeal–material notion of the face.

One of the most graphic examples of the gestural–functional meaning of the face is found in the Cain and Abel narrative.

> Gen. 4.5 *But on Cain and his offering he did not look with favour. And Cain was very angry and he scowled.*

This is rather a free translation, for in Hebrew we find: (*wayyipp*lû pānâw*) *And his face fell down.* This literal translation indicates what is meant here far more pronouncedly (in English: 'his face fell' is an expression which is used to this day, mostly to express disappointment): Cain's reaction can be read clearly from his expression. The face, therefore, is a means of communication. Here Cain's state of mind is reflected immediately.

The face mirrors a person's state of mind and his or her intent. The face, therefore, communicates. Old Testament texts do not solely dwell on the party transmitting the message, as in the example with Cain. The receiving party can also 'read in his face' as we see in the narrative of Jacob and Laban.

> Gen. 31.2 [When Laban allowed Jacob to leave] *And Jacob saw Laban's countenance and behold it was not towards him as before.*

The 'colours/tones' exuded by the face of a happy/positive person are described in the Old Testament as *bright/radiant* (Prov. 15.13, Qoh 8.1). We can read any number of feelings from a face: fear/dread (Jer. 30.6), shame

---

[17]Cf. Hartenstein, *Das Angesicht JHWHs*; A. Wagner, Körperbegriffe als Stellvertreterausdrücke der Person, in: id. (ed.), *Beten und Bekennen: über Psalmen* (Neukirchen-Vluyn: Neukirchener Verlag, 2008), pp. 289–317.

(blush, cf. Ps. 34.6), horror (to turn pale, cf. Joel 2.6) and so on. When the face does not express any feeling then it is *hard* (Deut. 28.50).

We can recognize further conventionalized gestures which are expressed by the 'communicative organ of the face':

- 'to turn to face somebody' is a positive movement/emotion/ atmosphere/attitude; in the narrative of the dedication of the temple, Solomon, who had been talking to God, turns his face to the assembly to bless them (1 Kgs 8.14);
- 'to turn your face away' is the negative aspect; it means to shut yourself off from any communication (1 Kgs 21.4 *Then Ahab went home, sullen and angry because Naboth the Jezreelite had said, I will not give you the inheritance of my fathers. And he lay on his bed and turned his face away and refused to eat.*);
- to cover your face is a sign of grief (2 Sam. 19.5);
- to bow your face to the ground is a sign of deference (1 Sam. 28.14, Ruth 2.10).

5.2.7 Synthetic spectrum of meaning for *eye*[18]

As far as the Old Testament is concerned, the eye is initially linked with the function of this organ – seeing.

Prov. 20.12 *Ears that hear and eyes that see, Yhwh made them both.*

Recent discussion on the eye, as the organ for seeing and for optical perception, has shown clearly that seeing in the Old Testament is not inferior to hearing.[19] How highly estimated seeing with the eyes is can be deduced from the association with understanding: in the story of Balaam, *unveiled eyes* are a leitmotif (cf. Num. 22.31, 24.4.16). In the paradise narrative in Gen. 3, the recognition of being naked is knowledge perceived by the eyes.

Gen. 3.7 *Then the eyes of both of them were opened and they realised that they were naked.*

Eyes or *seeing* enable knowledge which is the prerequisite for examining, sorting and judging:

Prov. 20.8 *A king who sits on his throne to judge, winnows out all evil with his eyes.*

---

[18]Cf. Wagner, *Körperbegriffe*, pp. 304–7.
[19]Wolff, *Anthropology of the Old Testament*, p. 75. Wolff argues strongly for the prevalence of hearing above seeing based on texts like Isa. 43.8–12. Cf.: Schroer and Staubli, *Body Symbolism in the Bible*, pp. 112–3. The authors point to the higher occurrence of *seeing* (ca. 1300 examples).

Ps. 139.23–24 *Search me, O God, and know my heart, test me and know my thoughts, and see if I am on the way of idols, and lead me in the way of Olam (the everlasting).*

If the eye no longer functions, it becomes dull and dim:[20]

Ps. 6.7 *My eyes have become dull with sorrow and dim, because of all my oppressors.*

Another function of the eye is active communication, looking at something, as we saw previously in section 4.3.

If the eye represents man, pars pro toto, then man, too, must be seen under the aspect of seeing, recognizing and looking. A nice example of this is found in Ps. 54.7.

Ps. 54.7 *For he has delivered me from all my troubles, and my eyes look down on my foes.*

If the proxy expression is deleted in the translation, then the 'I' of the supplicant takes its place. We then lose the specific statement which the anthropological proxy had incorporated. 'I' becomes the general subject and the focus on the eye and the supplicant's chance and ability to understand is no longer evident.[21]

The efficacy of the 'eye' and of 'looking' is also indicated, not least by the many amulets and so on, in the form of an eye, which ward off the evil eye and exercise similar protective functions.

'One of the most common types of amulet in ancient Egypt was the Eye of Horus … [see Figure 5.5] According to the myth the eye [*sic!*] of Horus was wounded by his brother Seth. His mother, Isis, who possessed magical lore, healed it. The symbol stands for regeneration and can protect and designate the widest variety of things'.[22]

5.2.8 Synthetic spectrum of meaning for *ear*

The Hebrew word *'ozæn* denotes initially the visible part of the body, the ear:

Exod. 21.5 *But if the slave declares: I love my master and my wife and my child, I do not want to be freed, 6 his master must take him before God*

---

[20]Similarly, Ps. 31a.10, 88a.10. In Psalm 31 we find three representative expressions next to each other: my eye, my næpæš, my body/stomach, evidently for the three differing aspects (communication/knowledge, intention, corporeality), which describe sorrowful mankind here; they are 'darkened' by affliction. Cf. Eberhard Bons, *Psalm 31. Rettung als Paradigma: eine synchron-leserorientierte Analyse* (FTS 48; Frankfurt: Verlag Josef Knecht, 1994), pp. 56–63, esp. p. 62.
[21]Cf. Wagner, *Körperbegriffe*, pp. 305–7.
[22]Schroer and Staubli, *Body Symbolism in the Bible*, p. 107.

FIGURE 5.5 *Amulet with the 'Eye of Horus'.*
Source: Schroer and Staubli, *Body Symbolism in the Bible*, p. 107, fig. 45.

and take him to the door or the door-post and pierce his ear with an awl and he will be his servant for life.

The fact that ears were understood as being a corporeal element is indicated not least by the fact that they can be adorned with earrings (Exod. 32.2, Isa. 3.19).

As was true for the eye, *ʾozæn* not only denotes the part of the body, but also its function. Therefore, *ʾozæn* also indicates the ability to hear or the sense of hearing. According to Ancient Oriental anthropology (and the Old Testament conforms to this), Ancient Oriental man did not conceive the function of the brain as we do today. Thinking was located in the heart. Retentiveness, too, was not associated with the brain. It was the concern of the ears! Consequently, the ears become the location of discernment. Ear and heart can, therefore, appear in parallel, complimentary but comparable functions:

Prov. 22.17 (function)

Turn your ear and listen to my words/and direct your heart towards them, to discern them.

An extract from the teaching of Ptahhotep (Egyptian Vizier and teacher of wisdom), 2350 BCE, allows an insight into the Ancient Oriental culture of hearing/listening:

A splendid thing is the obedience of an obedient son; he cometh in and listeneth obediently.

Excellent in hearing, excellent in speaking, is every man that obeyeth what is noble; and the obedience of an obeyer is a noble thing.

Obedience is better than all things that are; it maketh good-will.

How good it is that a son should take that from his father by which he hath reached old age (Obedience).

That which is desired by the God is obedience; disobedience is abhorred of the God.

Verily, it is the heart that maketh its master to obey or to disobey; for the safe and sound life of a man are his heart.

It is the obedient man that obeyeth what is said; he that loveth to obey, the same shall carry out commands.[23]

The functions of the ear are hearing, understanding and recognizing. In this, the Old Testament does not differ from the Ancient Orient.

Where the Old Testament does differ is revealed by reflection on who is responsible for hearing and understanding, through the creation of the ear. According to the conviction of many Old Testament texts it was Yhwh:

Ps. 40.6 *Sacrifice and offering you did not desire, but my ears you have gouged/pierced ...*

By means of this divine entry gate, mankind is capable of discerning God's announcements: the prophet's ear is opened by Yhwh (Isa. 50.4–5). The prophet cries 'in [Israel's] ears' or, as in Jer. 2.2, in Jerusalem's ears. The people, however, can refuse to hear God's announcements: Ezek. 12.2 *they have eyes so that they could see but do not want to see, and ears so that they could hear, but do not want to hear; for they are a house of dissent.* As Ezek. 12.2 shows, the perception of the ear stands side by side with that of the eye. They are complimentary, and the perception of the ear is not dominant.[24]

Perhaps this last circumstance, that the ear is the gateway to God's word, is the reason why the ear is more important in Old Testament texts than in pictorial representations as we had noticed previously when we saw that the ear is often missing in depictions. All in all, the texts come rather towards the end of Israel's religious development and, in view of the increasing formation of the canon, they postulate that they contain Yhwh's word, which should be 'heard'. Mankind is therefore often present as the 'hearing man' in the texts. Depictions are utilized in a quite different context, in which the ear plays a lesser role.

---

[23]B.G. Gunn, *The Wisdom of the East. The Instruction of Ptah-Hotep and the Instruction of Ke'Gemni: The Oldest Books in the World* (Transl. from the Egyptian with an Introduction and Appendix, London: John Murray, Albemarle Street, 1906), p. 57.
[24]These two senses of perception point to different facets: Hearing to the announcement of God's word and seeing to the perception of God's deeds. In this way, the two main aspects of Old Testament anthropomorphism are again encompassed, cf. esp. section 5.3.

5.2.9 Synthetic spectrum of meaning for the *nose*

There can be no doubt of the corporeal meaning of the Hebrew word *ʾap*. It refers, initially, to the nose as part of the body: Prov. 30.33 … *whoever blows his nose too hard, produces blood* … and in extreme cases the nose can be cut off (Ezek. 23.25). Often the word is used twice; this refers then to the two nostrils.

The nose is the organ for the sense of smell (Amos 4.19) and for breathing. As the organ for breathing it is associated with the breath of life (Isa 2.22); according to Gen. 2.7, God blew the breath of life into the nose at creation.

The nose, too, has gestural meaning:

- A nose like a tower was mentioned previously (cf. section 4.3)
- As a pars pro toto for the face, the nose has similar verbalized gestures to those of the face: Gen. 19.1 *and he [Lot] bowed [lit.] both his nostrils to the ground.*

The term *ʾap* often has the meaning wrath/fury.

> Gen. 30.2 *Jacob's nose (=anger) flared in fury over Rahel = Jacob became very angry with Rahel and said: but I am not God, who withholds the fruit of the womb from you.*

It is not difficult to connect 'snorting with fury or wrath' with the organ of the nose. The result is that the Hebrew word *ʾap* also means 'fury'. Through the spoken word, however, the corporeal term is always present too – *ʾap* means 'wrath' and 'nose'. If translations only use the term wrath, then this nuance is missing. Therefore, '*ʾap*/nose/fury' is therefore a sort of 'organ for expressing emotion' and belongs to the communicative elements of the body.

5.2.10 Synthetic spectrum of meaning for *mouth*

To describe the mouth as a part of the body is not so easy since it is, to begin with, an 'opening' into the inner body. The opening is surrounded by the lips and bordered by the gums/palate, and the tongue is located inside. And so, we find a structure which includes various functions. The use of one part emphasizes a particular aspect of the diverse functions present in the structure: The palate is connected with taste, the lips speak and kiss and so on.

Schroer and Staubli justifiably accentuate the multi-functionality of the mouth, for a multitude of meanings are combined in the mouth: eating (Qoh 6.7), laughing (Job 8.21), kissing (Song 1.2), tasting and so on.[25]

---

[25]Schroer and Staubli, *Body Symbolism in the Bible*, p. 134.

One of the most noble functions of the mouth is speaking. Moses experiences God's assistance when God succours his mouth:

Exod. 4.12 *So go: I will be with your mouth and teach you what to say.*

In Gen. 24.57, we hear that 'her [Rebecca's] mouth' should be asked; the aspect of communication therefore also plays a role:

Gen. 24.57 *Then they said: Let us call the girl and ask what she has to say, lit. call and ask her mouth.*

And lastly the mouth is the organ for praising God:

Ps. 51.15 *Lord, open my lips, and my mouth will declare your praise.*

5.2.11 Synthetic spectrum of meaning for *throat/neck*[26]

It is helpful to approach the term *næpæš*[27] from its basic meaning. In Hebrew the verb *npš* (pi.) denotes breathing (Exod. 23.12, 31.17, 2 Sam. 16.14). From the meaning of the deverbal noun *breath* (1 Kgs 17.17ff, parallel to *n°šāmāh*/breath), further transferred meanings result: 'location of breathing' = *throat, gullet, windpipe, neck.*

Isa. 5.14 *therefore the Scheol/underworld widens its næpæš, opens its jaws/gullet without limit*

Ps. 105.18 *They forced his feet into fetters, his næpæš was put in irons*

---

[26]This chapter is based on the section about *næpæš*, in: A. Wagner (ed.), 'Les différentes dimensions de la vie: Quelques réflexions sur la terminologie anthropologique de l'Ancien Testament', in: *Revue des Sciences Religieuses* 81 (2007), pp. 391–408.
[27]Cf.: W. H. Schmidt, 'Anthropologische Begriffe im Alten Testament', in: *EvTh 24* (1964), pp. 375–388. see fn. 7; Wolff, *Anthropology of the Old Testament*, pp. 10–25; H. Seebass, 'נֶפֶשׁ *næfæš*', ThWAT V (1986), col. 531–55; C. Westermann, 'נֶפֶשׁ *næfæš* Seele', THAT[3] II (1984) col. 71–96; R. Lauha, *Psychophysischer Sprachgebrauch im Alten Testament. Eine strukturalsemantische Analyse von 'לֵב', 'נֶפֶשׁ' und 'רוּחַ'* Vol. 1: Emotionen (Annales Academiae Scientiarum Fennicae. Dissertationes humanarum litterarum 35, Helsinki: Suomalainen Tiedeakatemia, 1983), R. Rendtorff, Die sündige *næfæš*, in: F. Crüsemann, C. Hardmeier and R. Kessler (eds.), *Was ist der Mensch...? Beiträge zur Anthropologie des Alten Testaments. FS Hans Walter Wolff zum 80. Geburtstag* (München: Chr. Kaiser, 1992), pp. 211–20; Schroer and Staubli, *Body Symbolism in the Bible*, pp. 56–67. K. Liess, 'Leben. II. Biblisch. 1. Altes Testament', RGG[4] 5 (2002), pp. 135–136; English: 'Life. II. Bible. 1. Old Testament', RPP 7 (2010), pp. 476–7; Janowski, *Konfliktgespräche mit Gott.*, pp. 188–98.

Throat, gullet, windpipe, neck can all be understood as the 'location of lust and desire', and from this the meaning wish, craving, desire, longing, develops.

> Prov. 16.26 *The labourer's næpæš travails for him, truly his mouth drives him on.*

> Deut. 23.25 *If you enter your neighbour's vineyard you may eat grapes according to your næpæš = your momentary desire*[28], *but you may not harvest anything into your vessel.*

In many texts (Prov. 8.35–36, Ps. 26.9, Jonah 4.3), *næpæš* means *life*. It is not clear whether this meaning is derived from the specific meaning of *throat, windpipe* or whether *life* (or rather *being alive*) should be understood as a whole bundle of expressions, such as striving, wishing, desiring – and perhaps this is not an alternative. [29]

If *næpæš* is a pars pro toto for the whole person, then (in general) a person is a being that has needs, wishes, cravings, desires, longings, aspirations and is governed by them. *næpæš* is man in the sense of 'intensive intentionality'.[30]

5.2.12 Summary of the meaning of the corporeal parts that occur regularly

The functions concentrated in the corporeal parts point out two areas which are central to Old Testament anthropology: communication and action. The aspect of action was focussed on in the summary at the end of 5.2.4. Our attention is then drawn to man as a creature who is active and can act purposefully.

---

[28]At this point, a gloss is attached to the Hebrew text which I have omitted in my translation; with it the text reads: *the repletion of your næpæš/your desire.*

[29]'The sentence "your n. will stay alive" should not be perceived as tautology; what is meant is: Your self, that loves and hates, is saddened and pleased, will live on. The type of usage here is to be understood as arising from a life situation marked by threat and hazard: It is threatened by death and reaching out after life n. that we mean here. For the most part, this n. can also be described through the use of the personal pronoun ...'.Westermann, 'נֶפֶשׁ', p. 84. *Næpæš* never neutrally denotes a person, and therefore always performs more than a personal pronoun. The 'translation' soul is therefore never correct if, according to the Greek trichotomy, it means a part of man alongside spirit and body. The generally accepted meaning *corpse* is an incorrect translation and is based on false text interpretation, Cf.: D. Michel, *næpæš als Leichnam?*, in: *ZAH* (7) (1994), pp. 81–4.

[30]Westermann, 'נֶפֶשׁ', 92; the phrasing is taken from Westermann's section on God's *næpæš*, but it also expresses the central aspect of the human *næpæš*, especially if we consider anthropological-anthropomorphic reflections.

In comparison with older attempts at definition, we arrive at a rather different view of what makes 'man' 'man' by investigating the body. In the twentieth century, the 'Hebrew man' was often sought, in analogy to the 'Greek man'. Under the influence of classical Greek philosophy, the 'Greek man' was considered to be a being with body and spirit, or rather body, spirit and soul. Since then this discussion has developed further. For one thing 'the' Greek image of man is more differentiated today, as far as the temporal origin and the varying models developed by individual philosophers and schools of thought are concerned.[31] It is also increasingly clear that a simple equation of core Greek terms with the respective Hebrew terms is not a suitable method for comprehending 'the' Hebrew image of man.[32]

In our reconsideration of what constitutes Hebrew man, or the Old Testament concept of man, various paths can be followed. One approach is to consider how many terms can be substituted for 'man'.[33] An investigation

TABLE 5.8 *Hebrew body words relating to the field of communication*

Parts of the body			Function
roʾš head			prerequisite for communication
	pānîm face		communication
		ʿayin eye	exercises communication
		ʾozæn ear	exercises communication
		ʾap nose	reactive, basis for action, exercises communication
		pæh mouth (lips)	exercises communication
næpæš throat, neck			prerequisite for communication

[31]Cf.: R. Schlesier, Die dionysische Psyche. Zu Euripides' backchen, in: C. Benthien et al. (eds.), *Emotionalität. Zur Geschichte der Gefühle* (Literatur – Kultur – Geschlecht. Kleine Reihe 16, Köln: Böhlau, 2000), pp. 21–41.
[32]The most recent detailed discussion: A. Wagner, Wider die Reduktion des Lebendigen. Über das Verhältnis der sog. Anthropologischen Grundbegriffe und die Unmöglichkeit, mit ihnen die alttestamentliche Menschenvorstellung zu fassen. in: id. (ed.), *Anthropologische Aufbrüche*, pp. 183–99.
[33]Cf.: Wagner, *Körperbegriffe*, pp. 289–317.

of the constitution of the inner and outer body also sheds some light on the question. The investigation of terms for the inner body will follow elsewhere. Here we are interested in the external appearance and its comparability with material images.

Aspects which are attached to the elements of the 'body' most frequently mentioned are of particular interest here. If we highlight mankind as a being who acts, then in my opinion we have hit on an aspect which, according to the Old Testament, reveals the essence of man (see Table 5.7). The active parts of the body indicate that the ability to act is an important aspect of the Old Testament human. We will see that the ability to act plays a central role for God, too. This correspondence between anthropology and anthropomorphism indicates that these are matters of great importance. The fact that anthropology and theology cannot be separated is a precept well known to theology. However, the analysis of the body in the Old Testament confirms this in a unique way. What constitutes the Old Testament God, and is therefore the subject of theology, entails all those points which constitute Old Testament anthropology. It would appear that the more the aspects of the one God come to the fore and everything is concentrated on the one God, the more 'his' characteristics crystallize through experience, the more important the corresponding anthropological aspects become for anthropology. The God who works so powerfully in history, who alone determines overt action in the world according to monotheistic thought, has as his counterpart acting 'man', who is solely responsible to his or her God for his or her actions. A person does not act for him or herself but acts vicariously for God in whose image he or she is made, as Gen. 1.1–2.4a explicitly explains (see Chapter 6).

The second group of most frequently occurring elements of the body points to an aspect that is quite as central as action is – communication (see Table 5.8).

The terms for these parts of the body reveal how central the aspect of communication is for man.

The ability to communicate is important for contact between people, but also for contact with God. Knowledge of God is not possible without the perception supplied by eyes and ears. The transfer of knowledge and experience, the creation of tradition and its transmission, understanding between peoples, both simultaneously and successively in chronological and locational terms, by mouth and in writing are inconceivable without the optical and acoustic ability of humans to communicate.

These two aspects, 'action' and 'communication', guide us to the core of Old Testament anthropology. Before we consider the correlation between anthropology and theology more closely, let us discuss God's body, as it appears in the Old Testament, in more detail.

5.3 God's body as a theological message[34]

5.3.1 The elements of the body (the external figure) which do *not* appear in anthropomorphism

In section 4.2, the principles underlying the construction and understanding of pictures were investigated. These will now be applied to an interpretation of the 'verbal image of God's body'. The choice of components for the composition of the whole picture is the first central point.

The pictures only include the aspects essential to the intended content. The wholeness of God in anthropomorphic images is constructed in the same manner, so that we can assume that only those 'aspects' of God considered to be pivotal (i.e. the central parts of the body) are included. The selection does not rely, therefore, on chance or inability but rather follows pictorial principles.

It corresponds, therefore, to a 'drafted' concept of God, similar to a systematic draft. The selection is made from a large field of possibilities. It is the criteria for this selection which interests us here, for it affords information about the Old Testament image of God.

The first important insight is delivered by the analysis of those parts of the body found in Old Testament terms, which are chosen for a depiction of the human body but never used for God.

Head: Parting, skull, bald head, bald pate, forehead, eyeball, eye socket, eye brow, earlobe, temple, hair, grey hair, forelock, curls, pigtails, fresh complexion, beard, moustache, jaw, cheek/chin, gum, teeth, set of teeth, gum, goitre, nape, gullet

Upper extremities: Elbow/forearm, armpit, shoulder, shoulder blade, shoulder joint, left side/left hand, thumb, handbreadth, cup of the hand, wrist, small finger

Groin: Loin, origin of menstrual bleeding, buttocks, hips, groin, pelvis, nakedness/pudency, nakedness, pudenda, genitals, penis, testicles, foreskin

Lower extremities: Knee, hollow of the knee, bones, thigh, calf/fibular, ankles, sole of the foot, joints, large toe, toes

Other terms: Countenance, bump, blister, pallor, bare foot, hairiness, figure, swelling, boil, skin rash, skin fleck, body, trunk, scar, scratch, scab, wound

---

The list reveals a clear but startling selection principle: Among the elements used often for representing God, none which refer to gender! In view of the high number investigated, this is very significant and certainly not coincidental. A first conclusion is apparent: The Old Testament avoids any definition of gender in its anthropomorphic representation of Yhwh.

---

[34]Cf. for this chapter: Baumann, *Das göttliche Geschlecht*, pp. 220–250. Schroer and Staubli, *Body Symbolism in the Bible*. The following list contains some further body parts that have not yet been considered in the discussion.

TABLE 5.9 *List of anthropomorphisms of the external body*

Elements of God's body		Number
Core elements:		
pānîm	*face*	598
ᶜayin	*eye*	123
ᵓozæn	*ear*	28
ᵓap	*nose*	162
pæh	*mouth*	57
næpæš	*throat, neck*	16
zᵉrôᵃᶜ	*arm*	42
yāmîn	*right hand*	34
yād	*hand*	218
rægæl	*foot/leg*	13
Marginal body parts (body parts mentioned less than 10 times)		
roᵓš	head	3
ᵓæṣbaᶜ	finger	3
qæræb	abdomen/abdominal cavity	1
lāšôn	tongue	1
ᵓēṣæl	side	1
śāpāh	lips	3
šēn	teeth	1
ᵓāhôr	back/backside	1
ᶜoræp	nape	1
ᶜāqēb	heel	1
ᶜapᶜappayim	eyelids	1
ᵓîšôn	pupil	1
kap	palm of the hand	4
kap raegael	sole of the foot	1
gew	back	1
ḥêq	bosom (in the sense of, grasping sb. in someone's arms)	2
hopæn	hollow of the hand	1
šoᶜal	hollow of the hand	1
måtnayim	hips/loins/lower back	1
mēᶜæh	lower abdomen (?)	1
śᵉmoᵓl	left side/left hand	2

5.3.2 Which parts of the body *do* appear in anthropomorphism?[35]

We can draw further conclusions from this list of anthropomorphisms of the external body which is presented in Table 5.9. Clusters of certain corporeal elements are visible here, too, which correlate with those for the human body – apart from the head which appears far less often in anthropomorphism. The interplay of the functions introduced into the corporeal image by the choice of corporeal elements is significant theologically. Before we discuss this in detail, let us first describe those parts of the body which determine Old Testament anthropomorphism. The core selection is determined by how often they occur, once they are found more than ten times.

5.3.3 The core elements of God's body

5.3.3.1 Preliminary remarks

Since the correlation between the human and the divine body is so striking, we will follow the same succession of corporeal parts. The one exception is the head, which is only included as a central element because of the many equivalents to the human body. The actual number does not actually justify its inclusion and God's head should only be considered 'central' with certain reservations. However, the anthropomorphic significance does not vary whether the head is included or excluded.

In anthropomorphism, the functional meaning is of great importance. An optical/visual interest in God's body (in the sense of individual bodily structure, etc.) cannot be found. We can only touch on these issues superficially here; detailed discussion must take place elsewhere but further literature is suggested.

5.3.3.2 God's hand/s

Just as the human hand can take formative action, so can God's hand/s. God's formative action can, however, reach as far as forming the whole of creation. The creation is the *work of his hands* (Ps. 19.2), Isa. 45.12 *I made the earth and created mankind upon it. I – (both) my hands spread out the heavens* ... The earth remains in the hands/power of God: Exod. 15.12 *As you stretched out your right hand it swallowed the earth.*

God's hand is found, as is God's arm/s, in phrases about leading Israel out of Egypt. The phrase 'with mighty hand and outstretched arm' is found in Deuteronomy (Deut. 4.34, 5.15, 7.19, 11.2, 26.8) and in texts based on

---

[35]Counted according to THAT and personal concordance work.

Deuteronomy (Jer. 32.21, Ps. 136.12). They all refer to the Exodus: Jer. 32.21 *And [you, Yhwh] brought your people Israel out of Egypt with signs and wonders, by a mighty hand and an outstretched arm and with great terror.* Ps. 136.12 is similar. Beyond this particular phrase, God's hand can be found 'acting' alone without being combined with his arm, for example Yhwh's great saving deed in Exod. 15.4 *Pharaoh's chariot and his power he has hurled into the sea. … 6 Your right hand, Yhwh, has done great wonders, your right hand has shattered the enemy.* This use of God's hand ties in with the theme of creation.

God's hand bestowed exceptional power on the prophets (1 Kgs 18.46) or made great knowledge available to them (Isa. 8.11, Ezek. 3.14).

God's hand can express protection, for example when it rests 'on the mountain' (Zion) as in Isa. 25.10. It can also 'enclose', as an enemy force enclosed a town in Ps. 139.5.

Those who recognize God's power/hand, know God, and receive a revelation: Deut. 3.24 *You, Yhwh, you have begun to reveal your greatness and your strong hand to your servant. For what God is there in heaven and on earth who can do the deeds and mighty works you do?* Texts like this do not aim at a visual perception of God's hand but at a perception of his acting in the world, his deeds for mankind, his power in the world.

God's hands express functional meanings very similar to human hands. We have 218 examples of the hand in anthropomorphism; the hand is the most frequent instrument for God's deeds.

However, the manner in which God's hands act in the Old Testament is fundamentally different to that of humans, for it goes far beyond the possibilities open to people. God's power is more or less almighty in late texts such as Ps. 139.

In the post-biblical Hellenistic context, we find a pictorial representation of God's hands in a fresco from a synagogue in Dura-Europos (ca. 250 CE).

Despite the fact that we never hear of 'God's left hand' in the Old Testament, we see both hands here, cf. Ps. 119.73 *(Both) your hands have made me …*

Since this is certainly not a cult image, an image of this sort is evidently possible in a more liberal interpretation of the prohibition of imagery.[36] Early Christendom was of the same opinion.[37]

---

[36]Cf.: G. Stemberger, 'Bild/Bilderverbot', in: *Lexikon der Bibelhermeneutik* (2009), pp. 97–98; M. Tilly, Antijüdische Instrumentalisierungen des biblischen Bilderverbots, in: Wagner, *Gott im Wort – Gott im Bild*, pp. 23–6.

[37]Cf.: F. W. Horn, Die Herrlichkeit des unvergänglichen Gottes und die vergänglichen Bilder der Menschen. Überlegungen im Anschluss an Röm 1,23, in: Wagner, *Gott im Wort – Gott im Bild*, pp. 55–7; K. Greschat, Gregor des Großen Auseinandersetzung mit Serenus von Marseille um die Frage der Bilder, in: Wagner, *Gott im Wort – Gott im Bild*, pp. 59–74, esp. pp. 59–60; V. Makrides, Ikonen/sakrale Bilder und ihre Bedeutung für eine vergleichende Kulturgeschichte des Christentums, in: Wagner, *Gott im Wort – Gott im Bild*, pp. 151–164, esp. p. 153.

FIGURE 5.6 *Wall-painting from a synagogue in Dura-Europos.*
Source: Schroer and Staubli, Body Symbolism in the Bible, p. 163, fig. 74.

5.3.3.3 God's foot/feet

In section 5.2.3, we saw how the image of a foot could express power structures. The person who steps on something, or stands on it, has power over it. What is underfoot is under my control.

God's feet are just the same. The Ark of the Covenant in 1 Chron. 28.2 is the footstool under his feet and thereby subject to Yhwh's power. Ps. 132.7 is similar:

Ps. 132.7 *Let us go to his dwelling-place and worship at his footstool.*

Two texts go a step further when they describe Zion as Yhwh's footstool:

Lam. 2.1 *How the Lord has deluged the daughter of Zion with his wrath! He has hurled down the splendour of Israel from heaven to earth; he has not remembered his footstool in the day of his anger.*

Ps. 99.5 *Exalt the Lord our God and worship at his footstool for he is holy.*

And finally, Isa. 66.1 says that the whole earth is God's footstool:

Isa. 66.1 *This what Yhwh says: the heavens are my throne and the earth is my footstool. ...*

Nothing on earth, therefore, can evade Yhwh's power. The totality of this notion is found in other pictures (including anthropomorphic ones) which,

FIGURE 5.7 *Threshold of the temple at ᶜAin Dara.*
Source: Schroer and Staubli, *Body Symbolism in the Bible*, p. 194, fig. 96.

although they are different, have a similar intention, and also in comparable later texts in the Old Testament, for example in Ps. 139.[38] We must note that with the help of anthropomorphic phrases, monotheistic statements tending towards omnipotence are made in texts which are ascribed to the exile era. The picture fostered by earlier generations of researchers, that Old Testament anthropomorphism is 'outdated' and increasingly replaced by a transcendental concept of God, is not accurate in my opinion (cf. section 5.5).

Not only power but also an emphasis on his presence belongs to the wider spectrum of meaning for God's feet:

Ezek. 43.7 *He said to me: Son of man, this is the place of my throne and the place of the soles of my feet; this is where I will live with the Israelites for ever …*

---

[38]Cf.: A. Wagner, 'Permutatio religionis' – Ps 139 und der Wandel der israelitischen Religion zur Bekenntnisreligion', in: *VT* 57 (2007), pp. 91–113.

God is present and tangible, therefore, amid the Israelites in the temple. This is a further important function of anthropological statements: they nourish God's comprehensibility, tangibility and presence.

This Old Testament text is reminiscent of an anthropomorphic testimony found not far from Ancient Israel, which has been known for some time. In the temple of ᶜAin Dara in Syria (ninth/eighth century BCE) there are huge footprints hewn into the threshold.

5.3.3.4 God's arm/s

Gestural and functional meanings for human arms facilitate our understanding of texts which speak of the arm or arms of God. Phrases which refer to God's arm express God's power and his protection.

Yhwh's arm assumes its most important meaning in the preservation and protection of his people of Israel. The phrase 'with mighty hand and outstretched arm' is found in Deuteronomy (Deut. 4.34, 5.15, 7.19, 11.2, 26.8) and in texts based on Deuteronomy (Jer. 32.21, Ps. 136.12). They all refer to the Exodus: Jer. 32.21 *And [you, Yhwh] brought your people Israel out of Egypt with signs and wonders, by a mighty hand and an outstretched arm and with great terror.*

Yhwh also raises his arm to do battle against the powers of chaos, to curb and conquer them: Ps. 89.10 *You crushed Rahab [one of the chaos dragons] like one of the slain with your strong arm.* ... God's arm is also found parallel to God's hand: Ps. 89.13 *You have a mighty arm, your hand is strong, your right hand is raised/exalted.* Cf. also Isa. 51.9. According to notions outside the Old Testament, the conflict with the powers of chaos is linked to the creation of the world and of mankind. This reference is also present in the Old Testament. The battle against chaos either refers to God's unique act of creation (*creatio*) or to the continuing struggle against the constant threat of chaos (*gubernatio*). This struggle is therefore part of God's providential action. God's providence created the world and order in the world. By this means mankind and everything in the world received life; a life which God maintains. In some cases, God's creative act is seen as the work of his arm and has nothing to do with the battle with chaos. Jer. 32.17 ... *you have made the heavens and the earth by your great power and outstretched arm.*

His achievements in battle reveal that Yhwh possesses a 'great/mighty arm' (Exod. 15.16, Ps. 79.11, Ps. 89.11.14). The 'gesture of battle' portrays Yhwh as a warrior (cf. Exod. 15), a concept which stretches back to the very beginning of the veneration of Yhwh, and it continued into later eras.

Yhwh's arm not only portrays God's deeds for mankind graphically, but it is also necessary to procure justice (Isa. 51.5).

In individual requests for help, for example in the Psalms, Yhwh's arm is irrelevant. With just a few exceptions (aid for David Ps. 89.22), Yhwh's arm is connected above all with collective assistance.

Revealing his arm – exposing the inner person – makes Yhwh visible and comprehensible to foreign peoples (Isa. 52.10). In Isa. 51.9, the arm is addressed like a person: *Awake, awake! Clothe yourself with strength, you arm of Yhwh! … .* Isa. 63.12 says that Yhwh sent *his glorious arm of power to be at Moses' right hand.*

God gathers the people into his arm (Isa. 40.11) as the shepherd does his flock (see the previous discussion). Deut. 33.27 is difficult to interpret: *The eternal God is your refuge, and underneath are the everlasting arms. He will drive out your enemy before you, saying, Destroy him!*

Altogether God's arm/s visualizes God's ability to act in the world and for mankind. However, God's capability to act goes far beyond that of humans.

Preliminary appraisal

As we concluded previously in 5.2.4:

> In Hebrew the exercise of power, powerful deeds etc., is very often expressed verbally in phrases which in their essence concentrate on the specific or functional meanings of the arm, hand and foot. This personalises the whole area of power and sovereignty, creating the impression that 'power' and 'powerful persons' are closely related, that power cannot exist without a powerful person.

As we have seen in 5.3.3.2–5.3.3.4, this relation not only applies to power structures in human society but also expresses our experience with divine powers, that is, with the might and power of God.

Right hand/

hand	function: execute deeds
arm	function: execute deeds
foot	function: execute deeds and power, presence

Together with statements about Yhwh/God's arm/s and foot/feet, phrases referring to his hand/s express what God *has done* for mankind and the world and *continues to do.*

It is understandable, therefore, that God is conceived as a bodily figure. How could 'he' act for mankind if 'he' had no arms or hands?

All these statements belong to a theological verbal/pictorial concept of God, which uses the conceptual background conveyed by the Old Testament-Ancient Oriental corporeal statements to communicate God's deeds to the world.

In contrast to mankind, God's power exceeds that of any person, even that of kings or queens. On the one hand, as far as the anthropomorphic construction is concerned, the power that intervenes in this world remains an important issue, on the other hand, God is not a human force but a divine one. The theologumenon of God's historical impact must be developed from Old Testament anthropomorphism, as must the emphasis on God's divinity.

5.3.3.5 God's head

God's head is mentioned in a vision in Dan. 7.9 and in Isa. 59.17 and Ps. 60.7 par. 180.8.

> Ps. 60.7 *[God has spoken in his sanctuary] Gilead is mine, Manasseh is mine, Ephraim is my helmet, Judah is my sceptre. (par. Ps. 108.8)*

Since God's head is not mentioned elsewhere, these texts appear to be isolated within the Old Testament. However, we may assume that in the many instances of Yhwh's face, eyes, ears and mouth, the anthropomorphic concept included his head. The small number of texts can probably be explained by the fact that gestural meanings presume social classification, from which God is exempted. It is also quite obvious that God cannot be counted 'per capita' and that his head cannot be hewn off and so on. 'Late apocalypticism is aware that those who have heavenly visions see God's head (1 Hen. 71.10, Rev. 1.14)'.[39]

In these texts, the corporeal aspect of the head is of no consequence. As with mankind, the head occupies a special position and is worthy of protection; it often represents the whole person and their dignity. Parallelism with the sceptre in Ps. 60.7 points us in this direction. That God has a head demonstrates clearly that God is a real counterpart. God's head is the prerequisite for communication, and it emphasizes the possibility of communication between God and man.

5.3.3.6 God's face[40]

In functional use, as we saw in section 5.2.6, the interpretations for *pānîm/* face are above all in terms of expression and communication. This is particularly striking in Prov. 16.15, where the king's favour and his good mood are reflected in his face.

> Prov. 16.15 *When a king's face brightens it means life, and his favour is like a rain cloud in spring.*

When a king's face shines, he is the source of benefaction; his wrath, however, is dangerous (cf. Prov. 16.14). Both can be read in his face. The functional statement 'his face shines' represents the nurture which one person can grant to another. Turning the face away, on the other hand, expresses disinterest and even depression (cf. 1 Kgs 21.4). Therefore, mentioning a person's *pānîm* means depicting this person in communication.

---

[39]H.-P. Müller, 'ראשׁ *ro'š Kopf*', THAT[3] II., (1984), col. 701–15.
[40]Cf. Hartenstein, *Das Angesicht JHWhs*; Cf. Wagner, *Körperbegriffe*, pp. 289–317.

The good deeds which a king or queen can do depend on their power to act, which of course exceeds that of a normal person. God's good deeds go far beyond those of mankind. The anthropomorphic expressions in the Old Testament describe this analogous to human bodily expression. God's shining face means 'loving regard' and 'granting specific gifts of salvation'.[41] Phrases to this effect are found in the Aaronic blessing and the psalms in particular:

> Num. 6 24 *The Lord bless you and keep you; 25 the Lord make his face shine upon you and be gracious to you; 26 the Lord turn his face towards you and give you peace.*

> Ps. 67.2 *May the Lord be gracious to us and bless us, and make his face shine upon us.*

> Ps. 80.3 *Restore us O God! make your face shine upon us, that we may be saved.*

> Ps. 80: *O God of the multitudes! Restore us! May your face shine upon us, that we may be saved.*

> Ps. 80.19 *Yhwh, God of the multitudes! Restore us! May your face shine upon us, that we may be saved.*

Other phrases also invoke God's face when they are concerned with communication and Yhwh's/God's care and attention for mankind:

> Ps. 51.11 *Do not cast me from your presence or take your Holy Spirit from me.*

It is generally favourable to see Yhwh's countenance, as the supplicant in Ps. 42.2 pleads:

> Ps. 42.2 ... *when can I come (to him) and see God's countenance?*

If Yhwh turns his face against someone, doom threatens:

> Jer. 21: *For I have turned my countenance against this city for harm and not for good, says the Lord. It will be given into the hands of the King of Babylon that he consume it with fire.*

Next to phrases in the second and third person we find phrases in which *pānîm* refers to the first person.[42]

---

[41]A. S. van der Woude, 'פָּנִים *pānîm*, *THAT* II., (1984), col. pp. 432–460, esp. 451.
[42]This observation can probably be explained with speech to and about God in most psalm texts: Also of importance in the psalter are the rare speeches by Yhwh in the first person; in these speeches we find phrases with *pānîm*, referring to the first person (Exod. 25.30, 2 Chron. 7.14, Hos. 5.15, Jer. 32.31.

A particularly lovely text, which can also be seen in comparison with Amos 5.4[43], is found in Ps. 27.8 *My heart says of you [remembers your word]: 'seek his face!' Your face, Yhwh, I will seek.*

The heart is the organ for sense and thinking in the Old Testament as in the Ancient Orient; it is the place and organ for deliberating on God. Memory, too, is available to the heart. The Psalmist remembers one of Yhwh's words which he had heard and learnt (*Seek my face!*) when he deliberates on God. Guided by this expression the supplicant begins his quest: *Your face, Yhwh, I will seek.* He seeks contact and a relation with God. The Old Testament supplies the phrase *Seek my face!* so that the functional meaning of the face immediately indicates that God's nurture is sought, that God may turn towards us in communication. A comparison with the related phrase in Amos 5.4 demonstrates this clearly:

Amos 5.4 *For this is what Yhwh said to the house of Israel: 'Seek me (and live) then you will live!'*

In comparison with Amos 5.4 where *pānîm* does not appear, Ps. 27.8 emphasizes Yhwh's countenance: this is clearly about individual communicative contact with Yhwh.[44] In Amos 5.4, the listener is invited to seek Yhwh; the search for God remains an open issue. In this prophetic context the emphasis lies on correct (collective) conduct towards Yhwh. The addition of *pānîm* in Ps. 27.8, however, intentionally changes the statement made. The aspect of individual communication is brought into play.

Even in cases where the use of *pānîm* does not indicate a communicative attitude or a personal act of communication, the use of *pānîm* instead of a pronoun or a noun always indicates that communication is a possibility.

Ps. 100.2 *Serve the Lord with joy, come before his countenance with gladness!*

Ps. 100.2 uses *pānîm* instead of the pronoun *him*, the noun *God* or the proper noun *Yhwh*. In this way the person (God) is portrayed in terms of (possible) communication. The verse says nothing about God's reaction or communicative attitude, it assumes implicitly that being glad before him will secure his goodwill. We do not hear that God's *pānîm* is stirred in any way. The use of *pānîm* indicates that a visible communicative statement is expected from God. This is a different nuance than a phrase with pronouns, nouns,

---

[43]Cf.: F.-L. Hossfeld and E. Zenger, *Die Psalmen: I. Psalm 1-50* (NEB 29; Würzburg: Echter Verlag, 1993), p. 175.
[44]The individual supplicant here prays a word of Yhwh which contains a plural demand. This word is employed in Ps. 27.8 for individual contemplation. This may be a development from collective older quotations of God's words to their use in a later, more individualized context.

or proper nouns would suggest. With such a turn of phrase, the emphasis would not be on communication: God would then be seen under the aspect of reactive deeds, or his majesty, or as creator and so on. The surrogate term *pānîm* immediately directs our attention to (possible) communication (in the relationship supplicant–God).

This is true for many texts in which *pānîm* is combined with a preposition; it disappears lexically in most translations.

5.3.3.7 God's eye/s

Eyes facilitate the absorption of information and aid communication. This applies to God, too.

> Ps. 94.9 *Does he who implanted the ear not hear? Does he who formed the eye not see?*

In Ps. 34.15 Yhwh's eyes – parallel to his ears – indicate that he notices human need:

> Ps. 34.15 *Yhwh's eyes are on the righteous and his ears are attentive to their cry.*

When God sees with his eye/eyes it can also be understood as testing. Ps. 139 refers to being seen when it describes a process, which the supplicant goes through in thought[45], of being tested by Yhwh.

> Ps 139.15 *My frame is/was not hidden from you, of whom it is said: I was made in secret, woven in the depths of the earth, 16 your eyes saw/see my embryo and they (my days?) are/were/will be written in your book ...*

God can also, however, keep his eye on mankind to protect him:

> Ezra 5.5 *But the eye of their God was watching over the eldest of the Jews, so that they were not opposed until the report could reach Darius and a reply be received.*

> Ps. 33.18 *Yhwh's eyes are on those who fear him, on those whose hope is in his unfailing love.*

Therefore, God's eyes are connected with the function of seeing. The eyes are an organ of communication and of contact. God's eye protects and examines. As with all other parts of God's body, he is not limited by time or space; he has the singular gift of seeing 'everything' and can see into

---

[45]Cf.: Wagner, *Permutatio religionis*, pp. 91–113.

FIGURE 5.8 *Bronze figure from Egypt.*
Source: Schroer and Staubli, *Body Symbolism in the Bible*, p. 109, fig. 47.

mankind. One bronze figure from Egypt has a material way of visualizing this superhuman ability:

This figure is studded with eyes, pointing to its extraordinary capacity to see; many eyes see more than two can. However, the distance between man and this numinous being widens immediately. Old Testament anthropomorphism takes a different track. It does not attribute God with many eyes but with another, greater form of vision. The two-eyed human figure makes it possible to conceive of God as a partner, while his enhanced vision emphasizes the distance between God and man.

5.3.3.8 God's ear/s

God's ears fulfil the purpose of hearing/answering mankind; this notion is widely found in the Old Testament:

Num. 11.18 *Consecrate yourselves for tomorrow, for then you will eat meat; it came to Yhwh's ears when you wailed, you who say: 'who will give us meat to eat? For it was well with us in Egypt'. Therefore Yhwh will give you meat to eat.*

Ps. 10.17 *You hear the desire of the afflicted, Yhwh; you will prepare their heart, your ear will listen.*

Ps. 116.2 *He turned his ear to me; therefore I will call on him as long as I live.*

A praying person can call on God directly (Ps. 116.2), so there is direct communication, and he or she can be heard. However, as Ps. 92.12 shows, God also hears what happens on earth without being addressed directly.

Ps. 92.11 *My eye has looked down on my enemies with joy and my ear has heard my evil foes who rise against me.*

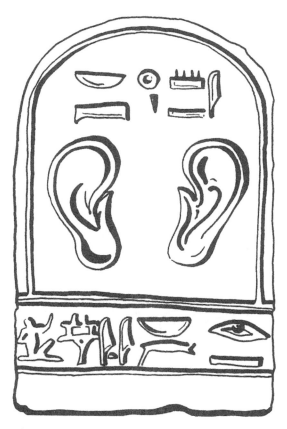

FIGURE 5.9 *Stele.*
Source: Keel, *The Symbolism of the Biblical World*, p. 192, fig. 263.

Viewed in this light – and in analogy to seeing with his eyes – he hears everything. A special theme is the cry of the afflicted and the destitute (Ps. 10.17–18) whose pleas reach God especially; they can be assured of God's help. Hearing is at the same time answering. There is an interesting material pictorial motif for the ear too: divine ears on stele.

The ears on the stele (see Figure 5.9), here the ears of Amun-Re, indicate that the requests of the supplicants have reached the ears of their respective God and have been answered.

Sometimes we find great numbers of divine ears in only one picture, see for example a limestone stele from Thebes (see Figure 5.10): 'Here the kneeling worshipper, named Bai, hopes that his prayer will be heard by the god Amun, depicted as a ram'.[46]

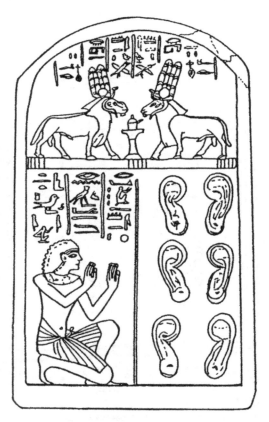

FIGURE 5.10 *Limestone stele from Thebes.*
Source: Schroer and Staubli, *Body Symbolism in the Bible*, p. 129, fig. 55.

---

[46]Schroer and Staubli, *Body Symbolism in the Bible*, p. 129.

The cumulative power of so many ears points to the god's exceptional ability to hear any given request.

The ears, as with the face and the eyes, stand for communication in the Old Testament: God hears mankind, and man can talk with God and communicate.

5.3.3.9 God's nose

As we saw previously, the nose is directly connected with 'wrath'. Although anthropomorphic texts with the nose also offer the sense of smell (Gen. 8.21), the greater focus is on God's wrath.

> Jer. 21.5 *And I will fight against you with an outstretched hand, with a mighty arm, with nose/anger and fury and with great wrath.*

According to Old Testament emotions, anger stands for God's reaction to the behaviour of mankind. The nose, therefore, is a further possibility for communication and a reason for action, and it can determine the relationship between God and humans. Although other organs mostly mark a positive aspect of the relationship between God and humans, wrath stands for a frightening, negative reaction on God's part. God's wrath may be justified as a reaction to human transgression, as the influence of Deuteronomical theology often suggests, but wrath causes fear in mankind and should cease as quickly as possible (Ps. 85.5 *Will you be angry with us for ever and will you prolong your anger through the generations?*).

5.3.3.10 God's mouth

The mouth is the part of the body which forms the prerequisite for active communication. Therefore, the mouth also enables God to speak to mankind:

> Isa. 55.11 *So shall it be with the word that comes out of my mouth: It will not return to me empty but will accomplish what I desire, and achieve all that I sent it out for.*

This verse also indicates clearly that there is a qualitative difference between the speech of God and the speech of people. God's word *'achieves all that I sent it out for'* – a characteristic not possessed by human speech.

The next text shows that the divine word has characteristics which differ from the human word:

> Prov. 8.29 *When he gave the sea its boundary so that the waters would not overstep his mouth/command, and when he marked out the foundations of the earth.*

The word of God, God's command, is law for the element of chaos; water. It is not only mankind that is subject to God's word. All things submit to the word of his mouth, as the battle of chaos imagery shows.

God's mouth, therefore, points out God's ability to speak/to communicate through language and allows God to perform certain deeds through speech which only God can perform.

5.3.3.11 God's throat/neck (life)

The meaning of the Hebrew word *næpæš* is not easy to determine, as we saw previously. All meanings are united in the external form of the word, but specific meaning comes from the context where the nuances of other meanings are always present. This makes an exact definition of God's *næpæš* difficult. It is hard to say where the focus lies in the following text: either it is on God's intention or on the throat, which turns towards us or is averted.

> Jer. 6.8 *Reform, Jerusalem, before my næpæš turns from you and I make you a desolate land, in which no-one can live!*

What is important here is that *næpæš* touches the aspect of 'self in its most intense intentionality'[47] for God as well. *næpæš* means that God lives, is alive, like mankind, that God has a will and acts intentionally. *næpæš* is a foundation for action, for God as well as for humans; in this, too, there is similarity between God and people, a common prerequisite for acting and communicating.

5.3.3.12 Conclusion

Two basic features have repeatedly come to our notice in this survey of the key (external) parts of God's body, which had already come to our attention in the previous description of parts of the human body. We cannot deny a certain analogy and indeed the analogy receives theological terminology in the Old Testament when we talk of being made in the image of God. We will take a closer look at this issue in Chapter 6. These two basic features are immediately evident from our survey of the function of God's body parts; they can be summarized under the aspects of 'communication' and 'action', as presented in Table 5.10.

Let us begin with a summary of the argumentation which led to our two basic features, communication and deeds, and then subsequently explore each of them in more detail.

---

[47]Westermann, נֶפֶשׁ, col. 92.

TABLE 5.10 *Overview of the primarily representative hebrew words for body parts correlating with the two basic aspects of 'action' and 'communication'*

Parts of the body	(Gestural) Functional/ abstract meaning	Functional aspect 'communication'	Functional aspect 'action'
roʾš head	personal counterpart	prerequisite for communication	
pānîm face	establish relationship, communicate face to face	communication	
ʿayin eye	see	practise communication	
ʾozæn ear	hear	practise communication	
ʾap nose	wrath, to be angry with	opportunity to react, practise communication	reason for action
pæh mouth (lips)	talk	practise communication	
næpæš throat, neck	life, living counterpart	prerequisite for communication	
zᵉrôᵃᶜ arm			exercise power and presence execute deeds
yād hand see for example: kap hand/ palm			execute deeds (word) and power
yāmîn right hand			as for hand, see the previous discussion
rægæl foot			exercise power and presence

a) Summary of argumentation

We must consider the parts of God's body as an ample verbal image and explore the principles of construction as we would investigate a material image (Chapter 2 and sections 4.1; 4.2 and 4.4). In our argumentation, we have narrowed the field to the external visible body, in accordance with the fact that material images depict the external body only. In this area, it is possible to analyse material and metaphorical images together and to compare them.

The prohibition of imagery refers to the prohibition of cult images and not to a prohibition of pictorial representations of God per se (section 2.1). As far as the construction of depictions is concerned, images of God do not have a special status and are constructed just like pictures of other 'objects'. Indeed, image construction follows universal rules.

The analysis of the (material and verbal) pictorial world in the Ancient Orient and in the Old Testament (Chapters 2 and 4) suggests that the elements most frequently chosen were not random; the choice followed the principles of aspect (section 4.2) in such a way that 'in material and verbal images' only the aspects central to the 'object depicted' were represented. Examples of body parts which are chosen for humans but not for God in the Old Testament are a clear indication that a conscious choice was made (sections 5.3.1 and 5.3.2).

According to the concept of the synthetic understanding of the body, the function and not the form of parts of the body is important (section 4.3). Therefore, the statement made by a material or verbal image includes the statement made by the functions; physical images in particular show that a photographically realistic depiction is not intended.

b) The testimony made by Old Testament images of God's body: a graphic vision of God in light of communication and action

The parts of the body chosen most frequently in the anthropomorphic verbal image of God are – to repeat the observation made previously – those which express communication (God has a close relationship with us and can contact us as we can God) and action (God acts in us and for us) according to the synthetic understanding of the body in the Old Testament.

The pictorial elements which the Old Testament presents do not intend to display form, the external figure of God; rather they present these two main features of the Old Testament God. When we abandon synthetic thought and the Ancient Oriental and Old Testament principles of pictorial construction and attempt to see visual forms of God's body in verbal images, we also abandon the testimony which the Old Testament with its construction of God's body had intended. Attempts at visualization, such as the Renaissance style, which attempted a visual depiction of God[48] diverge widely from the intended Old Testament statement. In the photographically realistic bodily rendition of the 'form/person' of God, they attempt to express something

---

[48]C. Wagner, Der unsichtbare Gott – Ein Thema der italienischen Renaissancemalerei? in: Wagner, *Gott im Wort – Gott im Bild*, pp. 113–42, esp. pp. 120–2.

that the Old Testament never intended, along the lines of their own principles of perspective.

A first systematic theological assertion about anthropomorphism in the Old Testament can now be made with the help of the insights presented by the graphic representation of God's corporeality. For mankind, God is a God who exercises power and a God who acts (in the world), a God capable of communication, like mankind, who thereby manifests himself as a partner in communication for mankind. Both these characteristics show that the Old Testament God is not a distant, unworldly God; instead a God who communicates with mankind and acts in the world.

His ability to communicate and to act are comparable to human ability, they have much in common. However, God's ability to act and to communicate goes far beyond man's; it is divine and not human. God's divinity is maintained, God is not human (Hos. 11.9 *For I am God and not man.*).

The accentuation of these two aspects, communication and acting, highlights a fact which is well-known to us from Old Testament texts: Yhwh is apostrophized again and again as the God who created the world, who guided Israel out of Egypt and through history (Pentateuch, the Book of History), as the God amenable to people's words and desires, as many Psalms indicate, but who imparts himself to humans through the word of the prophets and the Scriptures.[49]

What, then, is the particular achievement of anthropomorphic assertions, when they are along the same lines as many textual statements? Their particular achievement lies in their manner of making theological statements – graphically! These central factors are not imparted in arid, abstract phrases but with an image of God's body that is woven into almost all of the Old Testament stories of faith. These highly eidetic pictures seep into the consciousness of listener and reader and exert their influence. Sometimes pictures, even verbal ones, are much more effective than words, terms and abstract concepts. Their vividness and verbal imagery is instantly comprehensible and does not, in view of the Old Testament and Ancient Oriental background, even require particular knowledge. The assertions made about God immediately create comprehension, conversance and closeness in each person. A direct relationship between God and man comes into being. The verbal image of God's body is like a net, thrown out over and again, refined and cultivated through reception and impact. God remains present, identifiable, a counterpart to humans but not restricted to a cult image.

---

[49]Cf.: D. Michel, Einheit in der Vielfalt des Alten Testaments, in: id. (ed.), *Studien zur Überlieferungsgeschichte alttestamentlicher Texte* (ed. by Andreas Wagner et al.; TB 93; Gütersloh: Kaiser, 1997), pp. 53–68, esp. p. 68; O. Kaiser, *Der Gott des Alten Testaments: Theologie des Alten Testaments*; O. Kaiser, *Der Gott des Alten Testaments: Theologie des Alten Testaments 2–3.*

The complete absence of sexual features in the representation of God's external body is striking (sections 5.3.1 and 5.3.2). Identifiable sexual features are found often in Old Testament representations of people; they are completely absent for God. This is true not only for the core terms but also for all terms used for the external body. It corresponds well with the observation that the images chosen to depict God in comparisons and metaphors come from both genders. An assignation of God to one gender is thus avoided.

Here we perceive a further theological assertion: Old Testament texts evidently desired to make it quite clear that the one God cannot and should not be assigned to one gender.

God's divinity is not to be challenged in any way. However similar God and people are, there is a great difference: God is not to be confined to one gender. In this I see a certain inner motivation for the prohibition of imagery. The creation of cult images in the late Israelite era was prevented by the impossibility of forcing the Old Testament Creator God, who had so evidently worked in history, into the restraining vessel of a cult image: the impossibility of depicting such a sexless God may well have played a role, too.

Therefore, Old Testament anthropomorphism does not intend to represent the person of God pictorially, nor is it a primitive attempt to humanize God. It unfolds assertions about God in a highly eidetic manner, which belong to the central experiences and insights of Old Testament faith.

5.4 Anthropomorphism in the pantheons of neighbouring religions

We have already observed some interesting parallels from Egypt, Mesopotamia and various other neighbouring religions in sections 5.3.3, and Chapters 2 and 4. An anthropomorphic concept of God was the rule for the religions with which Israel was temporally and geographically surrounded.[50]

A comparison with Old Testament anthropomorphism, however, reveals crucial differences.

a   The gods in the neighbouring polytheistic religions were multiple. Therefore, characteristics emerge which we recognize from human gatherings and groups. The gods behave and act like humans: they celebrate parties, they eat together and so on. We find both male and female divinities and relationships between the various deities result.

---

[50]Cf.: Porter, *What is a God?*; Wagner, *Menschenkörper – Gotteskörper*, pp. 1–28.; Nunn, *Mesopotamische Götter und ihr Körper in den Bildern*, pp. 51–66; Machinist, *Anthropomorphism in Mesopotamian Religion*, pp. 67–99; Smith, *Ugaritic Anthropomorphism, Theomorphism, Theriomorphism*, pp. 117–40; Niehr, *Körper des Königs und Körper der Götter in Ugarit*, pp. 141–67.

It is obvious that the Old Testament God – at the very least in the late stage of Israelite religion where Yhwh was the only conceivable God – did not behave in such a manner. In neighbouring religions, we do not find any gods who consequently avoid being prescribed to one particular gender in their external appearance. As far as I know, this is only found in the Old Testament concept of God.

b   Cult images were of great importance to Israel's surrounding religions. I will not go into this further here. These cult representations can be anthropomorphic or have abstract forms.[51] In Chapter 2, I have already pointed out some anthropomorphic examples. The wide spread anthropomorphic cult images visualize the human concept of a divine form found in surrounding religions.[52]

c   A phenomenon almost unknown for the Old Testament God exists among the gods in neighbouring religions: animal and hybrid forms. Compounds between gods and animals, and also animal-human mixed forms, are a common phenomenon, above all in Egypt. Without intending to provide a deeper analysis of these phenomena, several examples of animal form are presented here merely to highlight this point:

Animal form, see Figure 5.11; mixed form, see Figures 5.12 and 5.13.

There are thousands of examples from Egypt alone. The fact that there are so many pictorial representations of gods in mixed and animal form allows insights into the neighbouring religions. This phenomenon evidently expresses something important for the divine concept in these religions.[53] Animal forms express the transcendental, non-human character of the gods: This is even more drastic in mixed forms.

Susanne Ris-Eberle summarizes the situation in Ancient Egypt in the following manner: 'As an animal surpasses mankind in some of its characteristics, the power of a god surpasses that of mankind so greatly that animals may be

[51]Cf.: B. Groneberg, *Die Götter des Zweistromlandes. Kulte, Mythen, Epen* (Düsseldorf: Artemis & Winkler, 2004); Berlejung, *Die Theologie der Bilder*, pp. 296–9; Nunn, *Mesopotamische Götter und ihr Körper in den Bildern*, pp. 51–66; Pongratz-Leisten, *Entwurf zu einer Handlungstheorie des altorientalischen Polytheismus*, pp. 101–16.
[52]K. van der Toorn, B. Becking and P. W. van der Horst (eds.), *Dictionary of Deities and Demons in the Bible* (2nd edn, Leiden: Brill, 1999).
[53]For Egypt cf.: D. Kessler, Tierische Missverständnisse: Grundsätzliches zu Fragen des Tierkultes, in: M. Fitzenreiter (ed.), *Tierkulte im pharaonischen Ägypten und im Kulturvergleich*, (IBAES IV; retrieved from Humboldt University, 2003, pp. 33–67: http://www2.rz.hu-berlin.de/nilus/net-publications/ibaes4/; cf. further articles in the same magazine; D. Kessler: *Die heiligen Tiere und der König*, Vol. 1: *Beiträge zur Organisation, Kult und Theologie der spätzeitlichen Tierfriedhöfe* (ÄAT 16,1; Wiesbaden: Harrassowitz, 1989); Erik Hornung, *Die Bedeutung des Tieres im Alten Ägypten*, in: StGen 20 (1967), pp. 69–84; Theodor Hopfner, *Der Tierkult der alten Ägypter nach den griechisch-römischen Berichten und den wichtigen Denkmälern* (DÖAW.PH 57,2; Wien: Hölder, 1913).

FIGURE 5.11 *The vulture goddess Nechbet from Elkab (18th Dynasty).*
Source: Hamann, *Ägyptische Kunst*, p. 64, fig. 68.

FIGURE 5.12 *God Anubis with the head of a jackal (18th Dynasty).*
Source: Hamann, *Ägyptische Kunst*, p. 62, fig. 65

FIGURE 5.13 *Granite statue of the goddess Sachmet (with the head of a lion).*
Source: Schäfer and Andrae, *Die Kunst des Alten Orients*, p. 328.

used to express it.'[54] This is true for deities completely in animal form, but also, perhaps even more, for deities which occur in mixed form. Characteristics which surpass the anthropomorphic are especially drastic in mixed forms.

Animals venerated as conveying divine powers included the following: the falcon, vulture, ibis, bull, cow, ram, lion, cat, baboon, ichneumon (Egyptian mongoose), shrew, snake, frog (toad), dung beetle, hippopotamus, canids (dogs, wolves, jackals etc.), eels and some types of fish. Almost every god is attributed with one, sometimes two or even three animals, while on the other hand a particular animal may be ascribed to several gods. Although not every god is recorded in every representational form, each god is found in many forms. Certain gods appear more often in particular forms, but there is no god for whom there is only one acceptable form.

The human form includes male (with extremities or 'mummy-shaped') and female bodies and male infants. If Thot appears as a man with a mummy-shaped body, and at the same time as a baboon or a man with

---

[54]S. Ris-Eberle, 'Tiere als Götter im Alten Ägypten?', in *Unipress* 122 (2004), pp. 50–53, esp. p. 50.

the head of an ibis then we may assume that his essence cannot be grasped in human or animal form. There is no form which adequately reveals his true essence. The divine image does not define God clearly. Therefore the gods appear in ever more forms; the image is not itself the god but the receptacle in which the deity dwells.[55]

The fickle inconsistency of the divine figure evades being tied to one form alone. This in turn maintains the divinity of the gods. Since feral aspects (which are threatening for mankind) are also included, fearfulness, unpredictability and a sense of distance on the part of the god (from mankind) are emphasized.

The inconstancy, the fluctuating forms of appearance and the combination with fearful aspects introduces a note, unknown in the Old Testament, to the relationship between gods and humans.[56]

The contrast with the very different concept of divinity in the neighbouring religions is a theologumenon which highlights the theological statement made by the consistency of the Old Testament God. God is consistently presented in human form in the Old Testament; he never assumes the form of an animal and certainly not a hybrid form, and he always remains a reliable counterpart for mankind in his body language (section 5.3).

5.5 Observations on the chronological development of anthropomorphism in the Old Testament

In previous exegetical generations, it was common to consider anthropomorphism as an 'old' phenomenon within the history of Old Testament religion which made way for a more transcendental concept of God by the late post-exile era. This has been discussed in Chapter 3.

However, as we have seen in sections 5.1–3, the 'components' of the image of God's body, that is the texts where these appear, are spread over the whole of the Old Testament. There is virtually no text, and certainly no larger group of texts or books, which is not included in this verbal image. We should be sceptical of the notion that anthropomorphism became increasingly insignificant as the Old Testament religion developed.

---

[55]Ris-Eberle, *Tiere als Götter im Alten Ägypten?*, p. 50.
[56]Against this background, it is interesting and indeed significant that the few theriomorphisms which can be found in the Old Testament belong on the whole to texts about 'Yhwh's wings'. Although their interpretations are not complete, they are concerned with positive functions for mankind (shade, protection, etc.). Therefore, it is clear that if the Old Testament uses animal comparisons at all to describe God, then it is always the positive and humanitarian aspects which emerge. Emphasis on unpredictability or fear has no priority. Cf.: E. Martin, (ed.), *Tiergestaltigkeit der Göttinnen und Götter zwischen Metapher und Symbol* (BThSt 129; Neukirchen-Vlyn: Neukirchner, 2012).

The development of the Old Testament into a collection of texts was a slow process. It became the unalterable canon that we know today sometime after the first century CE. This process began in the pre-exile era and was rooted in the traditions of Old Testament prophesy.[57]

Israel's religion underwent profound change through the experience of exile and the deep incisions caused by the loss of monarchy, land, temple and unity, and through the destruction of Jerusalem and the Southern Kingdom of Judah in 587 BCE. This dramatic process of transformation began in exile and continued into the post-exile era. The result of this process is the Old Testament religion, which was so formative for Judaism and Christianity.

In the post-exile era, the Old Testament, as a collection of texts, became the foundation of the religion. We can, therefore, speak of a 'religion of the book'. The 'truth' of the religion is found in the book; through the encounter with the text, an encounter with God takes place.

Four aspects of the image of God, which were formative in the post-exile era, must be emphasized in a description of this religion:[58]

- the one and only God as the counterpart to mankind, who is to be revered without any cultic images (monotheism and the prohibition of imagery);
- the only God, who is the creator and keeper of mankind and the whole world (the creator God);
- the only God, who is the Lord of history;
- the God who, however, demands obedience from humans in their life and their actions (God as the source of the law).[59]

These four aspects continually come to the fore when we read the Old Testament at the canonical level. By this we mean the youngest text form, which has hardly been changed and is the basis for later reception and for all translations. These basic statements clarify many other texts, which are somewhat ambivalent concerning monotheism and the prohibition of imagery and so on.

In the Decalogue, for example, it says: Exod. 20.3/Deut. 5.7 *You shall have no other gods before me.* This phrase intends that God alone should be revered. It does not deny the existence of other gods and is thus not monotheistic. On the basis of other, definitely monotheistic statements (Deutero-Isaiah), such texts are later understood as saying that, apart

---

[57]Cf.: A. Wagner, *Prophetie als Theologie: die "so spricht Jahwe"-Formeln und das Grundverständnis alttestamentlicher Prophetie* (FRLANT 207; Göttingen: Vandenhoeck & Ruprecht, 2004), pp. 317–25.

[58]Cf.: D. Michel, *Einheit in der Vielfalt des Alten Testaments*, in: A. Wagner et al. (eds.), *Studien zur Überlieferungsgeschichte alttestamentlicher Texte* (Festschrift für Diethelm Michel; Gütersloh: C. Kaiser, Gütersloher Verlagshaus, 1997), pp. 53–68, esp. p. 68; Kaiser, *Der Gott des Alten Testaments*; Kaiser, *Der Gott des Alten Testaments*.

[59]A. Wagner (ed.), *Primäre und sekundäre Religion als Kategorie der Religionsgeschichte des Alten Testaments* (BZAW 364; Berlin: deGruyter, 2006), pp. 3–19, here p. 11.

from Yhwh, no other gods exist. Exegesis, over centuries, confirms this. As far as the body of Yhwh is concerned, we cannot find any system of reinterpretation. The figure of God remains present to the last stage of the canon. Indeed, the concentration on the canonical texts, read repeatedly and in their entirety, makes this concept more dynamic than ever.

If an abstract concept of God had developed in the wake of monotheism, and become increasingly 'allergic' to anthropomorphism, then many anthropomorphic texts would certainly have been deleted from the canonical text. There is no indication of such a process. The monotheistic concept of God appears, therefore, to be compatible with the concept of a human form. Perhaps the human figure was even necessary.

In my opinion, the inner theological reasons for this lie in the nature of the Old Testament God. A monotheistic God who is more or less almighty could easily lose connection with the world. The figural concept of God and the functions attached to the various parts of the body indicate to the very last corner of the canon that God's power and greatness should not characterize the image of God alone. Although there is only one God and although he is to be venerated even without imagery, our concept of God is deeply rooted in the fact that he can act, with hands, arms and feet. Moreover, God's connection with mankind and with the world does not come to an end; God can communicate with eyes, ears and mouth and the connection with each individual is maintained without the mediation of priest, cult or temple. God remains tangible and accessible. It is almost as if anthropomorphism balances the dangers presented by a monotheistic image of God and sustains the comprehensibility of the Old Testament God, albeit a God that is still at a great distance from mankind. Perhaps this is why anthropomorphic concepts, intensified by monotheism, appear so strongly in later texts such as Psalm 139.

Anthropomorphism is certainly an old tradition, shared by neighbouring religions, but it is also a phenomenon which, with its own specific character, remains important until the end of the Old Testament period and indeed gains in importance.

These basic observations admittedly only sketch a framework within which we must then investigate the specific treatment of the body of God in individual books, texts and text categories. Various approaches are conceivable. On the one hand, lines can be drawn through the whole biblical canon and beyond to older, contemporary cultures and to Hebrew post-biblical literature and tradition (LXX, Qumran, literature from the Jewish-Hellenistic field), starting from one part of the body and questioning how the hand, arm, or eye are treated, on the other hand, the 'body theology' of individual texts and books must be investigated.[60]

---

[60]There are some generic studies, for example Janowski, *Konfliktgespräche mit Gott*; D. Bester, *Körperbilder in den Psalmen: Studien zu Psalm 22 und verwandten Texten* (FAT 24; Tübingen: Mohr Siebeck, 2007); Florian Markter, *Transformationen. Zur Anthropologie des Propheten Ezechiel unter besonderer Berücksichtigung des Motivs 'Herz'* (FzB 127; Würzburg: Echter, 2013).

6

The picture of God in the Old Testament and of mankind made in the image of God[1]

Old Testament examples of mankind made in the image of God are rare. In the whole of the Old Testament, there are three explicit examples: Gen. 1.26f, Gen. 9.6 (see chapter 5.1) and Gen. 5.3 (chapter 5.2). The striking sparsity indicates that this concept is not of central importance in the Old Testament. Compared to the number of texts concerning the Exodus, the covenant or creation, there are very few texts about humans in the image of God. This does not mean that the concept does not have an important place in the Old Testament or its origin, the Priestly Source. It merely indicates that it is not a main topos of Old Testament theology.

Gen. 9.6, in which it is forbidden to commit murder, refers to Gen. 1.26f, and justifies the prohibition with the fact that man is made in God's likeness. Gen. 5.3 likewise refers to Gen. 1.26–27, but in quite a different way:

Gen. 5.1–3 *When God created man, he made him in the likeness (dᵉmût) of God 2 and he created them, male and female, and blessed them and called them 'man' at the time they were created. 3 When Adam was 130 years old he had a son in his own likeness (ṣælæm) and in his own image and called him Seth.*

---

[1]For more see: A. Wagner, *Die Gottebenbildlichkeitsvorstellung der Priesterschrift zwischen Theomorphismus und Anthropomorphismus*, in: J. Luchsinger, H. -P. Mathys and M. Saur (eds.) *der seine Lust hat am Wort des Herrn!* (Festschrift Ernst Jenni zum 80. Geburtstag) (AOAT 336; Münster: Ugarit Verlag, 2007), pp. 344–63; A. Wagner, *Verkörpertes Herrschen. Zum Gebrauch von 'treten' / 'herrschen' in Gen 1,26–28*, in: G. Etzelmüller, A. Weissenrieder (eds.), *Verkörperung als Paradigma einer theologischen Anthropologie* (TBT, 172, Berlin: deGruyter, 2016), pp. 127–41.

Being made in likeness to God was not only true for the first people on earth, as Gen. 5.3 explains, but through procreation, it is a basic truth for all mankind.

The foundation for the likeness of humans to God is laid out in Gen. 1.26–27. It belongs to the great creation text Gen. 1.1–2.4, with which one of the most important parts of the Pentateuch, the Priestly Source, begins.[2] I do not intend to discuss this highly complex text here, but a rough outline of the structure and the themes discussed indicates immediately that the likeness of mankind to God is not at the core of this text either.[3] The core is found in v. 26–27; the creation of humans is the culmination of the work of creation.

---

[2]Gen. 1.1–2.4a is attributed to the Priestly Source; apart from Gen. 2.4a there is consensus on this; Genesis 1 is the fount of this great work P; the historical draft begins here; important theological and anthropological groundwork starts here. For discussion on P and the limits of the text, cf. (selective literature): H. Gunkel, *Genesis: übersetzt und erklärt von Hermann Gunkel.* (Göttinger Handkommentar zum Alten Testament 1; Göttingen: Vandenhoeck & Ruprecht, 1901). English: *Genesis. Translated and Interpreted by Hermann Gunkel* (trans. M. E. Biddle; Macon, GA: Mercer University Press, 1997); von Rad, *Das erste Buch Mose.* English: *Genesis. A Commentary*; W. H. Schmidt, *Die Schöpfungsgeschichte der Priesterschrift: zur Ueberlieferungsgeschichte von Genesis 1,1–2,4a und 2,4b–3,24* (Wissenschaftliche Monographien zum Alten und Neuen Testament, 17; Neukirchen-Vluyn: Neukirchener Verlag, 1967); C. Westermann, *Genesis: Teilbd. 1. Genesis 1–11* (BK 1.1, Neukirchen-Vluyn: Neukirchener Verlag, 1974); O. H. Steck, *Der Schöpfungsbericht der Priesterschrift. Studien zur literarkritischen und überlieferungsgeschichtlichen Problematik von Genesis 1,1–2,4a.* (FRLANT 115; Forschungen zur Religion und Literatur des Alten und Neuen Testaments, Göttingen: Vandenhoeck und Ruprecht, 1975); T. Pola, *Die ursprüngliche Priesterschrift: Beobachtungen zur Literarkritik und Traditionsgeschichte von P^g.* (Wissenschaftliche Monographien zum Alten und Neuen Testament 70; Neukirchen-Vluyn: Neukirchener-Verlag, 1995); H. Seebass, *Genesis I: Urgeschichte (1,1–11,26)* (Neukirchen-Vluyn: Neukirchener-Verlag, 1996); M. Witte, *Die biblische Urgeschichte. Redaktions- und theologiegeschichtliche Beobachtungen zu Genesis 1,1–11,26* (BZAW 265; Berlin, New York: deGruyter, 1998); B. Janowski, *Sühne als Heilsgeschehen: Traditions- und religionsgeschichtliche Studien zur Sühnetheologie der Priesterschrift.* (Wissenschaftliche Monographien zum Alten und Neuen Testament, 55; Neukirchen-Vluyn: Neukirchener Verlag, 2000); R. G. Kratz, *Die Komposition der erzählenden Bücher des Alten Testaments* (Göttingen: Vandenhoeck & Ruprecht, 2000), pp. 230–48. English: *The Composition of the Narrative Books of the Old Testament* (trans. J. Bowden; London: T. & T. Clark 2005); M. Kessler and K. A. Deurloo, *A Commentary on Genesis: The Book of Beginnings* (New York: Paulist Press, 2004); U. Neumann-Gorsolke, *Herrschen in den Grenzen der Schöpfung. Ein Beitrag zur alttestamentlichen Anthropologie am Beispiel von Psalm 8, Genesis 1 und verwandten Texten* (Wissenschaftliche Monographien zum Alten und Neuen Testament, 101; Neukirchen-Vluyn: Neukirchener Verlag, 2004); A. Schüle, '*Der Prolog der hebräischen Bibel: Der literar- und theologiegeschichtliche Diskurs der Urgeschichte (Gen 1–11)*', (AThANT 86, Zürich, 2006); M. Arneth, '*Durch Adams Fall ist ganz verderbt ... : Studien zur Entstehung der alttestamentlichen Urgeschichte*', (FRLANT 217; Göttingen: Vandenhoeck & Ruprecht, 2007); P. Weimar, *Studien zur Priesterschrift* (FAT 56; Tübingen: Mohr Siebeck, 2008); S. Shectman and J. S. Baden, (eds.), '*The Strata of the Priestly Writings: Contemporary Debate and Future Direction*', (AThANT 95; Zürich: Theologischer Verlag Zürich, 2009); F. Hartenstein and K. Schmid (eds.), *Abschied von der Priesterschrift? Zum Stand der Pentateuchdebatte* (VWGT 40; Leipzig: Evangelische Verlagsanstalt, 2015).

[3]Cf.: Seebass, *Genesis I*, pp. 79–80: 'The motif is restricted to P, is brought up for the last time in 9.6 and is only indirectly reflected in Ps. 8.5ff. The unusual importance attached to it for centuries cannot be explained by the exegetical situation (Westermann) and is a great burden to the discussion'.

TABLE 6.1 *Structure of Gen. 1.1–2.4a*

1.1	title
1.2–2.1	creation
1.2	before creation
1.3–5	Day 1, separation of light and darkness
1.6–8	Day 2, separation of the water, below and above the 'expanse' (heaven)
1.9–13	Day 3, sea and land, the vegetation
1.14–19	Day 4, sun, moon and stars
1.20–23	Day 5, animals (above the earth, in the water)
1.24–25.26–31	Day 6, animals (on the earth), man
1.24–25	the land should produce living creatures
1.26–27	*creation of man*
1.28	*God blesses his creation, his injunction to multiply, to fill the earth and to subdue it, to rule over the living creatures*
1.29	*plants as food*
1.30	*plants are given to the animals as food, too*
1.31	*God saw that it was all good*
2.1	heaven and earth are complete
2.2–3	end: rest on Day 7
2.4a	a signature (non-P?)

The concept that man was created in the likeness of God is one of the 'additional concepts' which P introduced, going beyond the pure act of creation. Let us take a closer look in order to understand this better. My draft translation contains Hebrew terms which I shall explain in the course of the discussion. Parts to be discussed are underlined:

Gen. 1.26–27
26 Then <u>Elohim</u> said:
let <u>us</u> make (a) ʾādām
as something like <u>our</u> ṣælæm corresponding[4] to <u>our</u> dᵉmût.
and they (mankind) shall <u>set their foot</u> on/rule over
*   the fish of the sea*

---

[4]Oddly, the prepositions *b* and *k* appear to have the same meaning; they are also found in Gen. 5.3, but *b* stands for *dᵉmût* and *k* for *ṣælæm*. The translation for *b* (as Beth essentiae) in Gen. 1.26 is found in E. Jenni, *Die hebräischen Präpositionen. Vol. 1: Die Präposition Beth* (Stuttgart, Berlin: W. Kohlhammer, 1992), p. 84. There is further literature on the topic on the same page.

the birds in the air
the livestock
and the whole earth
and over all the <u>crawling</u> <u>creatures</u> that move along the ground.
27 *And so <u>Elohim</u> created (<u>br</u>ᵓ (spoken: <u>bara</u>)) man as something like*
his ṣælæm, as something like his ṣælæm he created (<u>br</u>ᵓ) him, <u>male and</u>
<u>female</u> *he created them (<u>pl.</u>).*

Elohim

Elohim is the name for God, which P uses in the Story of Creation. As a
denotation for God (appellative noun) it corresponds to the English word
God and is set apart from the proper name for the Hebrew God, Yhwh
(proper noun). P uses the name Yhwh from Exodus 6 onwards. Elohim is a
plural form but is often (cf. Gen. 1.27) constructed with verbs in the singular,
an indication that Elohim is generally not understood as a plural. This is
further reflected in the synonymous use of the non-plural short form El.

let us make

The combination of *Elohim* in Gen. 1.26 with a clearly plural context
is therefore all the more surprising: once with a cohortative (1. Pers. Pl.
cohortative, *let us make*)[5], twice with the plural suffix which defines the
words (*our*) *ṣælæm* and (*our*) *dᵉmût*. This is an unequivocal *we*; indeed, if
we take the introduction into account *Elohim* speaks as, or for, *we*. How
can this be explained?

One explanation often given presupposes that God is accompanied by his
council, the gathering of the sons of God (*benê-ᵓelîm*), the crown council.[6]

---

[5]The cohortative of Gen. 1.26 also has further features: In the context of Gen. 1.1–4a, it is
unparalleled that Elohim begins a work of creation with an invitation. Usually, works of creation
begin with a command (*let it be…, may the earth bring forth*, etc.). This is a further argument for
the importance attached to the creation of man among all the other works of creation. A second
feature concerns the communicative situation; God speaks to himself! This, too, is unique within
Gen. 1.1–2.4a; its function is to underline the singularity of the creation of man.
[6]The reference to possible echoes of Ancient Oriental concepts of creation does not explain the
plural adequately. Even if the following text forms the background to Gen. 1.26, we would still
have to explain why P adopted the plural:
   The gods ask:
   'What shall we change, what shall we create?
   Oh Annunaki, you great gods,
   What shall we change, what shall we create?'
   (answer in cohortative):
   'We shall slaughter N.N. (name of a deity), the twin god,
   and create mankind from his blood.'
Seebass, *Genesis I*, p. 79. A genuine plurality of gods as in this Assyrian text is not found in P!

Descriptions of such councils are in fact found in the Old Testament several times:[7]

Ps. 29.1–2

1 *A Psalm of David.*
Give to Yhwh, you sons of God, give to Yhwh glory and strength.

2 *Give to Yhwh the glory due to his name, worship Yhwh in the beauty of his holiness.*

Job 1.6
There was a day when the sons of God came and presented themselves to Yhwh, and Satan also came among them.

Cf. Gen. 6.2 and so on.

If we bring this explanation into play, then the sons of God are called upon here to make mankind. The crucial problem with this explanation, however, is that there are no further examples of *bᵉnê-ʾelîm*, the sons of God, within P and no related concepts. Is it likely that this concept appears just this once and is then immaterial for the rest of P?

Another explanation could be to assume a binary God, who creates mankind like itself, male and female. A pair of Gods therefore. However, there are no further texts of this sort in P or in the Old Testament, so that this solution is also out of the question.[8]

The most probable solution is that the plural must be understood as *pluralis majestatis*. Other examples of this royal linguistic form are found in the Old Testament, but only from the beginning of the Persian era.

Ezra 4.17+18

17 *The King* (the Persian King Artaxerxes) *sent the following reply: To Rehum, the chancellor and to Schimshai the secretary and their other associates who live in Samaria and elsewhere in Trans-Euphrates: Peace to you! 18 The letter which you sent to us has been read to me word for word.*

Persian influence is plausible for the late- and post-exile era. Since P originated in the late exile or early post-exile era this explanation is compatible with the origins of P. This solution, therefore, is the most plausible. It is possible

---

[7]Cf.: H. D. Neef, *Gottes himmlischer Thronrat: Hintergründe und Bedeutung von sôd JHWH im Alten Testament* (Stuttgart: Calwer Verlag, 1994).
[8]A *pluralis deliberationis* was also discussed. In 2 Sam. 24.14, we find a deliberation formulated in the plural. In Gen. 1.26, however, there is no hint of deliberation: the decision is announced in the *we*-form.

that we find a hint of polemic here: Yhwh who uses *we* but is not a king, is the lord, the sovereign over his likenesses![9]

ʾādām

In Hebrew, *ʾādām* means the collective human being (as species), mankind, people. Therefore, it is quite correct when Luther translates this as: Let us make man (*Lasst uns Menschen machen!*). The individual is *bæn-ʾādām*. Hebrew uses *ʾādām* for humanity beyond all social, political and familial borders.[10] As a result, Westermann can say that *ʾādām* is in fact located in the History of Creation (Gen. 1–11), for here we are concerned with the basic facts of humanity and fundamental experiences: Creation, expulsion, floods, preservation, dispersal (guilt and punishment reveal the limitations of humanity).

ʾādām is synonymous with the basic Old Testament conception of humanity: mankind is related to God from the moment of his conception, there is no humanity outside this relationship. 'Man cannot be defined nor understood without accepting that he exists as God's counterpart.'[11]

brʾ/to create

Most examples of *brʾ*, *to create, to bring into being*, are found in P and in Deutero-Isaiah, that is, quite explicitly in the exile era. The subject of statements formed with *brʾ* is always God (Yhwh or Elohim), and solely the God of Israel, not foreign gods. This term for the act of creation is reserved for the Israelite God alone: other gods and mankind are clearly excluded from the act of creation.

Since there are no analogies, the essence of creation remains untouched – how does God do it – *how* remains in the dark, a secret beyond human conception. God creates new things which were not there before. Therefore *brʾ* denotes God's free, sovereign, unbound act of creation.

male and female

This characteristic of newly created man is presented quite tersely: mankind (humanity, man) is only available as man and woman, male and female.

---

[9]Seebass conjectures a polemic against the human – non-Israelite – Kings: 'Yhwh, not a king, is the lord of those made in the image of God'. Seebass, *Genesis I*, p. 79.
[10]C. Westermann, Art. אדם *ʾādām*, THAT I (1984), col. 50–1.
[11]Westermann, Art. אדם *ʾādām*, col. 50–1.

Since P is otherwise patrilinear (cf. genealogies) and even androcentric, it is all the more remarkable that man and woman are made equally in the likeness of God and do not differ in their relationship with him. This is truly the embryo of the worldwide concept of the equality of all mankind.

'The differentiation between male and female prevents mankind from comparing itself with the unique God of Israel, who reserved sexuality for his creation'.[12]

This coincides with our findings on the 'image of God' in the Old Testament.

In the following discussion of *ṣælæm* and *dᵉmût*, we will focus on the nature of the relationship between God and mankind as a mirror image. For the creation of mankind as male and female casts a light on our image of God: According to the principle of similarity which lies behind *dᵉmût*, this bisexuality is reflected on to our image of God. This corresponds with the picture found in chapter 5.3.3.12b of a God who cannot be assigned to one particular gender by the parts of the body with which he is explicitly accorded. Gen. 1.27 suggests that both genders are reflected and that consequently God encompasses both genders.[13] This concept, too, is difficult to portray along the lines of Ancient Oriental principles of imagery and can, therefore, be classified under the many other statements which contradict the assignation of God to one gender.

ṣælæm (pronounced: zäläm)

ṣælæm is one of the pivotal terms in Gen. 1.26–27. The interpretation of this word is crucial for our understanding of the likeness of God. It is of great importance (more than *dᵉmût?*) since it is taken up two more times in this text.

To analyse the meaning of a Hebrew term, we must investigate its use in the Old Testament. In general, the context delivers the basic meaning of a word. The more texts we consult, the more stable the result will be. We cannot consider all the texts here, but a few are enough to clarify the meaning of *ṣælæm*.

A verb similar to the root verb from which the noun *ṣælæm* is derived would give a good clue. Although Hebrew does not have such a verb, Arabic has the verb *ṣlm* = to cut off, to hew, to cut, to carve. Since Semitic languages are related, Arabic can deliver the first clue.

2 Kgs 11.18 (=2 Chron. 23.17). (Joash becomes king in Judah, measures taken by the priest Jehoiada)

---

[12]Seebass, *Genesis I*, p. 82.
[13]Cf.: T. Gudbergsen, '*God consists of both the male and the female genders: A short note on Gen 1:27*' in: VT 62.3 (Leiden: Brill 2012), pp. 450–3.

All the people of the land went to the house (temple) of Baal and tore down the altars. And they smashed all his ṣælamîm (pl. of ṣælæm) thoroughly and killed Mattan the priest of Baal in front of the altars.

The meaning of *ṣælæm* can be deduced easily from this context. Since something is smashed, it must be material. And since it is a cult object from the temple (altars were mentioned) and the Arabic verb indicates something that has been carved, manufactured or hewn, there is every indication that *ṣælæm* in this case means the statue of a god, an idol. The same is true for Ezek. 7.20:

Ezek. 7.20 (from a vision about the end of the world)

They used their noble (precious metal) jewels for arrogance and used it to make ṣælamîm their idols and vile images. Therefore I will make it all into an unclean thing for them.

Ezek. 7.20 could indicate, as Num. 33.52 clearly does, that *ṣælamîm* also includes the cult image, an idol, cast in metal:

Num. 33.52 (Yhwh's commission to the Israelites before they passed into the Land of Canaan)

Drive out all the inhabitants of the land before you and destroy all their (painted, cf Lev. 26.1) sculptures and all their cast ṣælamîm and demolish all their sacrificial places/heights.

Other similar texts, Amos 5.26 (although this text is not quite so reliable); Ezek. 16.17 and 23.14, refer to a (wall-) painting of men.

1 Sam. 6.5 expresses a 'theurgic' relation between an object and its depiction; here, too, it means artisan sculptures:

1 Sam. 6.5 (tale told of the ark, when the Philistines returned it)

Make models of your tumours/bubo (pestilential bubo, at any rate signs of illness) and your mice which have destroyed your country, and pay honour to Israel's God. Perhaps he will lift his hand from you and your gods and your land. ... 11 They placed the ark of Yhwh on a cart and with it the chest with the golden mice and the ṣælamîm of their tumours.

We can summarize that *ṣælæm* means finely wrought pictures, custom-built artefacts, objects made from various materials as representations. Emphasis lies in some cases on the object (cult image) and sometimes on the depiction.[14]

---

[14]The meaning of *ṣælæm* is quite different in:
  Ps. 39.5–7.
  5 Yhwh, teach me to know that my end will come and that my life has a goal and that I must leave.

What, however, does *ṣælæm* mean in Gen. 1.26–27? Is the cult image of more importance or the depiction? What exactly does *ṣælæm* mean? We will consider this question again once we have taken a look at *dᵉmût*.

dᵉmût

The abstract form *dᵉmût* is derived from the verb *dmh/resemble*, which is widely found in biblical Hebrew. Corresponding to the meaning of the verb, the abstract form *dᵉmût* indicates the state of sameness, likeness. L. Köhler's suggestion that *dᵉmût* could be translated as *something like* is fitting.[15]

dᵉmût also refers to depictions/figurative representations 'and emphasises their equivalence to the model'.[16] Two aspects of *dᵉmût* are especially important:

- The figure has *external visible* similarity
- Similarity does *not* make it *identical*!

This is important for our understanding of man-made in the image of God: Man and God are *similar* (at least in a certain sense) but *not identical*!

What concept of likeness corresponds to both *ṣælæm* and *dᵉmût* as in Gen. 1.26–27?

The first important observation is the combination of *ṣælæm* and *dᵉmût*. The terms seem to be a pair which express the whole of man as God's (pictorial) counterpart. The concurrence of the two terms is decisive here, the thing which must be depicted is approached from two sides. We can indeed call this a merism, a linguistic metaphor which expresses an entity by naming two aspects.[17]

---

6 *See, my days are a handbreadth with you and my life is as nothing before you.*
(Every man at his best state is [apparently] but a breath).
7 *Every man goes to and fro as a ṣælæm*
Meaning: Shadow, see also Ps. 73.20 (the fate of the godless).
As a dream when one awakes, Lord, when you awake you will despise their ṣælæm.
Meaning: Transient picture.

[15]Cf.: E. Jenni, *Art.* דמה *dmh gleichen*, in: THAT I (1984), col. 451–6.
[16]Jenni, *Art.* דמה *dmh gleichen*, col. 452.
[17]Cf.: J. Krasovec, *Der Merismus im Biblisch-Hebräischen und Nordwestsemitischen* (Rome: Biblical Institute Press, 1977); W. Bühlmann and K. Scherer, *Sprachliche Stilfiguren der Bibel: von Assonanz bis Zahlenspruch. Ein Nachschlagewerk* (Gießen: Brunnen, 1994), p. 84; T. Longman III, *Art.* Merism, in: T. Longmann III and P. Enns (eds.), *Dictionary of the Old Testament: Wisdom, Poetry and Writings* (Downers Grove, Ill Nottingham: IVP Academic Inter-Varsity Press), pp. 464–6.

Ps. 89.12	*heaven and earth*	= the universe, the world
Exod. 10.9	*young and old*	= everyone
Gen. 24.50	*good and bad*	= everything
Ps. 8.8	*sheep and cows*	= (small livestock and heavy livestock)
		= all domestic animals
Gen. 1.26	*ṣælæm* and *dᵉmût*	= the whole likenesses

In Old Testament merisms, it is not unusual for the two components to be introduced with (the same or different) prepositions.

Ps. 57.12,	*Be exalted, O God, above (preposition ᶜal) the heavens and let your glory be above (preposition ᶜal) the whole earth*	= the whole world
Ps. 113.6	*Who is like Yhwh … 6 … in (preposition bᵉ) heaven and on (preposition bᵉ) earth*	= the whole world
Isa. 1.6	*From (preposition min) the sole of your feet to (preposition ᶜad) (the top of) your head*	= the whole person
Ps. 72.8	*from (preposition min) sea to (preposition ᶜad) sea, from (preposition min) the river to (preposition ᶜad) the ends of the earth*	= the whole earth

ṣælæm and *dᵉmût* should not be considered separately, their synergy is the essence. Similar to parallelism,[18] the message conveyed by a merism is the sum of the individual statements. The individual statements are not superseded by the whole but remain present and act as the 'boundary' of the 'whole'.[19]

---

[18]Cf. On parallelism and its noetic function, where both partial statements augment each other to form a new statement: A. Wagner, *Der Parallelismus membrorum zwischen poetischer Form und Denkfigur*, in: A. Wagner (ed.), *Parallelismus membrorum* (OBO 224, Fribourg: Academic Press; Göttingen: Vandenhoeck & Ruprecht, 2006), pp. 1–26.

[19]The merismic construction makes fine differentiation possible: In Gen. 5.3 for example, *dᵉmût* begins the merism; this, combined with the variance to Gen. 1.26, forms an emphasis; which is prepared by Gen. 5.1, where Adam is introduced as God's *dᵉmût – dᵉmût* without *ṣælæm* – as the first in the genealogy; the question of human genealogy is inevitably connected with likeness (family similarity through the generations) indicating that likeness to God is passed on from generation to generation. Therefore, similarity between man and God is of more importance than in Gen. 1.26-28, which is more concerned with representation (it is not an accident that P uses *ṣælæm* and not *dᵉmût* in Gen. 1.27). Cf.: H. -P. Müller, *Eine neue babylonische Menschenschöpfungserzählung*, in: H.-P. Müller, *Mythos - Kerygma - Wahrheit: gesammelte Aufsätze zum Alten Testament in seiner Umwelt und zur biblischen Theologie* (Berlin, New York: deGruyter 1991), pp. 43–67, here p. 52. P quite consequently uses only *ṣælæm* in Gen. 9.6, since the issue of human murder could be a threat to God's representation and similarity is not important.

The second observation refers to what follows *ṣælæm* and *dᵉmût*. A verb form in a preformative conjunction (not a narrative!) is added with the help of the conjunctive *waw*, thus opening a further field of meaning. While it is linked to the previous statement (with the help of *waw/and*), it need only be connected explicitly if this is a necessity. Initially, *ṣælæm* and *dᵉmût* stand in their own right and round off the statement *let us make man*. In a second step, further information on the mandate for sovereignty is added. The mandate of sovereignty is not a backup for *ṣælæm* and *dᵉmût*. It is an additional statement, a specification, consequence and so on. (as is the syntactic construction with *wᵉ*-PK in a consecutive tense). If it was the real meaning of *ṣælæm* and *dᵉmût*, these terms would not be needed. The mandate for sovereignty is only awarded to mankind because they are created in the *ṣælæm* and *dᵉmût* of God.

ṣælæm was defined previously as the term for a finely wrought cult image. If we assume this meaning for Gen. 1.26, then it means that man is created as a cult image of God. Although this statement links in to the concept of cult images, it does not take it very literally. A cult image is a static, inanimate object, even when a close relation to the respective god is assumed, as was normal in the Ancient Orient. Humans do not otherwise appear as 'cult images'. However, here P transfers the cult image to mankind; the statement aims at a correlation of the picture with what it represents. As the cult image represents a god, according to the Ancient Oriental concept, so too does a human, according to P (i.e. in the Israelite context), represent God. In the world, man takes the place of God.[20] This is associated with the concept of a close relation between humans and God which does not necessitate any intermediary (next to slight polemic undertones against foreign cult images). The relationship exists between God and each person (*ʾādām* as a collective term! Cf. Gen. 5.3); therefore, each person is God's representative. There are no differences between man and woman in this point, as v. 27 shows. The concept of likeness with God is found above all in Egypt, where the Egyptian Pharaoh is the likeness of God. In the Old Testament, likeness with God is promised to each human. It is often said that P raises mankind to a sovereign rank. Royal characteristics from Egypt are accorded to all mankind in the Old Testament.[21]

---

[20]Cf.: B. Janowski, *Die lebendige Statue Gottes: zur Anthropologie der priesterlichen Urgeschichte*, in: M. Witte (ed.), *Gott und Mensch im Dialog* (Festschrift Otto Kaiser zum 80. Geburtstag; BZAW 345, Bd. 1; Berlin, New York: 2004), pp. 183–214, here p. 185; Neumann-Gorsolke, *Herrschen in den Grenzen der Schöpfung*; R. Oberforcher, *Biblische Lesarten zur Anthropologie des Ebenbildmotivs*, in: A. Vonach and G. Fischer (eds.), *Horizonte biblischer Texte* (Festschrift für Josef M. Oesch zum 60. Geburtstag; OBO 197, Fribourg: Academic Press; Göttingen: Vandenhoeck & Ruprecht, 2003), pp. 131–68. W. Gross, *Gen 1,26.27; 9,6: Statue oder Ebenbild Gottes? Aufgaben und Würde des Menschen nach dem hebräischen und griechischen Wortlaut*, in: I. Baldermann et al. (eds.), *Jahrbuch für Biblische Theologie Bd. 15* (Neukirchen-Vlyn: Neukirchener, 2000), pp. 11–38.

[21]Waschke, E.-J., *Die Bedeutung der Königsideologie für die Vorstellung der Gottesebenbildlichkeit des Menschen*, in: A. Wagner (ed.), *Alttestamentliche und interdisziplinäre Zugänge zur historischen Anthropologie* (FRLANT 232; Göttingen: Vandenhoeck & Ruprecht, 2009), pp 235–52.

ṣælæm also means depiction of an object. What a cult image looks like is not an arbitrary matter. This aspect is substantiated by dᵉmût: Man is not only a representative, God's mandatary (G. v. Rad); his figure is of the same kind.

We should approach the concept of similarity not from the familiar concept of form, but from Old Testament synthetic thought. To us, picture means form. But this puts us on a false track. Although we start with the figure of the body, it is not in view of the form but of the function of the various parts of the body. They are there to express equality; the point is that God and man are equal (but not identical) in their ability to communicate and to act (see the previous discussion). Our analysis of the representation of the body of God and of man pointed to the ability to communicate and to act.

This is not P's invention. Our comparison of the anthropomorphic depiction of God and the concept of the human body have shown that correspondence between the two exists for the whole period in which Old Testament texts were produced. P. explicitly utilizes this existing objective relationship theologically, using creation to make statements about man.

Being made in the likeness of God enables dominion, and this in turn is formulated by P as a mandate which humans have to fulfil. Only when humans can act and communicate like God, can they also rule.

We may summarize all this as follows in Table 6.2:

TABLE 6.2 *Summary: Representation and formal-functional similarity*

Man as God's ṣælæm	*Man as God's dᵉmût*
Emphasizes what was made, produced, man is God's cult image and therefore represents him, his (figurative) representative function is present in ṣælæm.	Emphasizes the similarity, above all of form; the figure/form cannot be understood without assuming synthetic concept; synthetic thought means the equality of form and of function: dᵉmût is aimed at the correspondence of man and God since both are designed for communication and action
→ Man in the likeness of God: Representation	→ Man in the likeness of God: Formal-functional similarity

These two statements, ṣælæm and dᵉmût, together shape the concept of similarity. Both partners, God and humans, are similar, but not identical. Since ṣælæm is connected with cult imagery, God is clearly superordinate to people, who are based on God. This preserves the disparity between God and humans. dᵉmût, on the other hand, emphasizes (figurative) equality as the basis of possible communication and action.

We found the same correspondence between God and man in the picture of the body of God and of humans. The prerequisite for this correspondence is not only the concept that humans are created, but also the corresponding functional-anthropomorphic 'image' of God.

rdh / tread on (rule)[22]

A further striking confirmation for the complex of concepts underlying Gen. 1.26–27, which are determined by the similar corporeal images of humans and God, is provided by the continuation of the principle of likeness in the mandate to rule.

Although Hebrew has at least two verbs commonly used to express rule, *mšl* and *mlk*, Gen. 1.27 uses yet another: *rdh/tread/trample on*.

This word is found in its literal sense in Joel 4.13 for trampling (with feet) in the wine press:

> Joel 4.13 *Grasp the sickle, for the harvest is ripe! Come and trample, for the wine press is full and the vats are overflowing, for their (the heathens) wickedness is great!*

Without doubt, *tread on* means *to rule* in Gen. 1.27, as it does in other texts too. It refers to the image of trampling on something with the feet. According to the functional meaning of parts of the body described previously, this quite evidently expresses dominion. *rdh/tread/trample on* not only fits in completely with this concept, it is also the best explanation.

It is evident that *rdh* is well on the way to meaning *rule*, for it is not of course possible to tread on the birds in the sky, nor to tread literally on the whole earth. But Joel 4.13 shows that the word has not been transferred completely into the figurative sense, it is still rooted in the 'body'. Indeed, a complete transfer into the figurative sense is unnecessary since feet, and the movement they make, have the functional meaning of *dominion*.

Summary

Humans are conceived to 'represent'. God's cult image *ṣælæm* is conceived to express similarity, *dᵉmût*. Together they constitute (a merism) the whole person in his relationship with God. Mankind wields dominion vicariously for God on earth (cf. the mandate to rule), as God's representative (B. Janowski), the mandatary (G. v. Rad). Communication between God and humans must work smoothly if the mandate is to be understood, and therefore similarity is a basic prerequisite. Secondly, humans must be able to act like God, less almighty and within the confines of human ability, but nonetheless capable of acting like God. Both these aspects, communication and the ability to act, lead us back to the similarity of the corporeal and functional images of God and humans, as described previously. P merely explicitly unites what was the core before and after P of the Israelite concept of the relationship between God and man.

---

[22]Cf.: Wagner, *Verkörpertes Herrschen*, pp. 127–41.

7

The theological significance of God's body in the Old Testament

7.1 Pictorial and corporeal concepts as prerequisites for understanding God's body in the Old Testament

The main thesis of this book is that the image of God's body, as it is drawn verbally in the Old Testament, must be comprehended along the lines of the Ancient Oriental/Old Testament understanding of images. Pictures in our modern world refer to visible objects, they are understood as portrayals of real objects. In the Ancient Orient, pictures referred to objects in their ideal, typical conceived form, more or less independent of their visible aspect. This is combined with a corporeal concept which diverges from ours, in which the body always stands for the functions it exercises. Figures in human form in the Ancient Orient can, therefore, be understood to indicate functions of the body quite independent of visibility, without referring to the visibility of the parts of the body depicted at all. Consequently, verbal images of the body of God in the Old Testament, the anthropomorphic figure, can express the functions connected with core elements of the body without indicating a visual figure.

A further thesis is that we must also take the foreign concept of the body found in the Old Testament texts into account. Reflection upon and comparison with other concepts of the body help us to distance ourselves from our own. When we recognize that our concept is relative, then we can try to grasp foreign concepts, such as the concept found in the Ancient Orient and the Old Testament. Portrayals of bodies and parts of the body do not depict individuals. It is their symbolic aspect, the functions connected with various parts of the body, which are of interest. According to conceptions in the Old Testament era, pictures do not express what we see; they express a concept of the body and what this then permits us to understand.

Old Testament texts draft their concept of the image of God's (external) body under these two premises, the pictorial and the corporeal concepts inherent to the Old Testament.

7.2 The complexity of body theology

It should be evident by now that the 'theology' behind statements on the body is not a naïve reflection of the human situation, but a complex way of expressing theological concepts of God. Impressions and ideas with which people in Old Testament times were familiar are 'implemented' in such theological concepts. This theology must, therefore, be understood and deciphered in light of its own time, as this book has done. Only then can the 'messages' contained therein be transferred into the present.

Biblical texts transport some of God's essential characteristics with the help of his corporeal picture, as far as they were important for the Old Testament image of God. Communication and the ability to act are the decisive factors, as is a corporeal concept which is not confined to one gender.

These are 'essentials' in the Old Testament concept of God and they are neither naïve nor slight. They are the core of the Old Testament experience of God.

Their common and extensive distribution in Old Testament texts ensures that in all the texts in which an element of God's body plays a role, part of the whole picture of God's body is present. Partial portrayals of God's body evoke, pars pro toto, the whole of his body and therewith all the central statements about God which are connected with his body. In this way, many texts are 'underlaid' with the theology of the body.

This can be 'implemented' today too, as it was in times gone by: Our very different understanding of the body and of pictures must, however, be taken into account.

7.3 Convergence with basic Old Testament theological statements

If we compare basic statements of the theology of God's body with other basic Old Testament statements, then the convergence is clear. This discussion takes place on a very abstract level at present. Greater depth could be achieved if the discussion was extended to include individual texts and books and their diversity.

Let us remain for the time being with central Old Testament statements that may be considered to be characteristic for the whole of the Old Testament canon. In chapter 5.5, the following essential statements were named:

- God's power in the course of history (deeds)
- The fact that God turns favourably towards mankind
- God's ability and intention to communicate

There is a striking correspondence of the these aforementioned essential statements with the two major aspects that are revealed by the theology of God's body:

- Communication
- The ability to act.

These statements accentuate the relation of God and humans. Although, in his being, God is always conceived as greater and different than man (see section 7.5), an element of partnership is retained

- God's action is directed towards humans and human action is directed towards God.
- God's ability to communicate, paired with a positive attitude to man, makes God tangible to humans.

Thus, God does not withdraw from man.

Here, too, convergent Old Testament theologumena indicate consonance. 'Covenant', for example, is a suitable convergent concept for the likeness to God. These are all concepts which were developed in the exilic/post-exilic Old Testament era. They are among the most influential legacies which the Old Testament can bestow.

7.4 God's body and monotheism

Historical impact and the orientation towards humanity displayed in creation and communication, belong to the essential shaping of the concept of God in the Old Testament. Monotheism must be placed in line with these developments.

In my opinion, it is surprising that monotheism employs the concepts of God's body unreservedly, in order to make statements linked to the monotheistic God, for example in Ps. 139 where God's hand can reach 'everywhere'.

The uniqueness of the one and only God could have led to conflict with the very human concept of the human figure of God. Instead, a form of anthropomorphism develops in monotheism, which makes God's human form so unique that it cannot be compared with any other form of anthropomorphism. This goes so far that the gender of God's external body cannot be determined (see section 7.5).

This is the greatest theological merit of the statements on God's body: This monotheistically conceived God remains close to mankind; the one and only God is always tangible and capable of communication and does not withdraw from mankind. The widespread distribution of texts, which mention elements of God's body, rooted all further statements in this fertile ground.

As long as there is a divine being as we know it in the world, we cannot forgo anthropomorphic concepts which relate mankind to God. Seen in terms of accommodation, anthropomorphism plays a central role; today, as in Old Testament times, it is the basis for communication with God.

7.5 God's divinity and his human figure

The unfolding picture of the body in the Old Testament reveals aspects of God's body which transcend the 'human body' and lack correspondence. They prevent a simple 'theology of corporeal correspondence'.

One of these aspects is the avoidance of gender: In his external form, God is neither male nor female. In comparative pictures, God is compared with both man and woman. Clearly, God cannot be restricted to one (human) gender. A simple equation God = man is thwarted.

The capacity of the functions expressed by the various parts of the body differs considerably between God and humans, and the difference between them is most evident here. Both have a hand and can act with it but their possibilities differ vastly.

The Old Testament states explicitly that God is not a human and that a human is not God (Ps. 8, and others). All these mechanisms[1] preserve the balance between God's proximity to man, expressed by the similarity of his body, and God's otherness, which is attributable to his divinity.

The lack of essential theriomorphisms in the Old Testament should be seen in this context, in my opinion.[2] Although animal and mixed forms can be used to express the otherness of the gods, the aspect of approachability would then be lost. In divine concepts which include animal and mixed forms,

---

[1] In anthropomorphism, the unavailability is emphasized by anthropopragmatisms, which must be investigated separately. If God continually breaches the logic of human action as a merciful God (the Flood in non-P sources) or as an (unfounded) angry God (Psalms), this underlines that God is different, God is not man.

[2] Reference to God's wings might possibly represent a certain exception (Ps 57:2 i.a.). However, given that a thorough investigation of this motive has not taken place, to ascertain whether the image comes from the sphere of animal forms (birds?) or whether it is a numinous figure, or indeed what statement it is intended to make, we should not refer to theriomorphism too hastily. If at all, it would be a case of theriomorph-anthropomorph hybridity.

the strangeness and otherness of the deity is so great that distance rather than approachability is emphasized. In this, too, there is correspondence with the content of other religions from Israel's vicinity. However, the relationship between God and man is completely different to that in the Old Testament. Mankind is far more exposed to the arbitrary behaviour of the gods, and a basic anthropology as positive as that found in Gen. 1:1–2:4a in the Priestly Source, is sought in vain.

7.6 Final comments

All in all, the theological achievement is highly sophisticated: The (mental) image of God's body has been retained while at the same time a prohibition of imagery (at least for statues) is conceived, and the whole is expressed in strictly monotheistic terms. In addition, the use of the human form visualizes God's superhuman omnipotence. This theological construction can be seen in the Old Testament as we know it. However, it is the result of a theological progression which unfolded during the long course of the development of the Israelite religion and our investigation of the various stages of this progression is only just beginning.

If we transfer the Old Testament concept of God's body into modern pictorial conceptions without any reflective process, then God is made visual in a manner quite foreign to the Old Testament. The criticism outlined in Chapter 3 of an anthropomorphism which makes God too substantial would then be justified. This, however, would be a modern misinterpretation of Old Testament intention. A new interpretation of anthropomorphism today must take into account the long gap in time and also the other prerequisites for understanding imagery and the body in the Old Testament.

If we take all this into account, then the conceptual framework of anthropomorphism can unfold: In the Old Testament concept, God remains on the one hand approachable, communicable and potent. On the other hand, he is inaccessible and preserves his divinity, even in human form. Understood in this way, imagery of God in human form cannot be relinquished, even today.

BIBLIOGRAPHY

Alt, Albrecht, *Die Ursprünge des israelitischen Rechts* (BUSAW 86,1, Leipzig: Hirzel, 1934). English: *Origins of Israelite Law* in: Alt, Albrecht (ed.), *Essays on Old Testament History and Religion* (Garden City, NY: Doubleday, 1966).

Anati, Emmanuel, *Höhlenmalerei. Die Bilderwelt der prähistorischen Felskunst* (trans. Dorette Deutsch; Düsseldorf: Albatros Verlag, 1997).

Arneth, Martin, '*Durch Adams Fall ist ganz verderbt...*': *Studien zur Entstehung der alttestamentlichen Urgeschichte* (FRLANT 217; Göttingen: Vandenhoeck & Ruprecht 2007).

Assmann, Aleida (ed.), *Positionen der Kulturanthropologie* (Stw 1724; Frankfurt: Suhrkamp, 2004).

Assmann, Jan, *Die Mosaische Unterscheidung: oder der Preis des Monotheismus* (Edition Akzente, München: Carl Hanser, 2003). English: *The price of monotheism* (trans. R. Savage; Stanford: Stanford University Press, 2010).

Assmann, Jan, *Monotheismus und Ikonoklasmus als politische Theologie*, in: E. Otto and J. Assmann (eds.) *Mose: Ägypten und das Alte Testament* (SBS 189; Stuttgart: Verlag Katholisches Bibelwerk, 2000), pp. 121–39.

Assmann, Jan, *Moses der Ägypter: Entzifferung einer Gedächtnisspur* (München: Hanser, 1998) English: *Moses the Egyptian: The Memory of Egypt in Western Monotheism* (Cambridge, MA: Harvard University Press 1997).

Aurelius, Erik, *Der Ursprung des ersten Gebotes*, in: *ZThK 100* (Tübingen: Mohr Siebeck, 2003), pp. 1–21.

Bätschmann, Oskar, *Einführung in die kunstgeschichtliche Hermeneutik: die Auslegung von Bildern* (5th edn, Darmstadt: Wissenschaftliche Buchgesellschaft, 2001).

Baumann, Gerlinde, *Das göttliche Geschlecht. JHWHs Körper und die Gender-Frage*, in: Hedwig-Jahnow-Forschungsprojekt (ed.), *Körperkonzepte im Ersten Testament: Aspekte einer Feministischen Anthropologie* (Stuttgart: Kohlhammer Verlag, 2003), pp. 220–50.

Baumann, Gerlinde, *Die 'Männlichkeit' JHWHs: Ein Neuansatz im Deutungsrahmen altorientalischer Gottesvorstellungen*, in: F. Crüsemann (ed.), *Dem Tod nicht glauben: Sozialgeschichte der Bibel* (Festschrift für Luise Schottroff zum 70. Geburtstag, Gütersloh: Gütersloher Verlag, 2004), pp. 197–213.

Behrens, Achim, *Verstehen des Glaubens: Eine Einführung in Fragestellungen evangelischer Hermeneutik* (Neukirchen-Vluyn: Neukirchener, 2005).

Belting, Hans, *Bild-Anthropologie. Entwürfe für ein Bildwissenschaft* (4th edn, München: Willhelm Fink Verlag, 2011). English: *An Anthropology of Images. Picture, Medium, Body* (trans. Th. Dunlap; Princeton: Princeton University Press, 2011).

Belting, Hans, *Bild und Kult: eine Geschichte des Bildes vor dem Zeitalter der Kunst* (7th edn, München: C.H. Beck Verlag, 2011). English: *Likeness and Presence: A History of the Image before the Era of Art* (trans. E. Jephcott; Chicago: University Of Chicago Press, 1997).

Benthien, Claudia, *Haut: Literaturgeschichte – Körperbilder – Grenzdiskurse* (Rohwolts Enzyklopädie 55626, Reinbek: Rowohlt Verlag, 1999).

Benthien, Claudia, *Im Leibe wohnen: Literarische Imagologie und historische Anthropologie der Haut* (Körper, Zeichen, Kultur 4, Berlin: Berlin Verlag, 1998).

Berlejung, Angelika, *Die Theologie der Bilder: Herstellung und Einweihung von Kultbildern in Mesopotamien und die alttestamentliche Bilderpolemik* (OBO 162; Göttingen: Vandenhoeck & Ruprecht, 1998).

Berlejung, Angelika (ed.), *Menschenbilder und Körperkonzepte im Alten Israel, in Ägypten und im Alten Orient* (ORA 9; Tübingen: Mohr Siebeck, 2012).

Bester, Dörte, *Körperbilder in den Psalmen: Studien zu Psalm 22 und verwandten Texten* (FAT 24; Tübingen: Mohr Siebeck, 2007).

Boardman, John (ed.), *Die griechische Kunst. Aufnahmen von Max Hirmer* (6th edn, München: Hirmer, 1992). English: *Greek Art* (4th edn, London: Thames & Hudson, 1996).

Boecker, Hans Jochen, *Recht und Gesetz im Alten Testament und im Alten Orient* (NStB 10; Neukirchen-Vluyn: Neukirchener, 1976). English: *Law and the Administration of Justice in the Old Testament and Ancient East* (trans. J. Moiser; London: Society für Promoting Christian Knowledge, 1980)

Boman, Thorleif, *Hebrew Thought Compared with Greek* (trans. J. L. Moreau; New York: W. W. Norton & Company, 1970).

Bons, Eberhard, *Psalm 31. Rettung als Paradigma: eine synchron-leserorientierte Analyse* (FTS 48; Frankfurt: Verlag Josef Knecht, 1994).

Bordreuil, Pierre, *Charges et fonction en Syrie-Palestine d'après quelques sceaux ouest-sémitiques du second et du premier millénaire*, in: *CRAI 130* (1986), pp. 290–307.

Braudel, Fernand, *Geschichte und Sozialwissenschaften. Die longue durée*, in: M. Bloch and F. Braudel (eds.), *Schrift und Materie in der Geschichte: Vorschläge zur systematischen Aneignung historischer Prozesse* (edition Suhrkamp 814, Berlin: Suhrkamp, 1977), pp. 47–85.

Bredekamp, Horst, *Bild – Akt – Geschichte*, in: GeschichtsBilder 46. Deutscher Historikertag vom 19.-22. September 2007 in Konstanz. Berichtsband, herausgegeben von Clemens Wischermann, Armin Müller, Rudolf Schlögl und Jürgen Leipold, Konstanz, 2007, S. 289–309.

Brunner-Traut, Emma, *Frühformen des Erkennens: Aspektive im Alten Ägypten* (3rd edn, Darmstadt: Wissenschaftliche Buchgesellschaft, 1990, ²1992, ³1996).

Bühlmann, Walter and Scherer, Karl, *Sprachliche Stilfiguren der Bibel: von Assonanz bis Zahlenspruch. Ein Nachschlagewerk* (Gießen: Brunnen, 1994).

Burda, Hubert (ed.), *The digital Wunderkammer: 10 chapters on the iconic turn* (München: Willhelm Fink Verlag, 2011).

Burda, Hubert and Maar, Christa (eds.), *Iconic turn. Die neue Macht der Bilder* (2nd edn, Köln: DuMont Buchverlag, 2004); http://www.iconicturn.de, Hubert Burda Stiftung (München).

Butler, Judith, *Bodies that Matter: On the Discursive Limits of "sex"* (New York: Routledge, 1993).

Butler, Judith, *Gender Trouble. Feminism and the Subversion of Identity* (New York: Routledge, 1990).

Camus, Albert, *The Myth of Sisyphus* (trans. [from French] J. O'Brien; UK: Hamish Hamilton, 1955).

Christ, Franz, *Menschlich von Gott reden: Das Problem des Anthropomorphismus bei Schleiermacher* (ÖTh 10; Einsiedeln: Gütersloh/Mohn, 1982).

Chrysippos, Frg. 1076 (SVF, II, 315).

Crüsemann, Frank (ed.), *Dem Tod nicht glauben: Sozialgeschichte der Bibel* (Festschrift für Luise Schottroff zum 70. Geburtstag, Gütersloh: Gütersloher Verlag, 2004).

Crüsemann, Frank, *Die Tora: Theologie und Sozialgeschichte des alttestamentlichen Gesetzes* (München: Chr. Kaiser, 1992). English: *The Torah. Theology and social history of Old Testament law* (trans. A. W. Mahnke; Minneapolis: Fortress Press, 1996).

Davies, Graham I., *Ancient Hebrew Inscriptions: Corpus and Concordance* (Cambridge: Cambridge University Press, 1991).

Deissler, Alfons, *Die Grundbotschaft des Alte Testaments* (Freiburg im Breisgau: Herder, 1995).

Delitzsch, Franz, *Hoheslied* und Kohelet (BC.AT 4.2; Leipzig: Dörffling und Franke, 1875).

de Hulster, Izaak J. and LeMon, Joel M. (eds.), *Image, text, exegesis. Iconographic interpretation and the Hebrew Bible* (LHB.OT 588; London and New York, Bloomsbury, 2014).

Diels, Hermann and Kranz, Walther (ed.), *Die Fragmente der Vorsokratiker* (Hamburg: Rowohlt, 1957).

Diesel, Anja A., *"Ich bin Jahwe": der Aufstieg der Ich-bin-Jahwe-Aussage zum Schlüsselwort des alttestamentlichen Monotheismus* (WMANT 110; Neukirchen-Vluyn: Neukirchener Verlag, 2006).

Diogenes von Babylon, Frg. 33 (SVF, III, 217).

Dohmen, Christoph, 'פסל psl,' ThWAT IV (1989), col. 688–97. vgl. S. 168: Ebeling, Jürgen in: RLA 1.

Dohmen, Christoph, *Das Bilderverbot: seine Entstehung und seine Entwicklung im Alten Testament* (BBB 62; Frankfurt: Athenäum, 1987).

Dohmen, Christoph, *Decalogue*, in: Th. B. Dozeman, C. A. Evans and J. N. Nohr (eds.), *The Book of Exodus: Composition, reception, and interpretation* (VT Suppl. 164; Leiden and Boston: Brill, 2014), 193–219.

Dohmen, Christoph, *Exodus 1–18/19–40* (HthKAT; Freiburg im Breisgau: Herder, 2004).

Dressel, Gert, *Historische Anthropologie. Eine Einführung* (Wien: Böhlau, 1996).

Duden, Barbara, *Geschichte unter der Haut. Ein Eisenacher Arzt und seine Patientinnen um 1730* (Stuttgart: Klett-Cotta, 1987). English: *The Woman Beneath the Skin. A doctor's patients in eighteenth-century Germany* (trans. T. Dunlap; Cambridge, MA and London: Harvard University Press, 1991).

Duden, Barbara, *Der Frauenleib als öffentlicher Ort. Vom Mißbrauch des Begriffs Leben* (Hamburg: Luchterhand, 1991). English: *Disembodying Women. Perspectives on pregnancy and the unborn* (trans. L. Hoinacki; Cambridge, MA and London: Harvard University Press, 1993).

Ebach, Jürgen, *Die Einheit von Sehen und Hören: Beobachtungen und Überlegungen zu Bilderverbot und Sprachbildern im Alten Testament*, in: R. M. E. Jacobi, B. Marx and G. Strohmaier-Wiederanders (eds.), *Im Zwischenreich der Bilder* (Schriften der Evangelischen Forschungsakademie NF Erkenntnis und Glaube 35, Leipzig: Evangelische Verlagsanstalt, 2004), pp. 77–104.

Ebach, Jürgen, *Gott ist kein Mann – aber warum?*, in: F. Crüsemann (ed.), *Dem Tod nicht glauben: Sozialgeschichte der Bibel* (Festschrift für Luise Schottroff zum 70. Geburtstag; Gütersloh: Gütersloher Verlag, 2004), pp. 214–32.

Egger-Wenzel, Renate and Corley, Jeremy (eds.), *Emotions from Ben Sira to Paul* (Deuterocanonical and Cognate Literature Yearbook 2011; Berlin and Boston: deGruyter, 2012).

Egidi, Margreth, et al. (eds.), *Gestik. Figuren des Körpers in Text und Bild* (Literatur und Anthropologie 8, Tübingen: Narr-Verlag, 2000).

Eichrodt, Walter, *Theologie des Alten Testaments, Teil 2* (Leipzig: J.C. Hinrichs, 1935). English: *Theology of the Old Testament Vol. II* (trans. J.A. Baker; The Old Testament Library; Bloomsbury Street London: S.C.M. Press 1967).

Feuerbach, Ludwig, *Das Wesen des Christentums* (Leipzig 1841) (E. Thies (ed.), *Ludwig Feuerbach. Werke in sechs Bänden*; Frankfurt: Suhrkamp, 1976). English: *The Essence of Christianity* (trans. G. Eliot; New York, Evanston and London: Harper & Row, 1957).

Fischer-Lichte, Erika and Fleig, Anne (ed.), *Körper-Inszenierungen: Präsenz und Kultureller Wandel* (Tübingen: Attempto Verlag, 2000).

Frevel, Christian, et al. (eds.), *Die Zehn Worte: der Dekalog als Testfall der Pentateuchkritik* (QD 212; Freiburg im Breisgau: Herder, 2005).

Frevel, Christian (ed.), *Biblische Anthropologie: Neue Einsichten aus dem Alten Testament* (QD 237; Freiburg im Breisgau: Herder, 2010).

Fritz, Volkmar, *Einführung in die biblische Archäologie* (Darmstadt: Wissenschaftliche Buchgesellschaft, 1985). English: *An Introduction to Biblical Archaeology*, in: *Journal für the Study of the Old Testament. Supplement Series 172* (trans. B. Mänz-Davies; Sheffield: Sheffield Academic Press, 1994).

Fritz, Volkmar, *Die Stadt im alten Israel* (Beck's Archäologische Bibliothek, München: Beck, 1990).

Frymer-Kensky, Tikva S., *Israel*, in: R. Westbrook (ed.), *A History of Ancient Near Eastern Law* (HdO 1, 72; The Near and Middle East; Leiden: Brill, 2003), pp. 975–1046.

Funk, Julika and Brück, Cornelia (eds.), *Körper-Konzepte* (Literatur und Anthropologie 5; Tübingen: Gunter Narr, 1999).

Gadamer, Hans-Georg, *Wahrheit und Methode. Hermeneutik I* (5th edn, Tübingen: Mohr Siebeck, 1986). English: Truth and Method (trans. W. Glen-Doepel; London: Sheed and Ward, 1979).

Gerleman, Gillis, *Ruth: Das Hohelied* (BK 18; Neukirchen-Vluyn: Neukirchener, 1965).

Gitler, Haim and Tal, Oren, *Coinage of Philistia of the 5th and 4th Centuries BC: A Study of the Earliest Coins of Palestine* (Collezioni Numismaticke 6, Milan and New York: Edizione Ennere and Amphora Books, 2006).

Giuliani, Luca, *Bild und Mythos: Geschichte der Bilderzählung in der griechischen Kunst* (München: C. H. Beck, 2003). English: *Image and myth. A history of pictorial narration in Greek art* (trans. J. O'Donnell, Chicago: University of Chicago Press, 2013).

Gombrich, Ernst Hans Josef, *Die Geschichte der Kunst* (16th edn, Berlin: Phaidon Press, 1996). English: *The Story of Art* (16th edn, trans. E. H. J. Gombrich; London: Phaidon Press, 1995).

Graf, Fritz, *Der Eigensinn der Götterbilder in antiken religiösen Diskursen*, in: G. Boehm (ed.), *Homo pictor* (München: K. G. Saur, 2001), pp. 227–43.

Graupner, Axel, *Die zehn Gebote im Rahmen alttestamentlicher Ethik*, in: H. G. Reventlow (ed.), *Weisheit, Ethos und Gebot: Weisheits- und Dekalogtraditionen in der Bibel und im frühen Judentum* (BThSt 43; Neukirchen-Vluyn: Neukirchener, 2001), pp. 61–95.

Greßmann, Hugo E. F. W. (ed.), *Altorientalische Bilder zum Alten Testament* (2nd edn, Berlin/Leipzig: deGruyter, 1927). (= *AOB*).

Greschat, Katharina, *Gregor des Großen Auseinandersetzung mit Serenus von Marseille um die Frage der Bilder*, in: A. Wagner, V. Hörner and G. Geisthardt (eds.), *Gott im Wort – Gott im Bild: Bilderlosigkeit als Bedingung des Monotheismus?* (2nd edn, Neukirchen-Vluyn: Neukirchener Verlag, 2008), pp. 59–74.

Groneberg, Brigitte, *Die Götter des Zweistromlandes. Kulte, Mythen, Epeen*, (Düsseldorf: Artemis & Winkler, 2004).

Gross, Walter, *Gen 1,26.27; 9,6: Statue oder Ebenbild Gottes? Aufgabe und Würde des Menschen nach dem hebräischen und griechischen Wortlaut*, in: I. Baldermann et al. (eds.), *Jahrbuch für Biblische Theologie 15* (Neukirchen-Vlyn: Neukirchener Verlag, 2000), pp. 11–38.

Gudbergsen, Thomas, *God Consists of Both the Male and the Female Genders: A Short Note on Gen 1:27*, in: *VT 62.3* (2012), pp. 450–3.

Gunkel, Hermann, *Genesis: übersetzt und erklärt von Hermann Gunkel* (HKAT 1; Göttingen: Vandenhoeck & Ruprecht, 1901). English: *Genesis. Translated and interpreted by Hermann Gunkel* (trans. M. E. Biddle; Macon, GA: Mercer University Press, 1997).

Gunn, Battiscombe, G., *The Wisdom of the East. The Instruction of Ptah-Hotep and the Instruction of Ke'gemni: The Oldest Books in the World* (trans. from the Egyptian with an Introduction and appendix; London: John Murray: Albemarle Street, 1906).

Habermas, Rebekka, Tanner, Jakob and Wagner-Hasel, Beate (eds.), *Thema: 20 Jahre Zeitschrift historische Anthropologie*, in: *Historische Anthropologie 20* (2012).

Hamann, Richard *Ägyptische Kunst: Wesen und Geschichte* (Berlin: Knaur, 1944).

Hamori, Esther J., *When Gods Were Men: The Embodied God in Biblical and Near Eastern Literature* (BZAW 384; Berlin: deGruyter, 2008).

Haraway, Donna J., *Primate Visions. Gender, Race and Nature in the World of Modern Science* (New York: Routledge, 1989).

Haraway, Donna J., *Simians, Cyborgs, and Women: The Reinvention of Nature* (New York: Routledge, 1990).

Hartenstein, Friedhelm, *Das Angesicht JHWHs: Studien zu seinem höfischen und kultischen Bedeutungshintergrund in den Psalmen und in Exodus 32-34* (FAT 55; Tübingen: Mohr Siebeck, 2008).

Hartenstein, Friedhelm, *Die unvergleichliche 'Gestalt' JHWHs: Israels Geschichte mit den Bildern im Licht von Dtn 4,1-40*, in: B. Janowski, N. Zchomelidse (eds.), *Die Sichtbarkeit des Unsichtbaren: Zur Korrelation von Text und Bild im Wirkungskreis der Bibel* (Stuttgart: Deutsche Bibelgesellschaft, 2002), pp. 49–77.

Hartenstein, Friedhelm and Schmid, Konrad (eds.), *Abschied von der Priesterschrift? Zum Stand der Pentateuchdebatte* (VWGT 40; Leipzig: Evangelische Verlagsanstalt, 2015).

Hedwig-Jahnow-Forschungsprojekt (ed.), *Körperkonzepte im Ersten Testament: Aspekte einer Feministischen Anthropologie* (Stuttgart: Kohlhammer, 2003).

Heinisch, Paul, *Der Einfluss Philos auf die älteste christliche Exegese (Barnabas, Justin und Clemens von Alexandria): ein Beitrag zur Geschichte der allegorisch-mystischen Schriftauslegung im christlichen Altertum* (Münster: Aschendorff, 1908).

Heinisch, Paul, *Theologie des Alten Testaments: Die Heilige Schrift des Alten Testaments Ergänzungsband 1* (Bonn: Hanstein, 1940).

Hempel, Johannes, *Die Grenzen des Anthropomorphismus Jahwes im Alten Testament*, in: *ZAW 57* (Berlin: deGruyter, 1939), pp. 75–85.

Hempel, Johannes, *Jahwegleichnisse der israelitischen Propheten*, in: *ZAW 42* (Berlin: deGruyter, 1924), pp. 74–104.

Herrmann, Christian, *Ägyptische Amulette aus Palästina / Israel: mit einem Ausblick auf ihre Rezeption durch das Alte Testament* (OBO 138; Fribourg/ Göttingen: Vandenhoeck & Ruprecht, 1994).

Hölscher, Tonio, *Die griechische Kunst* (Beck'sche Reihe 2551, München: Verlag C.H. Beck, 2007).

Hopfner, Theodor, *Der Tierkult der alten Ägypter nach dem griechisch-römischen Berichten und den wichtigen Denkmälern,* (DÖAW.PH 57, 2; Wien: Hölder Verlag, 1913).

Horn, Friedrich Wilhelm, *Die Herrlichkeit des unvergänglichen Gottes und die vergänglichen Bilder der Menschen*, in: A. Wagner, V. Hörner and G. Geisthardt (eds.), *Gott im Wort – Gott im Bild: Bilderlosigkeit als Bedingung des Monotheismus?* (2nd edn, Neukirchen-Vluyn: Neukirchner Verlag, 2008), pp. 43–57.

Hornung, Erik, *Die Bedeutung des Tieres im Alten Ägypten*, in: *Studium generale* 20 (Berlin: Springer-Verlag, 1967), pp. 69–84.

Horst, Johannes, Art. 'οὖς', ThWNT V (1954), col. 543–58.

Hossfeld, Frank-Lothar and Zenger, Erich, *Die Psalmen: I. Psalm 1-50* (NEB 29; Würzburg: Echter Verlag, 1993).

Hübler, Axel, *Das Konzept 'Körper' in den Sprach- und Kommunikationswissenschaften* (UTB 2182, Tübingen and Basel: Francke, 2001).

Hübner, Ulrich, *Archäologie. II. Biblische Archäologie*, RGG⁴ 1 (1998), pp. 709–11. English: *Archaeology. II. Biblical Archaeology*, RPP 1 (2007), pp. 354–6.

Hurrelmann, Bettina, Kinder und Medien, in: K. Merten, S. J. Schmid and S. Weischenberg (eds.), *Die Wirklichkeit der Medien. Eine Einführung in die Kommunikationswissenschaft* (Opladen: Springer VS, 1994) , pp. 377–407.

Jacobi, Rainer M. E., Marx, Bernhard and Strohmaier-Wiederanders, Gerlinde (eds.), *Im Zwischenreich der Bilder* (EuG 35; Leipzig: Evangelische Verlagsanstalt, 2004).

Janowski, Bernd, *Der Ganze Mensch: Zur Anthropologie der Antike und ihrer europäischen Nachgeschichte* (Berlin: Akademie Verlag, 2012).

Janowski, Bernd, *Die lebendige Statue Gottes: zur Anthropologie der priesterlichen Urgeschichte*, in: M. Witte (ed.), *Gott und Mensch im Dialog* (Festschrift Otto

Kaiser zum 80. Geburstag; BZAW, 345, Bd. 1; Berlin, New York: 2004), pp. 183–214.

Janowski, Bernd, *Konfliktgespräche mit Gott: eine Anthropologie der Psalmen* (2nd edn, Neukirchen-Vluyn: Neukirchener Verlag, 2006). Englisch: *Arguing with God: A Theological Anthropology of the Psalms* (trans. A. Siedlecki; Louisville, KY: Westminster John Knox Press, 2013).

Janowski, Bernd, *Sühne als Heilsgeschehen: Traditions- und religionsgeschichtliche Studien zur Sühnetheologie der Priesterschrift* (Wissenschaftliche Monographien zum Alten und Neuen Testament, 55; Neukirchen-Vluyn: Neukirchener, 2000).

Janowski, Bernd and Liess, Kathrin, *Der Mensch im alten Israel: Neue Forschungen zur alttestamentlichen Anthropologie* (Freiburg im Breisgau: Verlag Herder, 2009).

Janowski, Bernd and Zchomelidse, Nino (eds.), *Die Sichtbarkeit des Unsichtbaren: Zur Korrelation von Text und Bild im Wirkungskreis der Bibel* (AGWB 3; Stuttgart: Deutsche Bibelgesellschaft, 2002).

Jenni, Ernst, Art. דמה *dmh gleichen*, in: E. Jenni (ed.), 'Theologisches Handwörterbuch zum Alten', *THAT* I (1984), col. 451–6.

Jenni, Ernst, Die hebräischen Präpositionen. Vol. 1: Die Präposition Beth (Stuttgart, Berlin [etc.]: Kohlhammer, 1992).

Jeremias, Jörg, *Der Prophet Hosea* (Göttingen: Vandenhoeck & Ruprecht, 1983).

Jüngel, Eberhard, *Gott als Geheimnis der Welt: zur Begründung der Theologie des Gekreuzigten im Streit zwischen Theismus und Atheismus* (Tübingen: Mohr Siebeck, 1977).

Kaiser, Otto, *Der Gott des Alten Testaments. Theologie des Alten Testaments 1: Grundlegung.* (UTB 1747; Göttingen: Vandenhoeck & Ruprecht 1993).

Kaiser, Otto, *Der Gott des Alten Testaments. Wesen und Wirken. Theologie des Alten Testaments 2: Jahwe, der Gott Israels, Schöpfer der Welt und des Menschen.* (UTB 2024; Göttingen: Vandenhoeck & Ruprecht 1998).

Kaiser, Otto, *Der Gott des Alten Testaments. Theologie des Alten Testaments 3: Jahwes Gerechtigkeit.* (UTB 2392; Göttingen: Vandenhoeck & Ruprecht 2003).

Keel, Othmar, *Corpus der Stempelsiegel-Amulette aus Palästina/Israel: von den Anfängen bis zur Perserzeit*, Vol. 1 (OBO.SA 10; Fribourg: Academic Press, 1995).

Keel, Othmar, *Deine Blicke sind Tauben: Zur Metaphorik des Hohen Liedes* (SBS 114/115, Stuttgart: Verl. Katholisches Bibelwerk, 1984).

Keel, Othmar, *Die Welt der altorientalischen Bildsymbolik und das Alte testament. Am Beispiel der Psalmen* (5th edn, Göttingen: V & R, 1996). English: *The Symbolism of the Biblical World. Ancient Near Eastern Iconography and the Book of Psalms* (trans. T. J. Hallett; New York: Seabury Press, 1978).

Keel, Othmar and Uehlinger, Christoph, *Altorientalische Miniaturkunst. Die ältesten visuellen Massenkommunikationsmittel: Ein Blick in die Sammlungen des Biblischen Instituts der Universitat Freiburg* (Darmstadt: P. von Zabern Verlag, 1990).

Keel, Othmar, *Warum im Jerusalemer Tempel kein anthropomorphes Kultbild gestanden haben dürfte*, in: G. Boehm (ed.), *Homo pictor* (Colloqium Rauricum 7, München: K. G. Saur, 2001), pp. 244–81.

Keel, Othmar and Uehlinger, Christoph, *Göttinnen, Götter, Göttersymbole. Neue Erkenntnisse zur Religionsgeschichte Kanaans und Israels aufgrund bislang unerschlossener ikonographischer Quellen* (5th edn, QD 134; Freiburg i. Br.: Herder, 2001). English: *Gods, Goddesses, and Images of God in Ancient Israel* (Minneapolis, MN: Fortress Press, 1998).

Kessler, Dieter, *Die heiligen Tiere und der König*, Vol. 1: *Beiträge zu Organisation, Kult und Theologie der spätzeitlichen Tierfriedhöfe*, (ÄAT 16,1; Wiesbaden: Harrassowitz, 1989).

Kessler, Dieter, Tierische Missverständnisse: Grundsätzliches zu Fragen des Tierkultes, in: M. Fitzenreiter, (ed.), *Tierkulte im pharaonischen Ägypten und im Kulturvergleich*, (IBAES IV, retrieved from Humboldt University, 2003), pp. 33–67: http://www2.rz.hu-berlin.de/nilus/net-publications/ibaes4/.

Kessler, Martin and Deurloo, Karel A., *A Commentary on Genesis: The Book of Beginnings* (New York: Paulist Press, 2004).

Knafl, Anne K., *Forming God: Divine Anthropomorphism in the Pentateuch* (Siphrut: Literature and Theology of the Hebrew Scriptures 12, Winona Lake, IN: Eisenbrauns, 2014).

Köckert, Matthias, *Die Zehn Gebote* (BSR 2430; München: C. H. Beck, 2007).

Köhler, Ludwig, *Theologie des Alten Testaments* (Tübingen: Mohr Siebeck, 1953).

Köhlmoos, Melanie, 'Denn ich, JHWH, bin ein eifersüchtiger Gott' Gottes Gefühle im Alten Testament, in: A. Wagner (ed.), *Göttliche Körper – göttliche Gefühle: Was leisten anthropomorphe und anthropopathische Götterkonzepte im Alten Orient und Alten Testament?* (OBO 270; Fribourg: Academic Press Fribourg; Göttingen: Vandenhoeck & Ruprecht, 2014), pp. 191–217.

Körtner, Ulrich H. J., Art. Anthropomorphismus VI. Dogmatisch, RGG[4] 1 (1998). English: *Anthropomorphism VI. Dogmatics*, RPP 1 (2007).

Krasovec, Joze, *Der Merismus im Biblisch-Hebräischen und Nordwestsemitischen* (Rome: Biblical Institute Press, 1977).

Kratz, Reinhard G., *Die Komposition der erzählenden Bücher des Alten Testaments* (Göttingen: Vandenhoeck & Ruprecht, 2000). English: *The composition of the narrative books of the Old Testament* (trans. J. Bowden; London: T. & T. Clark 2005).

Krüger, Thomas, *Das menschliche Herz und die Weisung Gottes. Studien zur alttestamentlichen Anthropologie und Ethik* (AThANT 96; Zürich: Theologischer Verlag, 2009).

Kuitert, Harminus M., *Gott in Menschengestalt: Eine dogmatisch-hermeneutische Studie über die Anthropomorphismen der Bibel* (BEvTh 45; München: Christian Kaiser Verlag, 1967).

Lakoff, George and Johnson, Mark, *Metaphors we Live by* (Chicago: University of Chicago Press, 1980).

Lauha, Risto, *Psychophysischer Sprachgebrauch im Alten Testament: eine strukturalsemantische Analyse von 'נפש', 'לב' und 'רוח'* (Annales Academiae Scientiarum Fennicae Dissertationes humanarum litterarum 35, Helsinki: Suomalainen Tiedeakatemia, 1983).

Lehmann, Reinhard G., *Friedrich Delitzsch und der Babel-Bibel-Streit* (OBO 133; Freiburg (CH): Universitätsverlag, Göttingen: Vandenhoeck & Ruprecht, 1994).

Liess, Kathrin, 'Leben. II. Biblisch. 1. Altes Testament', RGG[4] 5 (2002). English: *Life. II. Bible. 1. Old Testament*, RPP 7 (2010), pp. 476–7.

Longman III, Tremper, Art. Merism, in: T. Longmann III and P. Enns (eds.), *Dictionary of the Old Testament: Wisdom, Poetry and Writings* (Downers Grove, IL Nottingham: IVP Academic Inter-Varsity Press, 2008), pp. 464–6.

Machinist, Peter, *Anthropomorphism in Mesopotamian Religion*, in: A. Wagner (ed.), *Göttliche Körper – göttliche Gefühle: Was leisten anthropomorphe und anthropopathische Götterkonzepte im Alten Orient und Alten Testament?* (OBO 270; Fribourg: Academic Press Fribourg; Göttingen: Vandenhoeck & Ruprecht, 2014), pp. 67–99.

Maier, Christl M., *Körperliche und emotionale Aspekte JHWHs aus der Genderperspektive*, in: A. Wagner (ed.), *Göttliche Körper – göttliche Gefühle: Was leisten anthropomorphe und anthropopathische Götterkonzepte im Alten Orient und Alten Testament?* (OBO 270; Fribourg: Academic Press Fribourg, Göttingen: Vandenhoeck & Ruprecht, 2014), pp. 171–89.

Makrides, Vasilios N., Ikonen / sakrale Bilder und ihre Bedeutung für eine vergleichende Kulturgeschichte des Christentums, in: A. Wagner, V. Hörner and G. Geisthardt (eds.), *Gott im Wort – Gott im Bild: Bilderlosigkeit als Bedingung des Monotheismus?* (2nd ed, Neukirchen-Vluyn: Neukirchener Verlag, 2008), pp. 151–64.

Markl, Dominik (ed.), *The Decalogue and its Cultural Influence* (HBM 58; Sheffield: Sheffield Phoenix Press, 2014).

Markter, Florian, *Transformationen. Zur Anthropologie des Propheten Ezechiel unter besonderer Berücksichtigung des Motivs 'Herz'* (FzB 127; Würzburg: Echter, 2013).

Martin, Evelyne (ed.), *Tiergestaltigkeit der Göttinnen und Götter zwischen Metapher und Symbol* (BThSt 129; Neukirchen-Vluyn: Neukirchener, 2012).

Matthiae, Paolo, *Geschichte der Kunst im Alten Orient; Die Grossreiche der Assyrer, Neubabylonier und Achämeniden: 1000-330 v.Chr* (Darmstadt: Wissenschaftliche Buchgesellschaft, 1999).

Meshel, Ze'ev, *Kuntillet 'Ajrud (Ḥorvat Teman): An Iron Age II religious site on the Judah-Sinai border* (Jerusalem: Israel Exploration Society, 2012).

Meyer, Rudolf, *Hebräische Grammatik* (Berlin and New York: deGruyter, 1992).

Michalowski, Kazimierz et al., *Die ägyptische Kunst* (3rd edn, Ars Antiqua VI/3, Freiburg im Breisgau: Herder, 2000).

Michel, Diethelm, *Israels Glaube im Wandel: Einführungen in die Forschung am Alten Testament* (Berlin: Verlag Die Spur, 1971).

Michel, Diethelm, 'næpæš als Leichnam?', in: *ZAH* 7 (1994), pp. 81–4.

Michel, Diethelm, *Einheit in der Vielfalt des Alten Testaments*, in: D. Michel and A. Wagner (eds.), *Studien zur Überlieferungsgeschichte alttestamentlicher Texte* (TB 93; Gütersloh: C. Kaiser, Gütersloher Verlagshaus, 1997), pp. 53–68.

Mitchell, William John Thomas, *Picture Theory: Essays on Verbal and Visual Representation* (Chicago: University of Chicago Press, 1994).

Mittmann, Siegfried, Das Symbol der Hand in der altorientalischen Ikonographie, in: R. Kieffer and J. Bergman (eds.) *La main de Dieu. Die Hand Gottes* (WUNT 94; Tübingen: Mohr Siebeck, 1997), pp. 19–47.

Mommer, Peter, Schmidt, Werner H. and Strauss, Hans (eds.), *Gottes Recht als Lebensraum* (FS für Hans Jochen Boecker, Neukirchen-Vluyn: Neukirchener, 1993).

Morawe, Günter, 'Turm', BHH III (1966), col. 2032–34.

Müller, Hans-Peter, 'ראֹש roʾš Kopf,' THAT³ II. (1984), col. 701–15.

Müller, Hans-Peter, *Eine neue babylonische Menschenschöpfungserzählung*, in: H. P. Müller, *Mythos – Kerygma – Wahrheit: gesammelte Aufsätze zum Alten*

Testament in seiner Umwelt und zur biblischen Theologie (Berlin, New York: deGruyter, 1991), pp. 43–67.

Müller, Hans-Peter, Kaiser, Otto and Loader, James Alfred, *Das Hohelied; Klagelieder; Das Buch Ester* (4th edn, ATD 16.2, Göttingen: Vandenhoeck & Ruprecht, 1992), pp. 1–90.

Müller, Katrin, Lieben ist nicht gleich lieben. Zur kognitiven Konzeption von Liebe im Hebräischen, in: A. Wagner (ed.), *Göttliche Körper – göttliche Gefühle: Was leisten anthropomorphe und anthropopathische Götterkonzepte im Alten Orient und Alten Testament?* (OBO 270; Fribourg: Academic Press Fribourg, Göttingen: Vandenhoeck & Ruprecht, 2014), pp. 219–37.

Müller, Peter, Dierk, Heidrun and Müller-Friese, Anita, *Verstehen lernen: Ein Arbeitsbuch zur Hermeneutik* (Stuttgart: Calwer, 2005).

Neef, Heinz-Dieter, *Gottes himmlischer Thronrat: Hintergründe und Bedeutung von sôd JHWH im Alten Testament* (Stuttgart: Calwer Verlag, 1994).

Neumann-Gorsolke, Ute, *Herrschen in den Grenzen der Schöpfung. Ein Beitrag zur alttestamentlichen Anthropologie am Beispiel von Psalm 8, Genesis 1 und verwandten Texten* (Wissenschaftliche Monographien zum Alten und Neuen Testament, 101; Neukirchen-Vluyn: Neukirchener, 2004).

Niehr, Herbert, Körper des Königs und Körper der Götter in Ugarit, in: A. Wagner (ed.), *Göttliche Körper – göttliche Gefühle: Was leisten anthropomorphe und anthropopathische Götterkonzepte im Alten Orient und Alten Testament?* (OBO 270; Fribourg: Academic Press Fribourg, Göttingen: Vandenhoeck & Ruprecht, 2014), pp. 141–67.

Nordhofen, Eckhard (ed.), *Bilderverbot: Die Sichtbarkeit des Unsichtbaren* (Ikon: Bild + Theologie, Paderborn: Schöningh Verlag, 2001).

Nunn, Astrid, *Der figürliche Motivschatz Phöniziens, Syriens und Transjordaniens vom 6. bis zum 4. Jahrhundert v. Chr.* (OBO 18; Freiburg: Universitätsverlag, Göttingen: Vandenhoeck & Ruprecht, 2000).

Nunn, Astrid, *Die Phönizier und ihre südlichen Nachbarn in der achämenidischen und frühhellenistischen Zeit – Ein Bildervergleich*, in: M. Witte et al. (eds.), *Israeliten und Phönizier: Ihre Beziehungen im Spiegel der Archäologie und der Literatur des Alten Testaments und seiner Umwelt* (OBO 235; Fribourg: Academic Press Fribourg, Göttingen: Vandenhoeck & Ruprecht, 2008), pp. 95–123.

Nunn, Astrid, *Körperkonzeption in der altorientalischen Kunst*, in: A. Wagner (ed.), *Anthropologische Aufbrüche: Alttestamentliche und interdisziplinäre Zugänge zur historischen Anthropologie* (FRLANT 232; Göttingen: Vandenhoeck & Ruprecht, 2009), pp. 119–50.

Nunn, Astrid, *Mesopotamische Götter und ihr Körper in den Bildern*, in: A. Wagner (ed.), *Göttliche Körper – göttliche Gefühle: Was leisten anthropomorphe und anthropopathische Götterkonzepte im Alten Orient und Alten Testament?* (OBO 270; Fribourg: Academic Press Fribourg, Göttingen: Vandenhoeck & Ruprecht, 2014), pp. 51–66.

Oberforcher, Robert, *Biblische Lesarten zur Anthropologie des Ebenbildmotivs*, in: A. Vonach and G. Fischer (eds.), *Horizonte biblischer Texte* (Festschrift für Josef M. Oesch zum 60. Geburtstag; OBO 196; Fribourg (CH): Academic Press, 2003), pp. 131–68.

Oberhuber, Karl, *Die Kultur des Alten Orients* (Frankfurt: Athenaion, 1972).

Oeming, Manfred: *Biblische Hermeneutik: Eine Einführung* (Darmstadt: Wissenschaftliche Buchgesellschaft, 1998). English: *Contemporary biblical hermeneutics: an introduction* (trans. J. F. Vette, Aldershot, England/Burlington, VT: Ashgate, 2006).

Otto, Eberhard, *Art. Anthropomorphismus*, in: *LÄ* 1 (1975), col. 311–18.

Otto, Eckart, *Dekalog. I. Altes Testament*, in: RGG⁴ 2 (1999), pp. 625–28. English: *Decalogue. I. Old Testament*, RPP 3 (2007), pp. 709–12.

Parrot, André, Chehab, Maurice H. and Moscati, Sabatino, *Die Phoenizier: Die Entwicklung der phönizischen Kunst von den Anfängen bis zum Ende des dritten punischen Krieges* (München: C.H. Beck, 1977). English: S. Moscati et al. *The Phoenicians* (London: I. B. Tauris, 2000).

Pfeiffer, Henrik, *Das Heiligtum von Bethel im Spiegel des Hoseabuches* (Göttingen: Vandenhoeck & Ruprecht, 1999).

Podella, Thomas, 'Bild und Text: Mediale und historische Perspektiven auf das alttestamentliche Bilderverbot', in: *SJOT* 15 (2001), pp. 205–56.

Podella, Thomas, *Das Lichtkleid JHWHs: Untersuchungen zur Gestalthaftigkeit Gottes im Alten Testament und seiner altorientalischen Umwelt* (FAT 15; Tübingen: Mohr Siebeck, 1996).

Pola, Thomas, *Die ursprüngliche Priesterschrift: Beobachtungen zur Literarkritik und Traditionsgeschichte von Pᵍ.* (Wissenschaftliche Monographien zum Alten und Neuen Testament 70; Neukirchen-Vluyn: Neukirchener, 1995).

Pongratz-Leisten, Beate, *Entwurf zu einer Handlungstheorie des altorientalischen Polytheismus*, in: A. Wagner (ed.), *Göttliche Körper – göttliche Gefühle: Was leisten anthropomorphe und anthropopathische Götterkonzepte im Alten Orient und Alten Testament?* (OBO 270; Fribourg: Academic Press Fribourg, Göttingen: Vandenhoeck & Ruprecht, 2014), pp. 101–16.

Porter, Barbara N., *What is a God? Anthropomorphic and Non-anthropomorphic Aspects of Deity in Ancient Mesopotamia* (Transactions of the Casco Bay Assyriological Institute 2; Winona Lake, IN: The Casco Bay Assyriological Institute/Eisenbrauns, 2009).

Preuss, Horst Dietrich, *Theologie des Alten Testaments Vol. I* (Stuttgart: Kohlhammer, 1991).

Pritchard, James B. (ed.), *The Ancient Near East in Pictures, relating to the Old Testament* (ANEP) (2nd edn, Princeton: Princeton University Press, 1969).

Rendtorff, Rolf, *Die sündige næfæš*, in: F. Crüsemann, C. Hardmeier, R. Kessler (eds.), *Was ist der Mensch..? Beiträge zur Anthropologie des Alten Testaments. Hans Walter Wolff zum 80. Geburtstag* (München: Chr. Kaiser, 1992), pp. 211–20.

Rendtorff, Rolf, *Theologie des Alten Testaments: Ein kanonischer Entwurf.* Vol.2 (Neukirchen-Vluyn: Neukirchener, 2001). English: *The Canonical Hebrew Bible: A Theology of the Old Testament* (trans. D.E. Orton; Tools for Biblical Study, 7; Leiden: Deo Publishing, 2005).

Renz, Johannes and Röllig, Wolfgang, *Handbuch der althebräischen Epigraphik, Vol. I* (Darmstadt: Wissenschaftliche Buchgesellschaft, 1995).

Ris-Eberle, Susanne, 'Tiere als Götter im Alten Ägypten?, in: *Unipress* 122 (2004), pp. 50–53.

Rudolph, Wilhelm, *Das Buch Ruth; Das Hohe Lied; Die Klagelieder* (3rd edn, KAT XVII 1–3, Gütersloh: Mohn, 1962).

Sarasin, Philipp, 'Körpergeschichte', *Historisches Lexikon der Schweiz 7* (2009), pp. 412–3.

Schäfer, Heinrich, *Von Ägyptischer Kunst, besonders der Zeichenkunst. Eine Einfürung in die Betrachtung ägyptischer Kunstwerke,* Vol. 2 (4th edn, Wiesbaden:

Harrassowitz, 1963). English: Schäfer, Heinrich, *Principles of Egyptian Art* (Rep. ed. E. Brunner-Traut, trans. by John Baines, Oxford: Griffith Institute, 1986).

Schäfer, Heinrich, *Von Ägyptischer Kunst: Eine Grundlage* (4th edn, Wiesbaden: Harrassowitz, 1963). English: *Principles of Egyptian Art* (3rd edn, trans. J. Baines; ed. E. Brunner-Traut; Oxford: Griffith Institute, 1986).

Schäfer, Heinrich, Die Kunst Ägyptens, in H. Schäfer and W. Andrae, *Die Kunst des Alten Orients* (Proplyäen-Kunstgeschichte II, Berlin: Propyläen-Verlag, 1925), pp. 9–122.

Schäfer, Heinrich and Andrae, Walter, *Die Kunst des Alten Orients* (Propyläen Kunstgeschichte II, Berlin: Propyläen-Verlag, 1925).

Schart, Aaron, *Die «Gestalt» YHWHs: Ein Beitrag zur Körpermetaphorik alttestamentlicher Rede von Gott*, in: *ThZ* 55 (1999), pp. 26–43.

Schleiser, Renate, Die dionysische Psyche. Zu Euripides' backchen, in: C. Benthien et al. (eds.) *Emotionalität. Zur Geschichte der Gefühle* (Literatur – Kultur – Geschlecht: Kleine Reihe 16, Köln: Böhlau, 2000), pp. 21–41.

Schmidt, Brian B., *The iron age pithoi drawings from Horvat Teman or Kuntillet 'Ajrud: Some New Proposals*, in: *JANER* 2 (2002), pp. 91–125.

Schmidt, Werner H., *Anthropologische Begriffe im Alten Testament*, in: *EvTh* 24 (1964), pp. 374–88.

Schmidt, Werner H., *Die Schöpfungsgeschichte der Priesterschrift: zur Ueberlieferungsgeschichte von Genesis 1,1-2,4a und 2,4b-3,24* (Wissenschaftliche Monographien zum Alten und Neuen Testament, 17; Neukirchen-Vluyn; Neukirchener, 1967).

Schmidt, Werner H. (perhaps: Schmidt, Werner; Holger Delkurt and Axel Graupner), *Die Zehn Gebote im Rahmen alttestamentlicher Ethik* (EdF 281, Darmstadt: WBG 1993).

Schmitz, Hermann, *System der Philosophie, Vol. 3.1 Der leibliche Raum* (Space of the Felt Body) (3rd edn, Bonn: Bouvier, 1998).

Schmitz, Hermann, *System der Philosophie, Vol. 3.2 Der Gefühlsraum* (The Space of Emotions) (3rd edn, Bonn: Bouvier, 1998).

Schmitz, Hermann, *System der Philosophie, Vol. 3.5 Die Wahrnehmung* (Perception) (2nd edn, Bonn: Bouvier, 1989).

Schmitz-Emans, Monika, 'Der Körper und seine Bindestriche: Zu Analysen der Ambiguität des Körperlichen und zur Dialektik seiner Modellierungen im wissenschaftlichen Diskurs der Gegenwart', in: *KulturPoetic* 1.2 (2001), pp. 275–89.

Schroer, Silvia, *Feministische Anthropologie des Ersten Testaments: Beobachtungen, Fragen, Plädoyers, lectio difficilior* 1 (2003). Available online: http://www. lectio. unibe.ch/03_1/schroer.htm.

Schroer, Silvia, *In Israel gab es Bilder* (OBO 74; Fribourg: Universitätsverlag, Göttingen: Vandenhoeck & Ruprecht, 1987).

Schroer, Silvia, 'Zur Deutung der Hand unter der Grabinschrifft von Chirbet el Qôm', in: *UF* 15 (1983), pp. 191–9.

Schroer, Silvia and Keel, Othmar, *Die Ikonographie Palästinas/Israels und der Alte Orient. Eine Religionsgeschichte in Bildern* (IPIAO), Vol. 1–4 (Fribourg: Academic Press Fribourg, 2005/2008/2011/2018).

Schroer, Silvia and Staubli, Thomas, *Die Körpersymbolik der Bibel* (2nd edn, Gütersloh: Gütersloher Verlagshaus, 2005). English: *Body Symbolism in the Bible* (trans. Linda M. Maloney; Liturgical Press: Collegeville, USA 2001).

Schroer, Silvia and Staubli, Thomas, *Menschenbilder der Bibel* (Ostfildern: Patmos, 2014).

Schüle, Andreas, *Der Prolog der hebräischen Bibel: Der literar- und theologiegeschichtliche Diskurs der Urgeschichte (Gen 1-11)*, AThANT 86 (Zürich: Theologischer Verlag Zürich, 2006).

Seebass, Horst, 'נֶפֶשׁ *næfæš*', ThWAT V (1986), col. 531–55.

Seebass, Horst, *Genesis I: Urgeschichte (1,1–11,26)* (Neukirchen-Vluyn: Neukirchener, 1996).

Sellin, Ernst, *Theologie des Alten Testaments* (Leipzig: Quelle & Meyer, 1933).

Shectman, Sarah and Baden, Joel S., (eds.), 'The Strata of the Priestly Writings: Contemporary Debate and Future Direction', AThANT 95 (Zürich: Theologischer Verlag Zürich, 2009).

Smith, Mark S., Ugaritic *Anthropomorphism, Theomorphism, Theriomorphism*, in: A. Wagner (ed.), *Göttliche Körper – göttliche Gefühle: Was leisten anthropomorphe und anthropopathische Götterkonzepte im Alten Orient und Alten Testament?* (OBO 270; Fribourg: Academic Press, Göttingen: Vandenhoeck & Ruprecht, 2014), pp. 117–40.

Sommer, Benjamin D., *The Bodies of God and the World of Ancient Israel* (Cambridge: Cambridge University Press, 2009).

Steck, Odil Hannes, *Der Schöpfungsbericht der Priesterschrift. Studien zur literarkritischen und überlieferungsgeschichtlichen Problematik von Genesis 1,1-2,4a.* (FRLANT 115; Göttingen: Vandenhoeck & Ruprecht, 1975).

Stemberger, Günter, *Bild/Bilderverbot*, in: *Lexikon der Bibelhermeneutik* (2009), pp. 97–98.

Tanner, Jakob, *Historische Anthropologie zur Einführung* (Zur Einführung 301, 2nd edn, Hamburg: Junius, 2008).

Tilly, Michael, *Antijüdische Instrumentalisierungen des biblischen Bilderverbots*, in: A. Wagner, V. Hörner and G. Geisthardt (eds.), *Gott im Wort – Gott im Bild*: *Bilderlosigkeit als Bedingung des Monotheismus?* (2nd edn, Neukirchen-Vluyn: Neukirchener, 2008), pp. 23–30.

Trillhaas, Wolfgang, *Dogmatik* (4th edn, Berlin: deGruyter, 1980).).

Uehlinger, Christoph, *Art. Bilderverbot, RGG⁴* 1 (1998), pp. 1574–77. English: *Prohibition of Images*, RPP 10 (2011), pp. 420–2.

Uehlinger, Christoph, Exodus, Stierbild und biblisches Kultbildverbot, in C. Harmeier, R. Kessler and A. Rume (eds.), *Freiheit und Recht* (Festschrift F. Crüsemann; Gütersloh: Gütersloher Verlagshaus, 2003), pp. 42–77.

van der Toorn, Karel, Becking, Bob and van der Horst, Pieter Willem (eds.), *Dictionary of Deities and Demons in the Bible* (2nd edn; Leiden: Brill, 1999).

van der Woude, Adam S., 'פָּנִים *pānīm*', THAT³ II. (1984), col. 432–460.

van Dülmen, Richard, *Historische Anthropologie. Entwicklung, Probleme, Aufgaben* (Köln: Böhlau, 2001).

van Oorschot, Jürgen (ed.), *Der Mensch als Thema theologischer Anthropologie. Beiträge in interdisziplinärer Perspektive* (BthSt 111; Neukirchen-Vluyn: Neukirchener, 2010).

van Oorschot, Jürgen and Wagner, Andreas (eds.), Anthropologie(n) des Alten Testaments (2nd edn, VWGT 42; Leipzig: Evangelische Verlagsanstalt, 2018).

Veijola, Timo, *Das fünfte Buch Mose: Deuteronomium* (ATD 8,1; Göttingen: Vandenhoeck & Ruprecht, 2004).

von Graevenitz, Gerhard et al. (eds.), *Die Unvermeidlichkeit der Bilder* (Literatur und Anthropologie 7, Tübingen: Gunter Narr Verlag, 2001).

von Rad, Gerhard, *Das erste Buch Mose* (Göttingen: Vandenhoeck & Ruprecht, 1987). English: *Genesis. A Commentary* (trans. J.H. Marks; The Old Testament Library; Bloomsbury Street London: SCM Press Ltd, 1963).

von Rad, Gerhard, *Theologie des Alten Testaments, Vol. 1* (EETh 1; München: Chr. Kaiser, 1987). English: *Old Testament theology. Vol. 1*, (trans. D. M. G. Stalker; London: S.C.M. Press, 196).

Vriezen, Theodoor C., *Theologie des Alten Testaments in Grundzügen* (Wageningen: Veenman & Zonen, 1956). English: *An outline of Old Testament theology* (2nd edn, Oxford: Basil Blackwell 1970).

Wagner, Andreas, *Alttestamentlicher Monotheismus und seine Bindung an das Wort*, in: A. Wagner, V. Hörner and G. Geisthardt (eds.), *Gott im Wort – Gott im Bild: Bilderlosigkeit als Bedingung des Monotheismus?* (2nd edn, Neukirchen-Vluyn: Neukirchener, 2008), pp. 1–22.

Wagner, Andreas, *Gottes Körper. Zur alttestamentlichen Vorstellung der Menschengestaltigkeit Gottes* (Gütersloh: Gütersloher Verlag, 2010).

Wagner, Andreas, *Anthropologie(n) des Alten Testaments im 21. Jahrhundert*, in: J. van Oorschot and A. Wagner (eds.), *Anthropologie(n) des Alten Testaments* (2nd edn, VWGT 42; Leipzig: Evangelische Verlagsanstalt, 2018), pp. 11–21.

Wagner, Andreas (ed.), *Anthropologische Aufbrüche. Alttestamentliche und interdisziplinäre Zugänge zur historischen Anthropologie* (FRLANT 232; Göttingen: Vandenhoeck & Ruprecht, 2009).

Wagner, Andreas, *Arm (AT)*, WiBiLex (2007), retrieved from Deutsche Bibelgesellschaft: https://www.bibelwissenschaft.de/stichwort/41407/.

Wagner, Andreas, *Hand (AT)*, WiBiLex (2007), retrieved from Deutsche Bibelgesellschaft: www.wibilex.de/stichwort/hand.

Wagner, Andreas, *Kopf (AT)*, WiBiLex (2007), retrieved from Deutsche Bibelgesellschaft: www.wibilex.de/stichwort/41419/.

Wagner, Andreas, *Heinrich Schäfer*, BBKL 8 (1994), col. 1518–31.

Wagner, Andreas, *Heinrich Schäfer*, NDB (2005), pp. 507–8.

Wagner, Andreas, *Das synthetische Bedeutungsspektrum hebräischer Körperteilbezeichnungen*, in: K. Müller and A. Wagner (eds.), *Synthetische Körperauffassung im Hebräischen und den Sprachen der Nachbarkulturen* (AOAT 416; Münster: Ugarit Verlag, 2014), pp. 1–11.

Wagner, Andreas, *Der Parallelismus membrorum zwischen poetischer Form und Denkfigur*, in: A. Wagner (ed.), *Parallelismus membrorum* (OBO 224; Fribourg: Academic Press, Göttingen: Vandenhoeck & Ruprecht, 2006), pp. 1–26.

Wagner, Andreas, *Die Gestalt(en) Gottes und der Mensch im Alten Testament*, in: B. Janowski and C. Schwöbel (eds.), *Dimensionen der Leiblichkeit.* (ThID 16; Neukirchen-Vluyn: Neukirchener, 2015), pp. 46–68.

Wagner, Andreas, *Die Gottebenbildlichkeitsvorstellung der Priesterschrift zwischen Theomorphismus und Anthropomorphismus*, in: J. Luchsinger, H.-P. Mathys and M. Saur (eds.), *... der seine Lust hat am Wort des Herrn!'* (Festschrift Ernst Jenni zum 80. Geburtstag, (AOAT 336; Münster: Ugarit Verlag, 2007), pp. 344–63.

Wagner, Andreas, *Emotionen, Gefühle und Sprache im Alten Testament*, (2nd edn, KUSATU 7, Spennern: Waltrop, 2011).

Wagner, Andreas, *Emotionen in alttestamentlicher und verwandter Literatur: Grundüberlegungen am Beispiel des Zorns*, in: R. Egger-Wenzel and J. Corley (eds.), *Emotions from Ben Sira to Paul* (DCL.Y 2011; Berlin and Boston: deGruyter, 2012), pp. 27–68.

Wagner, Andreas (ed.), *Göttliche Körper – göttliche Gefühle: Was leisten anthropomorphe und anthropopathische Götterkonzepte im Alten Orient und Alten Testament?* (OBO 270; Fribourg: Academic Press, Göttingen: Vandenhoeck & Ruprecht, 2014).

Wagner, Andreas, *Körperbegriffe als Stellvertreterausdrücke der Person*, in: id. (ed.), *Beten und Bekennen: über Psalmen* (Neukirchen-Vluyn: Neukirchener, 2008), pp. 289–317.

Wagner, Andreas, *Körperteile (AT)*, WiBiLex (2013), retrieved from Deutsche Bibelgesellschaft: https://www.bibelwissenschaft.de/stichwort/64672/.

Wagner, Andreas, Menschenkörper – Gotteskörper: Zur Einführung, in: A. Wagner (ed.), *Göttliche Körper – göttliche Gefühle: Was leisten anthropomorphe und anthropopathische Götterkonzepte im Alten Orient und Alten Testament?* (OBO 270; Fribourg: Academic Press, Göttingen: Vandenhoeck & Ruprecht, 2014), pp. 1–28.

Wagner, Andreas, 'Permutatio religionis' – Ps 130 und der Wandel der israelitischen Religion zur Bekenntnisreligion, in: *VT* 57 (2007), pp. 91–113.

Wagner, Andreas (ed.), Primäre und sekundäre Religion als Kategorie der Religionsgeschichte des Alten Testaments, (BZAW 364; Berlin: deGruyter, 2006).

Wagner, Andreas, Primäre/sekundäre und Bekenntnis-Religion als Thema der Religionsgeschichte, in: Id. (ed.), *Primäre und sekundäre Religion als Kategorie der Religionsgeschichte des Alten Testaments (BZAW 364)*. Berlin/New York, 2006, S. 3–19.

Wagner, Andreas, *Prophetie als Theologie: die 'so spricht Jahwe'–Formeln und das Grundverständnis alttestamentlicher Prophetie* (FRLANT 207; Göttingen: Vandenhoeck & Ruprecht, 2004).

Wagner, Andreas, *Sprechakte und Sprechaktanalyse im Alten Testament: Untersuchungen im biblischen Hebräisch an der Nahtstelle zwischen Handlungsebene und Grammatik* (BZAW 253; Berlin/New York: deGruyter, 1997).

Wagner, Andreas, Verkörpertes Herrschen. Zum Gebrauch von „treten' / „herrschen' in Gen 1,26-28, in: G. Etzelmüller and A. Weissenrieder (eds.), *Verkörperung als Paradigma einer theologischen Anthropologie* (TBT, 172; Berlin: deGruyter, 2016), pp. 127–41.

Wagner, Andreas, Wider die Reduktion des Lebendigen: Über das Verhältnis der sog. Anthropologischen Grundbegriffe und die Möglichkeit, mit ihnen die alttestamentliche Menschenvorstellung zu fassen, in: id. (ed.), *Anthropologische Aufbrüche: Alttestamentliche und interdisziplinäre Zugänge zur historischen Anthropologie* (FRLANT 232; Göttingen: Vandenhoeck & Ruprecht, 2009), pp. 183–99.

Wagner, Andreas, 'Les différentes dimensions de la vie: Quelques réflexions sur la terminologie anthropologique de l'Ancien Testament', in: *Revue des Sciences Religieuses* 81.3 (2007), pp. 391–408.

Wagner, Andreas, Hörner, Volker and Geisthardt, Günter (eds.), *Gott im Wort – Gott im Bild: Bilderlosigkeit als Bedingung des Monotheismus?* (2nd edn, Neukirchen-Vluyn: Neukirchener, 2005).

Wagner, Christoph, Der unsichtbare Gott – Ein Thema der italienischen
    Renaissancemalerei?, in: A. Wagner, V. Hörner and G. Geisthardt (eds.), *Gott im*
    Wort – Gott im Bild: Bilderlosigkeit als Bedingung des Monotheismus?
    (2nd edn, Neukirchen-Vluyn: Neukirchener, 2008), pp. 113–42.
Waschke, Ernst-Joachim, Die Bedeutung der Königstheologie für die Vorstellung
    der Gottesebenbildlichkeit des Menschen, in: Wagner, Andreas (ed.),
    Anthropologische Aufbrüche. Alttestamentliche und interdisziplinäre Zugänge
    zur historischen Anthropologie (FRLANT 232). Göttingen, 2009, S. 235–52.
Weimar, Peter, 'Studien zur Priesterschrift' (FAT 56; Tübingen: Mohr Siebeck,
    2008).
Weippert, Helga, *Palästina in vorhellenistischer Zeit* (Handbuch der Archäologie:
    Vorderasien 2, Vol. 1, München: Beck, 1988).
Weippert, Helga, Seybold, Klaus and Weippert, Manfred, *Beiträge zur*
    prophetischen Bildsprache in Israel und Assyrien (OBO 64; Göttingen:
    Vandenhoeck & Ruprecht, 1985).
Westermann, Claus, Art. אָדָם *ʾādām, THAT* I, (1984), col. 41–57.
Westermann, Claus, 'נֶפֶשׁ *næfæš* Seele', *THAT*[3] II, (1984), col. 71–96.
Westermann, Claus, *Genesis: Teilbd. 1. Genesis 1–11* (BK 1.1; Neukirchen-Vluyn;
    Neukirchener, 1974).
Witte, Markus, *Die biblische Urgeschichte. Redaktions- und theologiegeschichtliche*
    Beobachtungen zu Genesis 1,1–11,26 (BZAW 265; Berlin, New York:
    deGruyter, 1998).
Wolff, Hans Walter, *Anthropologie des Alten Testaments, mit Zwei Anhängen neu*
    herausgegeben von Bernd Janowski (München: Chr. Kaiser 1973; Gütersloh:
    Gütersloher Verlagshaus, 2010). English: *Anthropology of the Old Testament*
    (2nd edn; trans. M. Kohl; Mifflintown, Pennsylvania: Sigler Press, 1996.
Wulf, Christoph, *Anthropologie. Geschichte, Kultur, Philosophie* (Rowohlts
    Enzyklopädie 55664, Reinbek: Rowohlt Taschenbuch Verlag, 2004).
Würthwein, Ernst, Das Hohelied, in: E. Würthwein, K. Galling, and O. Plöger
    (eds.), *Die fünf Megilloth* (2nd edn, HAT I/18, Tübingen: Mohr Siebeck, 1969),
    pp. 25–71.
Wunn, Ina, Die Entstehung der Götter, in: A. Wagner (ed.), *Göttliche Körper –*
    göttliche Gefühle: Was leisten anthropomorphe und anthropopathische
    Götterkonzepte im Alten Orient und Alten Testament? (OBO 270; Fribourg:
    Academic Press, Göttingen: Vandenhoeck & Ruprecht, 2014), pp. 31–47.
Xenophanes, B 15, FVS, Nr. 21.
Zimmerli, Walther, Grundriß der alttestamentlichen Theologie (7th edn, Stuttgart:
    Kohlhammer, 1999, 1972).
Zwickel, Wolfgang, 'Überlegungen zur wirtschaftlichen und historischen Funktion
    von Kuntillet ʿAǧrūd', in: *ZDPV* 116 (2) (2000), pp. 139–42.

INDEX

INDEX OF REFERENCES